"You may think that it doesn't matter to you what color a guy's hairplugs are, but Shapiro shows that there are seven crucial image factors that can predict who will occupy the White House in 2008. What a fun book!"

Ann Coulter, Author,
If Democrats Had Any Brains, They'd be Republicans

"Great fun from a promising young observer of the political scene. Washington meets Hollywood."

Susan Estrich, syndicated columnist and author of
Soulless: Ann Coulter and the Right-Wing Church of Hate

"Witty, insightful, surprising, and consistently entertaining, Ben Shapiro's irreverent history of Presidential image-making will delight both political junkies and the bemused general public."

Michael Medved, nationally syndicated radio talk show host
and author of *Right Turns*

"An entertaining and illuminating romp through the politics of symbolism and personality in our presidential politics. If you're thinking of running for president, read this book before you spend a dime on a political consultant."

Rich Lowry, *National Review*

"Think Hillary Clinton's hair doesn't matter? Think again. As Ben Shapiro demonstrates in *Project President*, image is everything in politics. Devastatingly witty and unendingly informative, *Project President* traces America's fascination with presidential image-making all the way back to George Washington—and charts the trends forward for the 2008 race. A must-read!"

Mark Levin, nationally syndicated radio host and author of the
New York Times bestseller, *Men In Black*

"Ben Shapiro's new book, with good humor and style, makes the case that the right image isn't always the best thing to have while seeking the Presidency, but it is way ahead of whatever is second. So, wash out your hair gel, take off your make-up, settle down in your bathrobe and explore how candidates and their opponents create portraits than can change the tide of history. Just don't be photographed looking that way if you ever want to be president."

Barry Lynn, Executive Director,
Americans United for Separation of Church and State

"Don't let Ben Shapiro's irreverent wit and page turning anecdotes fool you. This is a massively researched, much needed, important work of modern history. This exposes our increasingly arcane system for choosing a president. As they say, 'The devil is in the details.'"

Doug Wead, former White House Staffer and author of the
New York Times bestseller, *All the Presidents' Children*

"Ben Shapiro's amusing romp through American history has a serious message: Image has always mattered in presidential politics, and yearning for an imaginary good old days gets us nowhere."

Dr. Marvin Olasky, editor-in-chief, *World*

"It takes a wise historian to know that small details can make up a more edifying tableau than the big picture. It takes a perceptive historian to know which details are most edifying. And it takes a good writer to present the details in a manner both witty and memorable. Congratulations to Ben Shapiro on all three accomplishments."

Eric Burns, author of *Infamous Scribblers*
and Fox News host

"Image, image, image! Ben Shapiro shows that elections have been that way from the start, but in our age of media manipulation, with candidates packaged like deodorant, we can be (and have been) sold a bill of goods. Shapiro's witty, dark comedy will make you laugh, but it should make you cry."

Ray Raphael, author of *Founding Myths*

"Ben Shapiro is one of the rising young stars in the conservative firmament, and Project President is yet another proof that his writing, his wit and his exhaustive research will be paying off for the conservative coalition for many years to come."

Jeff Babbin, editor of *Human Events* and
author of *In The Words of Our Enemies*

"Project President is laugh out loud fun. It's a welcome read during a glum political season. If you want to get to know Abe, Ron, Bill, Jimmy, and Dick up close and personal, this is the book for you."

Peter Schweitzer, *New York Times* bestselling author
and Hoover Institute Fellow

"Ben Shapiro's political analysis, always thoughtful and provocative, puts him in the very small circle of young writers whose work will shape our historical view of current events for decades to come. As part of the new vanguard of historians, Shapiro's *Project President* is an important book, and a delightful read from start to finish."

Russ Smith, founder of *New York Press*
and *Baltimore City Paper*

★ Project President ★

*Bad Hair and Botox on the Road
to the White House*

BEN SHAPIRO

THOMAS NELSON
Since 1798

NASHVILLE   DALLAS   MEXICO CITY   RIO DE JANEIRO   BEIJING

Published in Nashville, Tennessee, by Thomas Nelson. Thomas Nelson is a registered trademark of Thomas Nelson, Inc.

Thomas Nelson, Inc. titles may be purchased in bulk for educational, business, fund-raising, or sale promotional use. For information, please e-mail SpecialMarkets@ThomasNelson.com.

Library of Congress Cataloging-in-Publication Data

Shapiro, Ben.
  Project President: Bad Hair and Botox on the Road to the White House / Ben Shapiro.
      p. cm.
  Includes bibliographical references.
  ISBN 978-1-59555-100-9
  1. Presidents—United States—Election. 2. United States—Politics and government—Humor. 3. Political campaigns—United States—History. I. Title.
JK528.S53 2008
324.973—dc22   2007023844

Printed in the United States of America

08 09 10 11 QW 9 8 7 6 5 4 3 2

★ Table of Contents ★

Introduction

S ENATOR JOHN F. KERRY (D-Massachusetts) had to feel good on the morning of April 27, 2004. Just four months before, Kerry's presidential hopes had seemed destined for the incinerator; former governor of Vermont Howard Dean held a seemingly insurmountable lead in several opinion polls in the weeks leading up to the January 19, 2004, Iowa caucuses. In the last week before the caucuses, however, polls saw a sudden spike in support for Kerry.

And the polls were accurate. On the night of January 19, 2004, John Kerry won a sweeping victory, taking 38 percent of the caucus vote. Howard Dean's presidential campaign was effectively over, crushed at birth; his self-immolation in the immediate aftermath of the Iowa defeat—"*Yeeaaargh!*"—would become instant campaign legend. Meanwhile, John Kerry would go on to win virtually every other Democratic primary, including a big victory in Pennsylvania on April 27, 2004.

Kerry had to be confident about his hopes in the general election. He was running as a Vietnam War hero, a champion for the little guy, and a man who could speak truth to power. And he was succeeding. He was, as he dubbed himself after his Iowa win, "comeback Kerry." General election polls had him running neck and neck with an incumbent president in a time of war—and this was before the late July Democratic National Convention, from which Kerry could expect a sizable bump.

The world was a marble in John Kerry's hand.

Until 12:59 p.m. Eastern Time on April 27, 2004.

Then disaster struck. For though Senator Kerry was campaigning as an old soldier, a man of principle, a tall, strong, masculine fellow who could outfight, outdebate, and outrank President George W. Bush, he had forgotten one all-important fact: he was an elitist. He could rewrite his resumé; he could obscure his Boston Brahmin accent. But he couldn't change the crucial fact that he was, to the naked eye, a cross between the muppet Beaker and the Marquis de Lafayette. John Kerry looked like a French aristocrat. He sounded like a French aristocrat. He acted like a French aristocrat.

And, at 12:59 Eastern Time, Matt Drudge of Drudgereport.com broke the most fateful story of the 2004 presidential campaign: John F. Kerry got his hair dressed like a French aristocrat.

"On the Friday before his *Meet the Press* appearance," Drudge reported, "Dem presidential hopeful John Kerry flew his Washington, DC, hairdresser to Pittsburgh for a touch-up, the *Drudge Report* has learned. Cristophe stylist Isabelle Goetz, who handles Kerry's hair issues, made the trek to Pittsburgh, campaign sources reveal. 'Her entire schedule had to be rearranged,' a top source explains. A Kerry campaign spokesman refuses to clarify if Goetz flew by private jet on April 16 or on the official Kerry for President campaign plane. The total expense for the hair touch-up is estimated to be more than $1,000, insiders tell *Drudge*."[1]

The Grey Poupon hit the fan.

Fox News quickly confirmed the $1,000 haircut, and Brit Hume reported on April 28: "In an incident reminiscent of one of the great embarrassments of the Clinton presidency, John Kerry managed to have his hair styled while out of town last week, and he got it done by the same hair salon the Clintons used. The former president, you may recall, kept *Air Force 1* waiting on the tarmac in Los Angeles, 11 years ago this month, while Christophe of Beverly Hills came aboard and cut his hair. Christophe later opened a salon in Washington and one of his stylists, French-educated Isabel [sic] Goetz, does Kerry's hair as well as Hillary Clinton's."[2] The French Clinton. Not quite what Kerry was going for.

The $1,000 haircut became juicy fodder for late-night comics. "John Kerry, does he support gay marriage? Here's a hint: He gets thousand-dollar haircuts," quipped Craig Kilborn.[3] Jay Leno jibed, "$1,000 for a haircut. Which sounds like a lot, but have you seen the size of John Kerry's head?"[4] And David Letterman joked, "The campaign for the White House is heating up with John Kerry taking heat for throwing his Vietnam medals away, getting a $1,000 haircut, and wearing a 1970s wig known as 'the Leno.' There are really two sides to this story. And America can't wait for Kerry to present both of them."[5]

For the next six months, John Kerry's hair—and by extension, his elitism—became the central focus of the 2004 presidential campaign. On June 1, the Republican National Committee released an online game entitled Kerryopoly. One of the squares on the board: John Kerry's $1,000 haircut. "Most Americans can't afford yachts, private planes, thousand dollar haircuts or homes in Nantucket. But they can when they play *Kerryopoly*," poked RNC communications director Jim Dyke.[6]

"John Kerry tries to put a bunch of fancy, fancy talk—tried to disguise that record, sort of like his fancy haircut, fancy manicure, tried to disguise the whole thing," remarked the vice president's wife, Lynne Cheney, at a Kerry/Bush debate-watching party in October. "But there is nothing you can do to really—to really obscure that record. You can try, though. And in Wyoming, we've got a saying for what it is when you keep trying to make something that's not so good look good, we call it putting lipstick on a pig."[7]

Unbelievably, Kerry continued to shoot himself in the Versace-covered foot throughout the campaign. After he chose immaculately coiffed Senator John Edwards (D-North Carolina) as his running mate, Kerry remarked, "We've got better ideas. We've got great plans. We've got a better sense of what's happening in America. And we've got better hair." Kerry repeated the joke in Ohio and Florida.[8] Apparently Karl Rove was now writing John Kerry's lines.

Rove was also designing Kerry's photo ops. In three disastrous weeks, Kerry laminated his status as the Cannes Film Festival's presidential pick. On July 30, the Kerry and Edwards couples visited a Wendy's to celebrate the Edwardses' wedding anniversary, down-home style. Except that both couples left after a few minutes of posing for the cameras and returned to the campaign bus, where they had gourmet food awaiting them—"shrimp vindaloo, grilled diver sea scallops, prosciutto-wrapped stuffed chicken—all prepared by a Culinary Institute of America–trained chef." The all-too-predictable Marie Antoinette–invoking headline from the *New York Post*: "Let Them Eat Ketchup."[9] "The Kerry's [sic] and the Edwards' [sic] went to Wendy's the other day for lunch," said Jay Leno. "They made a big deal, oh, 'we're regular people going to Wendy's. We're going to go to Wendy's.' But when they got back they secretly had a gourmet meal delivered from a nearby yacht club. So I guess there really are two Americas, and they just don't like the food in the poorer one. That's basically the problem."[10]

Then, on August 11, Kerry visited Pat's Steaks in Philadelphia and ordered a Philly cheesesteak. With Swiss cheese.[11] Which is like ordering a hot dog at a ballgame with caviar on the side.

And, finally, the kicker. Kerry was a windsurfer. In January 2004, Kerry campaigners began handing out copies of a 1998 *American Windsurfer* magazine with Kerry on the cover.[12] This was already about as smart as handing out photographs of Kerry wearing a beret and sipping absinthe at a small café off of the Champs-Élysées. But Kerry wasn't done. The week of August 10, Kerry *again* had his hairdresser flown across the country, from Washington, D.C., to Portland, Oregon, in order to prepare Kerry for a windsurfing photo op. The photo op blew over, but Kerry would later go ahead with a similar photo op, his giant, French-pouf hair flying in the wind.[13] Pictures of Kerry windsurfing were plastered all over the Internet. He strongly resembles a slightly frazzled and thoroughly wet Pepé Le Pew.

On November 2, Senator John Kerry lost the presidential election by a hair.

★★★

MANY PEOPLE BELIEVE that our style of campaigning is broken. "Why," they ask, "should John Kerry's $1,000 haircut decide who holds the most powerful office on the face of the earth? Shouldn't politics be about *politics*? Shouldn't policy be the crux of our campaigns and elections? What does it matter if Barry Goldwater looked kooky in glasses or if Michael Dukakis looked goofy in a tank?"

It matters. Just ask Goldwater or Dukakis. These things have *always* mattered. We live in a visual world. As did the physiogamists of old, we like to think we can read a person's character by looking at him. A person's character is written "all over him." But isn't true beauty on the inside? As Jim Carrey puts it in *Liar, Liar,* "That's just something ugly people say."

When we vote, we vote not for a platform but for a person. And we judge our presidential candidates the same way we judge everyone else: based on the whole package.

Science says we make decisions about people within seconds of meeting them. According to a series of experiments by Princeton University psychologists Janine Willis and Alexander Todorov, people make hair-trigger judgments—we typically judge whether people are attractive, likable, competent, trustworthy, and aggressive all within less than one tenth of one second. Those judgments rarely change, even after people take more time to reconsider.[14]

Willis's and Todorov's findings are seconded by Michael Sunnafrank of the University of Minnesota, Duluth. Sunnafrank's research showed that we often decide whether we like or hate people within minutes of meeting them. "It happens so rapidly it's amazing," said Sunnafrank. "It just astounded me that after all that opportunity [to reconsider], there was such a continuing strong impact of those first impressions."[15]

This doesn't mean that impressions can't change over time—after all, Richard Nixon *was* elected in 1968. And it doesn't mean that policy doesn't matter—George Clooney could run for president tomorrow and lose big.

It does mean, however, that presidential candidates may only have one shot to convince voters that they should be president. To do so, they must package their background, positions, and looks into a convincing whole. And they must sell that image every hour of every minute of every day. As Roger Ailes, the former campaign aide to victorious presidential candidates Richard Nixon (1968), Ronald Reagan (1984), and George H. W. Bush (1988) put it, "You can have the greatest head of hair in the world, or the greatest smile, or the greatest voice, or whatever, but after two minutes you're going to be looked at as a whole person. All of those impressions of your various parts will have been blended into one complete composite picture, and the other person will have a feeling about you based on that total impression. Enough of that image has to be working in your favor for you to be liked, accepted, and given what you want."[16]

It is this necessity to "package the whole" that makes electoral campaigning such a long, arduous—and necessary—process. No man can hide who he is for months on end. Who the candidate is comes across clearly in speeches, in television ads, and at meet-and-greet dinners. When Jimmy Carter tried to portray Ronald Reagan as a radical extremist, he failed miserably—not because Reagan's politics were all that different from Barry Goldwater's, but because Ronald Reagan was a *different person* than Barry Goldwater. After Reagan's election, campaign advertising historian Kathleen Hall Jamieson reported that a Hollywood producer approached Carter media advisor Gerald Rafshoon and told him "that he should have known better than to try to portray Reagan as dangerous and insensitive. 'Let me tell you something,' said the producer. 'Ronald Reagan is not a good actor. I've known him for years and he's not a good actor. But he played in fifty-nine movies and in all but one he played the same role and that was of a sincere guy. Now, as I say, he is not a great actor but he knows how to play sincere people. And you should have known better. If you play sincere people in fifty-nine roles, it's got to rub off.'"[17]

The producer had it exactly backward. Reagan played sincere people because he *was* a sincere person. Every biography tells the same story about Ronald Reagan—he was a man who got along well with people, who generally said what he thought. Ronald Reagan was genuine and the American people got it. They voted based on it.

You could not build a winning campaign around Jimmy Carter's niceness, Barry Goldwater's tact, or Michael Dukakis's status as a "people person." The total picture candidates create must be different for each. Bill Clinton's "Man from Hope," rags-to-riches, likable uncle shtick wouldn't have worked for John Kerry; Kerry has a long reputation for elitism. Aside from Kerry's checkered marital past and Brahmin family history, Kerry is widely seen as an arrogant fellow. Such an impression is not without basis. Humorist Dave Barry told of the time he met Senator Kerry:

> Kerry once came, with his entourage, into a ski rental shop in Ketchum, Idaho, where I was waiting patiently with my family to rent snowboards, and used one of his lackeys to flagrantly barge in line ahead of us and everybody else, as if he had some urgent senatorial need for a snowboard, like there was about to be an emergency meeting, out on the slopes, of the Joint Halfpipe Committee.[18]

Kerry, in other words, is not the sort of candidate who could "feel your pain."

Similarly, Senator Bob Dole (R-Kansas) couldn't borrow Ronald Reagan's campaign playbook when he ran in 1996. While Reagan campaigned as a warm and genial father figure, Dole's caustic wit and less than polished appearance came off as more grandfatherly than fatherly. Dole, as former Clinton campaign manager James Carville put it, was "a candidate without luck or charm."[19]

There is no magic formula to victory. But candidates know that they are the product. If they market themselves badly, they end up next to New Coke in the garbage bin.

★★★

IT HAS ALWAYS BEEN THIS WAY. The politics of personality didn't begin with the Nixon-Kennedy debates of 1960 or even the advent of television campaigning in the 1952 Eisenhower-Stevenson race. From the very genesis of the American republic, Americans have cared about the *person* they were electing (of course at the *very* beginning, many voters cared mostly about the ale the candidates provided). George Washington campaigned subtly; Adams and Jefferson battled it out in the press. Had Adams looked like Jefferson and vice versa, the 1800 election might have fallen in Adams's favor. Had John Quincy Adams been a western military man rather than an eastern intellectual, perhaps Andrew Jackson never would have been president. Had handsome Franklin Pierce been dour James Buchanan's lost twin, Pierce would have remained an obscure former brigadier general.

Our most important presidents have reshaped voters' perceptions of personality—and appearance. Had Lincoln been clean-shaven rather than bearded, perhaps presidents Grant through Harrison would have looked less like refugees from a ZZ Top concert. Had Woodrow Wilson not looked like a banker, perhaps presidents Harding through Eisenhower would have looked less like the managers convention at Bank of America. Had John F. Kennedy not looked like a matinee idol, perhaps there would be no taboo on presidential baldness.

That is not to say that we elect candidates simply because they look like JFK (sorry, Teddy!). We elect them based on their positions, their personal histories, their personalities. Ugliness can sometimes be an asset, as it was for Lincoln, who famously turned his ugliness to his advantage in an 1858 debate with Stephen A. Douglas. After Douglas called him two-faced, Lincoln replied, "I leave it to you. If I had another face, do you think I would wear this one?"[20] Advanced age can sometimes help rather than harm; Reagan probably won the 1984 election when during a debate with Walter Mondale, he remarked, "I will not make age an issue of this campaign. I am not going to exploit for political purposes my opponent's youth and inexperience."[21] Great masters of politics can turn seeming weaknesses into advantages.

★★★

IF THERE IS NO MAGIC FORMULA for presidential victory, what should candidates do? One school of thought says that voters have an idea of the "ideal candidate"—Mr. President Right—and that if candidates can pattern themselves after that "ideal candidate," they can win. Shelves of books have been written attempting to define Mr. President Right. In 1959, *CBS News* journalist Eric Sevareid identified the ideal candidate as the candidate who could

> appear, in other words, to be the universal man, for we are a complex federation, we Americans, of different ethnic strains, economic conditions and geographical identifications, and to all of us he must somehow appeal. What American voters really want in their hearts is a man with whom they can personally identify, yet one who is a little better than they. One who is of them, but yet above them.[22]

It would be difficult to find a more vague definition of Mr. President Right than this. Not even Superman and Captain America rolled up into one could embody such a broad characterization.

If there is no Mr. President Right in theory or practice, we're left with our impressions. We gather those impressions from incidents like John Kerry's $1,000 haircut. The American public has a quick, keen eye for character; we want likability, toughness, charm, grit, honesty, energy, competence, sugar, spice, and everything nice. Most candidates don't have it all. But, as the old joke goes, candidates don't have to outrun the bear—they just have to outrun their opponents. Each candidate has one shot to prove to the public that their personality makes them the right person to claim the most powerful position on the face of the earth. How candidates parlay that shot into victory or defeat is the story of *Project President*.

★ 1 ★
Suits vs. Boots

WILLIAM HENRY HARRISON of Ohio was not a particularly strong candidate for the presidency of the United States in 1840. A "minor military figure,"[1] the sixty-eight-year-old former governor of the Indiana Territory was an able politician. He had won the Whig nomination for president by outlasting such giants as Henry Clay and Daniel Webster, but he had not been chosen for his superior intellect or political acumen. He had been chosen because he, like Andrew Jackson before him, was a general. He had also been chosen because he, unlike Webster in particular, had rural support; the Whigs had run three presidential candidates in 1836, with Harrison representing the West.

Most of all, Harrison had been chosen because he had no political convictions whatsoever. As campaign biographer Robert Gray Gunderson wrote, Harrison had wholeheartedly adopted Nicholas Biddle's 1835 advice:

> If Gen. Harrison is taken up as a candidate it will be on account of the past, not the future. Let him then rely entirely on the past. Let

him say not one single word about his principles, or his creed—let him say nothing—promise nothing. Let no Committee, no Convention—no town meeting ever extract from him a single word, about what he thinks now, or what he will do hereafter. Let the use of pen and ink be wholly forbidden as if he were a mad poet in Bedlam.[2]

Harrison embodied the Marcel Marceau theory of politics: keep quiet and you can silently mimic laughter all the way to the ballot box.

Harrison could afford to run on an invisible platform (the Whigs literally had no party platform in 1840)[3]—he was running against the unpopular, unattractive, and unsuccessful incumbent Democrat president Martin Van Buren. While Harrison was no natural beauty, he could invoke his long career of military service; Van Buren, ten years younger than Harrison and a lifelong politician, had no way to dismiss his shortness (five-feet-six inches), baldness, and general resemblance to Mr. Magoo. Van Buren was the Karl Rove of his day, except with more personal ambition; Harrison was Dwight D. Eisenhower, 112 years early.

Still, the election was not going to be a cakewalk for Harrison. Van Buren was Andrew Jackson's successor, and possibly the cleverest politician of his day. He had outmaneuvered Southern firebrand and former vice president John C. Calhoun years earlier, earning his nickname "The Little Magician."[4] He was a master of "efficient party organization," a mastery he used to triumphant effect in the election of 1836.[5]

It would take something special for Harrison to knock the "Red Fox" from the White House.

It would take pizzazz.

It would take sparkle.

It would take . . . logs and cider.

Harrison's campaign managers had scoured the earth for the right campaign imagery. They had labeled Harrison "Old Tippecanoe," reminding voters of Harrison's somewhat inconsequential military victory against Tecumseh in 1811. In 1834, a Whig newspaper had labeled Harrison "Old Buckeye," using his Ohio roots to link him with Andrew Jackson's similarly woodsman-oriented nickname, "Old Hickory."[6] It wasn't quite good enough.

Then, on December 11, 1839, one week after the Whig National Convention, Harrison's campaign strategy suddenly presented itself. A Democrat newspaper, the *Baltimore Republican,* suggested that if the American people truly wanted to get rid of Harrison, they should "give him a barrel of hard cider, and settle a pension of two thousand a year on him, and my word for it, he will sit the remainder of his days in his log cabin by the side of a 'sea coal' fire, and study moral philosophy."[7]

Two of Harrison's advisors, Thomas Elder and Richard S. Elliott, immediately seized upon the log cabin and cider imagery. If Van Buren was going to campaign against Harrison's western, hardscrabble, pioneer credentials, they thought he would lose and lose big. "Within the month," wrote Gunderson, "cabins, coons, and cider became symbols of resurgent Whiggery."[8]

Harrison supporters toted model log cabins around the country. Whig songs glorified log cabins and hard cider. Horace Greeley's pro-Harrison campaign newspaper was entitled *Log Cabin*.[9] Harrison took to using the log cabin and hard cider imagery in his speeches. In a speech at Fort Meigs, Harrison apologized for his oratorical shortcomings by referencing his identity as "an old soldier and a farmer," then guzzled down hard cider.[10]

Van Buren's own image contributed mightily to the Harrison campaign. Van Buren had an unfortunate weak spot: he was a dapper gent. And he was not merely a dapper gent: he was a *northern* dapper gent—a New Yorker. Even worse than that, he was a dapper gent from New York during a depression—a depression he had likely aggravated by refusing to support the National Bank.

It was only a matter of time before Whigs began using Van Buren's taste for shopping at Tiffany's against him. On April 14, 1840, Rep. Charles Ogle of Pennsylvania took to the floor of the House of Representatives to denounce Van Buren's lavish proclivities. The speech reads like a transcript from *Lifestyles of the Rich and Famous*. "The 'site' of the Presidential palace is perhaps not less conspicuous than the King's house in many of the royal capitals of Europe," Ogle railed.

> Martin Van Buren—plain, republican, hardhanded-democratic-locofoco Martin Van Buren—has [the East Room] now garnished with gold framed mirrors 'as big as a barn door,' to behold his plain republican self in . . . in my opinion, it is time the people of the United States should know that their money goes to buy for their plain hard-handed democratic President, knives, forks, and spoons of gold, that he may dine in the style of the monarchs of Europe . . . What has Martin Van Buren ever done? . . . Placed by the side of Harrison, what is he?[11]

Though much of the speech was false, Whigs quickly reprinted it and used it in the anti-Van Buren campaign.[12]

Other descriptions of Van Buren made Ogle's seem tame by comparison. Davy Crockett said that Van Buren "is laced up in corsets, such as women in town wear, and, if possible, tighter than the best of them . . . It would be difficult to say from his personal appearance, whether he was man or woman, but for his large *red* and *gray* whiskers."[13] John Quincy Adams, no rustic backwoodsman he, stated that Van Buren was "an amalgamated metal of lead and copper" with a "tincture of aristocracy."[14]

Whigs also took to song to express the contrast between "Golden Spoon" Van Buren and "Log Cabin" Harrison. One song carried these lyrics:

> Old Tip he wears a homespun coat
> He has no ruffled shirt-wirt-wirt.
> But Mat he has the golden plate
> And he's a little squirt-wirt-wirt.[15]

Another, to the tune of *Auld Lang Syne,* went like this:

> No ruffled shirt, no silken hose,
> No airs does Tip display;
> But like "the pith of worth," he goes
> In homespun "hoddin' gray."
> Upon his board there ne'er appeared
> The costly "sparkling wine,"
> But plain hard cider such as cheered
> In days of old lang syne.[16]

It wasn't exactly Cole Porter, but it got the message across.

Of course, the message was largely wrong. William Henry Harrison was hardly a poor boy from the wrong side of the tracks; his log cabin was rather plush, his birthplace was a two-story brick house in Virginia, and he also owned a "palatial Georgian mansion in Vincennes, Indiana."[17] And, according to Lincoln, Van Buren spent less on upkeep for the White House than any other president.[18]

The truth didn't end up mattering very much. On Election Day, William Henry Harrison won a resounding victory over Martin Van Buren, carrying nineteen of twenty-six states, including most of the Northeast.

Harrison gave a two-hour inauguration address in bitter cold weather, during which he did not swig hard cider. He should have. One month later, William Henry Harrison died of pneumonia, brought about by a cold he contracted during the address.[19]

★★★

AMERICANS LOVE FARMERS AND COWBOYS, rough and tumble characters from rural areas, candidates who work fields instead of crowds and wear boots instead of suits. We always have. Our roots are in the soil, not in the big cities; our hearts are with those who civilize the wilderness. Show us a candidate shoeing a horse, and our hearts palpitate; show us a candidate who walks the floors of the New York Stock Exchange, and we grow restless. Cowboy boots trump Armani suits.

In the battle between suits and boots, the boots have the upper hand. Presidents from non-northeastern states have an immediate advantage, particularly since the end of JFK's tenure: only Nixon, running nominally from New York, has emerged from the Northeast.

After we factor in the images of the candidates themselves, the suits versus boots divide becomes even more apparent. Boots aren't restricted to the South and the West, and suits aren't restricted to the Northeast. Eisenhower ran from New York and Adlai Stevenson from Illinois in both 1952 and 1956, but it was Stevenson, not Eisenhower, who came off as the suit. Reagan was from California and Mondale was from Minnesota, but Mondale came off like a high school principal. Wearing the boots in a presidential campaign is like putting Roger Clemens on the mound to face Gwyneth Paltrow. Except more one-sided.

A northeastern candidate has not won the presidency since John F. Kennedy in 1960; we've had three elected presidents from

Texas, two from California, one from Arkansas, and one from Georgia. Every one of them campaigned as a weathered wilderness man with a rags-to-riches story—or at least as a man who can ride a horse.

Meanwhile, suits have fared poorly in presidential elections. Candidates who appear too buttoned-down or intellectual annoy the public. In recent elections, such candidates have been Democrats; when such Democrats lose, the media portrays them as high-minded citizens unable to get in touch with an ignorant populace. But the problem isn't with the American people—it's with a Democratic Party unwilling to adopt a winning strategy. Like Republicans, when Democrats cultivate the boots image, they facilitate victory.

★★★

THE SUITS VERSUS BOOTS DIVIDE has been a factor in presidential elections since the very beginning. Leading up to the election of 1796, Jefferson carefully maintained his image as a philosopher-farmer in the mode of the ancients. As historian John Ferling put it, "Jefferson wrote letter after letter proclaiming his contentment . . . Jefferson claimed that his days were so absorbed with farming that he had time for little else, including reading out-of-state newspapers or books or reflecting on public matters." As Ferling also pointed out, Jefferson was apparently unoccupied enough to write 220 letters during 1794 and 1795.[20]

Jefferson's farmer image wasn't enough to win him the presidency in 1796; John Adams was George Washington's handpicked successor. But in 1800, Vice President Thomas Jefferson used his image as a Virginia farmer to great effect against former Massachusetts lawyer and incumbent president John Adams. While Jefferson disingenuously protested that his "private gratification

7

would be most indulged" if events would "leave me most at home"—at idyllic Monticello—he simultaneously campaigned vigorously against Adams.[21]

The Jefferson campaign consistently championed Jefferson's farming background, citing his *Notes on the State of Virginia*,[22] in which Jefferson wrote, "Those who labour in the earth are the chosen people of God, if ever he had a chosen people, whose breasts he has made his peculiar deposit for substantial and genuine virtue."[23] As a farmer, Jefferson certainly knew how to spread the horse manure.

Meanwhile, the Jefferson campaign labeled Adams an elitist and closet monarchist. Though Adams was also a farmer (his farm can still be visited in Braintree, Massachusetts), he was unable to counter charges of elitism. Jefferson's faux boots triumphed over Adams's manufactured suit.

★★★

JEFFERSON'S BOOTS SQUASHED ADAMS; Andrew Jackson's squashed Adams's son. Andrew Jackson ran in 1824 and in 1828 as the boots candidate against Adams's son, John Quincy Adams. Secretary of State J. Q. was a learned diplomat, a keen philosopher, a brilliant fellow. Jackson was a general, the former military governor of Florida, a rough-and-tumble character. In both 1824 and 1828, Jackson defeated J. Q. in the popular vote, campaigning largely on the basis of his own wilderness credentials and against J. Q.'s hoity-toity resumé.

"Old Hickory" campaigned as a wilderness man. And he had the most sought-after qualification in presidential politics: he had been born in a log cabin. He had made his reputation for intestinal fortitude at age thirteen, when he refused to clean a British officer's boots during the Revolutionary War. The British officer retaliated by cutting Jackson's face and hand with his sword; Jackson retained the scars.[24]

Now the victor of the Battle of New Orleans was setting his sights on the presidency. And he had backing from the common people. Jackson's supporters in Philadelphia, for example, pledged not to "surrender to a self-constituted aristocracy," but rather to back Jackson, "a statesman and a warrior . . . a friend to the *rights of man* and *universal suffrage.*"[25]

J. Q. Adams was similar in style, temperament, and appearance to his father. He was perceived as aristocratic and monarchical. During the 1824 campaign, he was mocked for his "slovenly dress and 'English' wife."[26]

Though Jackson won the popular vote in 1824, Adams became the president through a series of political machinations culminating in Henry Clay's decision to throw his supporters to Adams. Adams's victory was to be pyrrhic, however; after Adams appointed Clay as his secretary of state, the public reacted by accusing Adams and Clay of engaging in a "corrupt bargain."

By 1828, Adams's fate had virtually been sealed. Like his father, Adams was accused of monarchic pretensions and spendthrift habits as president. A Jackson election handbill with the list of Jacksonian candidates carried the message, "No 'favored few, booted and spurred, ready to ride us legitimately by the grace of God'"—an oblique reference to J. Q. Adams.[27] Adams was labeled a "pimp and a gambler"—at the time, an insult—and bizarrely accused of "[procuring] an American girl for the Czar of Russia when he was minister to that country."[28]

And just as in 1824, Jackson's campaign portrayed him, in the words of historian Paul Boller, "as a man of the soil who dropped his tools in the field like Cincinnatus of old to respond to his country's call to duty in time of crisis."[29]

This time Jackson won both the popular vote and the presidency.

And the beauty of the boots strategy was that Jackson did not need to fear being labeled an aspiring dictator or power-hungry boor. When he ran again in 1832 against Henry Clay, one Republican newspaper headlined, "The King upon the Throne: *The People in the Dust!!!*"[30]

Nice try. Jackson destroyed Clay—trampling him, like Adams, under boot.

★★★

ABRAHAM LINCOLN TOOK ADVANTAGE of his wilderness roots in 1860. Though Lincoln was running against two western candidates in Stephen Douglas and John Bell, and a southern candidate in John Breckinridge, Lincoln recognized the value of his dirt-poor upbringing. Lincoln was no political slouch; he had campaigned for William Henry Harrison in 1840, and had seen firsthand the value of the boots strategy. During the 1840 campaign, for example, he debated Colonel Dick Taylor. Taylor accused the Whigs of "foppery." Lincoln, who was already known as "the Rail Splitter" and was fond of wearing blue jeans,[31] moved toward Taylor . . . then, in a move Justin Timberlake would reenact a century and a half later, Lincoln suddenly ripped open Taylor's coat. Underneath, Taylor was wearing a ruffled shirt, velvet vest, and gold watch chain.

Lincoln quickly took advantage, contrasting Taylor's childhood full of "ruffled shirts" and "kid gloves" with his own Spartan lifestyle. He had "only one pair of breeches," he said, "and they were buckskin . . . Now if you know the nature of buckskin when wet and dried by the sun, it will shrink," Lincoln continued. "[And] whilst I was growing taller they were becoming shorter, and so much tighter that they left a blue streak around my legs that can be seen to this day. If you call this aristocracy," Lincoln quipped, "I plead guilty to the charge."[32]

Lincoln's supporters would use his wit and "hick from the sticks" reputation to similar effect in the 1860 election. At the Republican state convention in Illinois, Lincoln's cousin introduced him by walking down the aisle carrying two fence rails with a sign attached: "The Rail Candidate for President in 1860. Two rails from a lot of 3,000 made in 1830 by Thomas Hanks and Abraham Lincoln . . ." Lincoln took the stage, then declined to identify the rails as his handiwork, musing, "It is possible I may have split these rails but I cannot identify them . . . I can only say that I have split a great many better-looking ones."[33]

Campaign songs citing Lincoln's rail-splitting prowess became the rage. One, to the tune of Stephen Foster's "Old Uncle Ned" (a virulently racist song, ironically enough), went like this:

> We've a noble rail splitter, and his name is Honest Abe,
> And he lives in Illinois, as you know;
> And he has all the tools there to carry on his trade,
> And the way he piles them up isn't slow.[34]

The cartoons of the 1860 campaign routinely depicted Lincoln as a man of humble origins—the Paul Bunyan of presidential candidates. One, entitled "Taking the Stump" or "Stephen in Search of His Mother," shows all the other presidential candidates decked out in suits. Meanwhile, Lincoln stands to the side, wearing a simple white shirt unbuttoned at the top, leaning against—you guessed it—a rail fence.[35] Another print, also Republican, shows Lincoln in the same simple white shirt, this time wearing work boots and carrying an axe for rail-splitting.[36]

Even Lincoln's opponents fell into the trap of connecting him with the rail-splitting imagery. One cartoon entitled "The Rail Candidate" portrays Lincoln riding a rail labeled "Republican Platform," carried by New York editor Horace Greeley and an African American. Lincoln is turning to Greeley and complaining, "It is true I have split Rails, but I begin to feel as if 'this' rail would split me, it's the hardest stick I ever straddled." The rail refers to the 1860 Republican platform plank opposing the extension of slavery to the territories.[37]

Lincoln wasn't elected specifically because of his rail-splitting, but it certainly didn't hurt. It is fortunate for our country that Americans of 1860 were just as fond of logs as Americans of 1840.

★★★

PRESIDENT THEODORE ROOSEVELT'S prospects for reelection looked excellent in 1904. Roosevelt had assumed office after the assassination of President McKinley in 1901; he had become McKinley's running mate in 1900, adding weight to the ticket as a Spanish-American War hero. Roosevelt wore the prototypical campaign boots—he owned a ranch in North Dakota and was a hunting fanatic. His fondness for wilderness was legendary.

And he knew how to campaign. During the presidential campaign of 1908, TR would advise his would-be successor, William Howard Taft, on how to cultivate a sufficiently rustic image: "Photographs on horseback, yes, tennis, no, and golf is fatal." When a concerned Illinois voter sent TR a letter warning that golf was a "dude's game" and that Taft should "cast aside golf and take an axe and cut wood," TR informed Taft of the request, adding, "It is just like my tennis. I never let a photograph of me in tennis costume appear."[38] The boots strategy in a nutshell.

During the 1900 campaign, cartoonists ubiquitously portrayed

TR in his Rough Rider outfit, so it wasn't as though Roosevelt needed to remind the public of his boots credentials in 1904, particularly while running against a judge from New York, Alton Parker. Nonetheless, with the help of cartoonist Clifford Berryman of the *Washington Post*, TR created a powerful personal myth combining new humanity with his already mythical toughness.

In 1902, TR went bear hunting in Mississippi. After an unsuccessful morning, TR headed back to camp. Suddenly TR's bear catcher, Holt Collier, signaled that he had captured a bear. When TR reached the bear, however, he was disappointed to see that it was a scrawny specimen, already concussed by Collier and tethered to a tree. TR didn't have the heart to shoot the bear and told Collier to "put it out of its misery." Collier obliged using his hunting knife.

This wasn't a particularly important event in TR's career.

Or was it?

Cartoonist Berryman certainly thought it was. Berryman parlayed TR's sportsmanlike refusal to shoot the bear into some of the most important presidential imagery in American history. His cartoon depicted Roosevelt virtuously sparing the life of a black bear that had been tied around the neck by a white hunter—the cartoon was an attempt to analogize TR's mercy toward the bear to TR's protection of Southern African Americans against white oppression.[39]

Washington Post readers may not have understood Berryman's racial point, but they were universal in their love of the bear. As Roosevelt biographer Edmund Morris put it, "Berryman obliged—again and again, as he realized he had hit upon a symbol the public adored. With repetition, his original lean bear became smaller, rounder, and cuter . . . it became the leitmotif of every cartoon he drew of Theodore Roosevelt."[40]

In fact, Berryman went to ridiculous lengths to include the bear in all of his cartoons of TR. Even when Berryman criticized TR, he included the bear. One famous Berryman cartoon from 1906 was designed to criticize TR's vacationing at his Pine Knot retreat in Virginia. The cartoon shows TR running into the woods—so far so good—but also has a cute little black bear following TR, bearing his suitcase and umbrella.[41] Note: criticizing a president by connecting him with adorable forest animals is not an effective editorial strategy.

The bear frenzy didn't end with Berryman's cartoons. Berryman had timed his imagery auspiciously for TR: toy stores in the United States began issuing plush toy bears just as Berryman coined his bear cartoons. These bears soon became known as "Teddy" bears—to the everlasting delight of children worldwide.[42]

Who could vote against the boot-wearing man for whom teddy bears were named? Certainly not the American public, which re-elected Roosevelt in a landslide.

★★★

FROM 1912 TO 1948, America developed a peculiar fondness for suits. The transition from boots to suits is a testament to the power of President Woodrow Wilson, who won the 1912 election only because TR ran a tremendous third-party campaign, splitting the vote with incumbent president William Howard Taft. Wilson was a high-minded fellow, a former president of Princeton University, and subsequent governor of New Jersey. And he had a bold new plan for the direction of American government: government as an administrative agency. Such a plan would require an energetic executive who could get things done—and that executive would require tremendous power. In Wilson's view, the president was the only true representative of the people as a whole, and as such, the president would lead the way from the murkiness of politics to the practical business of administration.

Though Wilson was born in Virginia, he was a prototypical suit. It wasn't just his academic background—it was his method of speaking, his mode of dress, his general holier-than-thou manner. Wilson described himself as "a vague, conjectural personality, made up more of opinions and academic prepossessions than of human traits and red corpuscles."[43] *Harper's Weekly,* which endorsed Wilson a full year before the 1912 election, portrayed Wilson alternatively as a bespectacled and suited businessman[44] and a robed and capped professor[45] in its editorial cartoons. As George E. Mowry wrote, "Wilson was easy to respect, but difficult to love. Had the times not been what they were—a product of progressivism's decade-long emphasis upon moral duty and righteousness—Wilson might never have been nominated."[46]

In 1912, Wilson did not run as the progressive ultra-reformer he turned out to be. But during the course of his presidency, Wilson changed the very notion of what the presidency meant. The role of the president changed from that of statesman to "visionary"; the president became the "embodiment of the public will," as Ronald Pestritto put it.[47]

And as the embodiment of public will, Wilson used the kind of rhetoric that would make Julius Caesar blush. H. L. Mencken described Wilson's speeches thus: "When Wilson got upon his legs in those days he seems to have gone into a sort of trance, with all the peculiar illusions and delusions that belong to a pedagogue gone *mashugga.*"[48]

In assuming his status atop a pedestal of his own making, Wilson destroyed his own popularity and the popularity of his party. He also created a powerful image—the image of the banker, self-assured, competent. Warren G. Harding would look the part, as would Calvin Coolidge and Herbert Hoover. FDR would fulfill the image best, combining the imagery of Wilsonian vision with the able administrator, and adding a common touch altogether foreign to Wilson.

★★★

WITH FDR's DEATH, however, the line of bankers ended. In the election of 1948, Harry Truman would bring back boots in a big way. Behind his spectacles and close-trimmed silver hair, Truman was a boots candidate. A former haberdasher, judge, and farmer from Missouri, Truman had assumed the vice presidency during the 1944 election and the presidency after FDR's death in 1945. His popularity waned during his first term, leading to the election of Republican House and Senate majorities in 1946. By 1948, most observers thought that the Republican nominee, New York governor Thomas Dewey, would win the presidency in a walk.

Truman had one advantage, however: he was a boots candidate, and Dewey was a suit. While Dewey remained aloof and distant from the voters, Truman engaged with them, beginning a two-month whistlestop tour that would crisscross the country, covering some twenty thousand miles and delivering 250 speeches. His speeches were "hard-hitting and frequently folksy," and Truman focused heavily on farming interests.[49]

Reading Truman's campaign speeches today, it is amazing how much he reaches out to rural interests, relying on his own Missouri past for legitimacy. In his nomination acceptance speech, for example, Truman referred to "the 26th day of July, which out in Missouri we call 'Turnip Day'" while pledging to call Congress back into session.[50] In a speech in Iowa in September 1948, broadcast to a national radio audience, Truman stated, "It does my heart good to see the grain fields of the Nation again. They are a wonderful sight."[51] He then launched into a full frontal assault on Republican farming policies, allying himself repeatedly with the folks of the earth.[52] Of course, cultivating the farm vote was part of Truman's basic strategy; a report composed by his campaign aides suggested that Truman would have to carry the "West and the farm vote" if he hoped to win the 1948 election.[53]

Truman's boots strategy wasn't a masquerade; the man was folksy by nature. During a campaign stop in Ardmore, Oklahoma, Truman saw a cowboy riding a palomino horse. Truman disembarked from the train, opened the horse's mouth, and declared it to be six years old. "Correct!" the cowboy said. "Truman Gets Right Dope from Horse's Mouth" read the headline across the country.[54] Apparently Truman repeated the routine in Texas, declaring the horse to be eight years old. "Who'd of thought that the president of the United States would know about horses?" exclaimed the young owner of the horse.[55]

And Truman wasn't just a gutsy campaigner—he was a smart campaigner. In 1952, when Adlai Stevenson was running for president against General Dwight D. Eisenhower, Stevenson asked Truman what he was doing wrong. Truman went to the hotel window and pointed to a man on the street. "The thing you have got to do is to learn how to reach that man," he told Stevenson.[56] Stevenson never learned, but Truman was a master.

While Truman got along famously with crowds—crowds of thousands would show up to yell, "Give 'em Hell, Harry!"— Thomas Dewey seemed largely mechanical. David McCullough wrote, "Dewey, it was cracked, was the only man who could strut sitting down."[57] Even Dewey's stilted exclamations—"Good gracious" and "Oh, Lord"—drew ire.[58]

Dewey generally refused to sling arrows at Truman and barely deigned to discuss policy during the campaign. His speeches were full of tautologies and generalities. Just as today's politicians do,

Dewey would meaningfully utter sentences like "America's future is still ahead of us,"[59] then wait for applause.

Dewey's suit strategy led him down the primrose path to electoral defeat—and afterward, he recognized it. While vacationing with his family after the 1948 election, Dewey "took off his coat, rolled up his sleeves, squatted in the dust, and began pitching pennies with his two boys," as Paul Boller described it. "When his wife warned that photographers might catch him in an undignified pose he told her: 'Maybe, if I had done this during the campaign, I might have won.'"[60]

★ ★ ★

"Eggheads of the world, unite! You have nothing to lose but your yolks!" So ran the most memorable slogan of 1952 and 1956 Democratic presidential nominee and former Illinois governor Adlai Stevenson, the biggest suit in the history of presidential politics. It is no wonder that Stevenson lost the 1952 election by nearly 11 percent and the 1956 election by a whopping 15 percent margin.

Yes, Stevenson was running against one of the best presidential candidates of all time in Dwight D. Eisenhower. But Stevenson personified stuffiness, stiffness, and stilted philosophizing. He tried to channel Woodrow Wilson; instead, he channeled Ben Stein.

Stevenson recognized that he was no boots candidate; he quashed the idea of a campaign biography by remarking, "I don't see how you're going to do it. My life has been hopelessly undramatic. I wasn't born in a log cabin. I didn't work my way through school, nor did I rise from rags to riches, and there's no use trying to pretend I did."[61]

Still, Stevenson never understood Eisenhower's appeal, or his own inability to reach the people. "If I talk over people's heads,"

Stevenson quipped during the 1952 campaign, "Ike must talk under their feet."[62] Of course, that was precisely his problem: talking over the people's heads—treating them like students—is what being a suit is all about. And Stevenson talked over the people's heads routinely. After one speech, a television executive stated, "How did he get to be so *sure* of everything? He speaks as though he just got a wire from God. Somebody should ask him, 'Tell me, Adlai, how are the apostles?'"[63]

Stevenson campaign stories abound. He constantly rewrote his speeches to the extent that he could not read them, so defaced were they with his notes.[64] Despite the fact that Stevenson's speechwriting team was one of the most star-studded in history—it included such notables as Arthur Schlesinger, John Kenneth Galbraith, Bernard DeVoto, Herbert Agar, John Fischer, etc.[65] —the speeches themselves were masterpieces of pretentiousness. Stevenson's 1952 nomination acceptance speech contains passages like this: "Let's tell them that the victory to be won in the twentieth century, this portal to the Golden Age, mocks the pretensions of individual acumen and ingenuity. For it is a citadel guarded by thick walls of ignorance and of mistrust which do not fall before the trumpets' blast or the politician's imprecations or even a general's baton."[66]

The nomination speech is replete with redundant synonyms and ostentatious rhetorical flourishes: "the hard, the implacable," "their comradeship and their fealty," "argued and disagreed," "disagreed and argued," "neither equivocates, contradicts, nor evades," "our party's record, its principles, and its purposes," "partisan denunciation, with epithets and abuse," and so on.[67] Stevenson may have been running for president, but he sounded as though he were running for thesaurus.

Stevenson's speaking difficulties were nothing compared to his trouble with that infernal television machine. In 1959, when Stevenson was again questing for the Democratic presidential nomination, Mary McGrory wrote:

> In campaigns Stevenson broods endlessly over substance but remains indifferent to form. He scorns to learn the simple lessons of effective television delivery . . . Stevenson would never so much as go to a television studio for a voice test. Nor can he ever be persuaded to take a nap or a walk during the hour before going on the air . . . The opening rally of the 1956 campaign in Harrisburg brought a traumatic experience with the teleprompter, a device that President Eisenhower used with the greatest ease. Stevenson, however, fell among technicians who put fierce lights between him and the prompting boards, with the result that he looked from one to another like a frantic spectator at a tennis match.[68]

In his television commercials, Stevenson is clearly ill at ease. One of his commercials from 1956 featured Stevenson talking about peace with a young senator from Massachusetts named John F. Kennedy. The two sit side-by-side in the commercial. But while Kennedy sits comfortably and explains the Democratic position, Stevenson shifts in his seat, gets up, walks around, then sits down again. Stevenson goes on and on like a runaway jukebox, interspersing his mind-numbing litany with a veritable panoply of "uh." An uninformed viewer could easily conclude that it was Kennedy running for president and Stevenson interviewing him.[69]

If only the Democrats had been that lucky.

★★★

THE 1980 ELECTION PITTED a former boots candidate, incumbent president Jimmy Carter, against the president who revitalized boots once and for all: Ronald Reagan. Carter was no suit. As the former governor of Alabama and a peanut farmer, Carter had all of his boots credentials in order. When he ran against incumbent president Gerald Ford in 1976, Carter ran strictly on a boots platform. Campaign commercials touted Carter's family history and rural roots. His biography ad bragged that his "folks have been farmers in Georgia for more than 200 years" and showed him standing in a peanut field wearing a plaid shirt and jeans; other shots depicted him in a jean shirt leaning against the proverbial log cabin.[70] His commercials look like clips from *The Waltons*.

During his presidency, Carter attempted to bring a down-home style to the White House. In an early presidential broadcast, he appeared in a cardigan sweater and said, "I've spent a lot of time deciding how I can be a good president."[71] Unfortunately for Carter, he lost his boots somewhere in Washington, D.C. He likely lost them when the country began thinking of him as incompetent and weak. Being a boots candidate has drawbacks for governance: the image of the tough guy in spurs and a ten-gallon hat vanishes if the cowboy ends up acting more like Grace Kelly than Gary Cooper in *High Noon*.

Carter had hardly been tough with regard to either domestic or foreign policy. His own 1980 campaign advisors saw that he had squandered the public trust. Carter media advisor Gerald Rafshoon wrote a campaign memo bluntly asserting, "The public is now convinced that Jimmy Carter is an inept man. He has tried hard but he has failed. He is weak and indecisive—in over his head. *We have to change peoples' minds.*"[72] And *Washington Post* columnist Richard Harwood wrote, "After only two years in the White House, Carter's competence had become something of an international joke."[73]

With Carter's boots credentials up for debate, the door was open for Ronald Reagan—a throwback cowboy. Reagan grew up in Illinois, attended Eureka College in his home state, and then moved to Hollywood to pursue his movie career. Eventually Reagan became governor of California. But throughout his life people thought of him as a spokesman for a simpler time, a more rugged and honest time. Nicknamed "Gipper," "Dutch," and "the cowboy,"[74] Reagan entered politics with his boots image in tow.

Reagan bolstered that image in 1974 when he bought the Rancho del Cielo—the "Ranch in the Sky"—that he renovated and tended himself.[75] In his autobiography, Reagan spoke fondly of Rancho del Cielo, which came to be known to the media as the White House West: "Over the next eight years, the ranch was a sanctuary for us like no other . . . at Rancho del Cielo, Nancy and I could put on our boots and old clothes, recharge our batteries, and be reminded of where we had come from."[76] Countless photo ops revolve around Reagan chopping wood, mending fences, and riding horses at Rancho del Cielo. The relatively modest ranch largely came to signify Reagan. And Reagan didn't object to that.

"This," Reagan said, "is who I really am."[77]

Reagan exploited his hardscrabble roots throughout the 1980 campaign. His 1980 commercials are masterpieces of personality politics. A late campaign commercial, "This Is a Man," describes Reagan's childhood "in America's heartland, small town Illinois. From a close-knit family a sense for the values of family, even though luxuries were few and hard to come by." The ad states that as an actor his "appeal came from his roots, his character . . . he appealed to audiences because he was so clearly one of them."[78]

Reporter Lou Cannon echoed this glowing characterization:

His values were shaped in a day when most Americans lived not in the great, cluttered urban landscapes of our time but in towns and small cities surrounding a more pastoral land. When he was trying out self-characterizations early in the 1980 campaign, Reagan briefly referred to himself as a "Main Street Republican," a phrase intended to show that he was not a boardroom candidate like John Connally or an Ivy Leaguer like George Bush. The phrase, quietly discarded after the primaries because Reagan's advisers thought it made the candidate seem partisan and out of date, was an appropriate description of Reagan. Like all persons, he is a product of his time and region, his experience and his culture.[79]

Reagan was often photographed at his ranch in California. One of his favorite jokes sprang from his horse-riding photo ops. Jimmy Carter, Reagan stated, had contacted him one day to ask him a question.

"Ronneh," asked Carter, "how can yew look younger every day when I see a new picture of yew ridin' horseback?"

"Jimmeh," Reagan replied, "I jes' keep ridin' older horses."[80]

As Reagan shored up his boots image, Carter continued to undermine his own. During the presidential debate with Reagan, Carter strangely invoked the authority of his twelve-year-old daughter, Amy, while discussing nuclear disarmament. "I think, to close out this discussion, it would be better to put into perspective what we're talking about," Carter said. "I had a discussion with my daughter, Amy, the other day, before I came here, to ask her what the most important issue was. She said she thought nuclear weaponry—and the control of nuclear arms."[81] Nothing like relying on the advice of a twelve-year-old girl to boost that image of presidential competence and strength.

When the election came around, voters gave Carter the boot. Reagan moved into 1600 Pennsylvania Avenue—Rancho del Cielo East.

★★★

No presidential candidate in history has had his luck shift as quickly or as precipitously as George H. W. Bush. In 1988, he received a terrific White House–warming gift from the Democratic Party in the form of Michael Dukakis. Then, in 1992, he had his boots license revoked by a hick from Arkansas named Bill Clinton and a big-eared hick from Texas named Ross Perot.

Bush was lucky in 1988. He was no boots candidate—his Ivy League credentials and Connecticut heritage precluded that. By his own admission, he was a "boring kind of guy."[82] And he didn't seem particularly tough to the general public. When he ran for the Republican presidential nomination in 1980, Lou Cannon and William Peterson sensed "a lingering hard-to-define uneasiness about the man, a sense that he lacked toughness and grit. It led his opponents and the press to dismiss him as a fragile, rich Ivy Leaguer, a Texan who didn't own a single cow . . . A Carter campaign aide captured the feeling with a tongue-in-cheek slogan for a Carter-Bush campaign: 'Why change wimps in the middle of the stream?' His quip captured the problems that would plague the Bush campaign."[83] Bush maintained his image as a "wimp" throughout the Reagan years. In the fall of 1987, *Newsweek* came out with a cover story featuring Bush. The title: "The Wimp Factor."[84]

Fortunately for Bush, his opponent in the 1988 election was Massachusetts governor Michael Dukakis, a suit of suits. Though Dukakis's campaign tried to play up Bush's suit-ness—former Texas governor Ann Richards told the 1988 Democratic National Convention that Bush had been "born with a silver foot in his mouth"—the campaign couldn't overcome their own suity candidate. Next to Dukakis, Bush looked like John Wayne. Dukakis was generally perceived as soft on defense, soft on crime, and socially liberal—a Massachusetts liberal. The Republicans could have run a small bunny rabbit against Dukakis and looked tough.

Bush was in the fortunate position of having been Reagan's vice president, which alleviated the suit problem. He was from Texas, even if only nominally. He was a generally genial fellow, in contrast to the cold Dukakis. And in going after Dukakis in a series of hard-hitting attack ads, Bush only strengthened his image. He looked tough, not mean, especially when he juxtaposed his attack ads with ads glorifying the Pledge of Allegiance and the American flag.[85]

Bush also benefited from the media attacks. As his campaign manager, Roger Ailes, stated, "I think George was dramatically undersold. By the time he got to the convention, he had been described as a wimp, a man who couldn't make a speech, and a man who would cave under pressure of the campaign. I think the public saw him at the convention do a good job and give a good speech. And they said once again the media have hoodwinked us; this guy is not as bad as everybody keeps telling us he is."[86]

By 1992, Bush's boots persona had been badly damaged. He had not gone all the way in Iraq. He had backed down on his pledge not to raise taxes. He was no rancher or cowboy.

Unfortunately for Bush, he was faced with two boots candidates in 1992: Bill Clinton and Ross Perot. Clinton was homey in the Jimmy Carter mode—except Clinton was more personable, warmer, and more likable. Clinton's campaign commercials featured him as the kid from Hope, growing up poor and living the American dream. In his nomination acceptance speech, Clinton rhetorically asked why the American people should trust him. His answer:

> I never met my father. He was killed in a car wreck on a rainy road three months before I was born, driving from Chicago to Arkansas to see my mother. After that, my mother had to support us, so we

lived with my grandparents while she went back to Louisiana to study nursing. I can still see her clearly tonight through the eyes of a three-year-old, kneeling at the railroad station and weeping as she put me back on the train to Arkansas with my grandmother. She endured that pain because she knew her sacrifice was the only way she could support me and give me a better life. My mother taught me. She taught me about family and hard work and sacrifice. She held steady through tragedy after tragedy, and she held our family—my brother and I [sic]—together through tough times. As a child, I watched her go off to work each day at a time when it wasn't always easy to be a working mother. As an adult, I watched her fight off breast cancer, and again she has taught me a lesson in courage. And always, always, always she taught me to fight.[87]

What this had to do with trust was never answered; what it had to do with hardscrabble roots was clear.

Meanwhile, Ross Perot campaigned on sheer Texan gall. He sounded like Jed Clampett and acted like a high school principal. His populist rhetoric caught on. During his debate with Clinton and Bush on October 19, 1992, he dismissed both candidates with his straight-talking style. He called Clinton's record in Arkansas "irrelevant," since Arkansas "has a population less than Chicago or Los Angeles, about the size of Dallas and Forth Worth combined . . . I could say, you know, that I ran a small grocery store on the corner, therefore I extrapolate that into the fact that I can run Wal-Mart. That's not true." And Bush was given no quarter; Perot grilled him about his handling of the Gulf War. Perot summed up his own appeal aptly: "Now, look, I'm just kind of a, you know, cur dog here; I was put on the ballot by the people, not special interests. So I have to stand up for myself."[88]

Bush could not emerge victorious against the combined boots

of Perot and Clinton. Clinton—the man who essentially campaigned as a hick, Jimmy Carter 1976–style—became president.

★★★

GEORGE W. BUSH LEARNED from his father's mistakes. Bush was far more of a Texan than his father; though he was born in Connecticut, he was raised in Texas, becoming first a part-owner of the Texas Rangers and then a two-term governor of the state. He looked comfortable in a cowboy hat and boots, announcing his candidacy wearing both[89] and routinely campaigning in the outfit. Even his political enemies recognized his boots authenticity. Molly Ivins said of him, "W does not have his daddy's goofy, upper-middle class, WASPy streak . . . Culturally, W is more of a Texan than his daddy was."[90]

Like Reagan, Bush bought a ranch, this one in Crawford, Texas, where many of his photo ops originated. While George H. W. Bush used a Houston hotel as his campaign headquarters, W used the ranch. During a media tour, Bush called the ranch his "little slice of heaven."[91] Most prominently, Bush used the ranch as a backdrop while choosing his running mate.[92]

Bush's 2000 opponent, Vice President Al Gore, also attempted to wear boots. Though Gore was from Tennessee, he was well-known as a calculator and manipulator—not genuine enough to capture America's heart and about as exciting as a block of wood. Throughout the campaign, Gore tried to change his image, adopting more cowboy-oriented attire. A story from *USA Today* on May 17, 1999, highlighted Gore's new strategy:

Vice President Gore unveiled a two-part strategy Sunday to regain his political footing for next year's presidential race: an education policy blueprint and black cowboy boots . . . And in a bid to shed his image as a stiff campaigner more comfortable in Harvard salons than Hawkeye living rooms, he donned a short-sleeve, blue knit shirt and cowboy boots as he hopscotched by bus across southeastern Iowa, stopping in small towns from Lamoni to Fort Madison.

In recent days, the article reported, Gore had also "lost the suit and tie to demonstrate that he can connect with voters."[93] The *New York Times* similarly reported on Gore's "unbuttoning," explaining that "he has shed his blue suit (as per President Clinton's instructions) for a green polo shirt, khakis, and cowboy boots."[94]

Unfortunately for Gore, his transformation from buttoned-up suit to buttoned-down boots candidate seemed manipulated. Out-cowboying Bush would be a difficult task to begin with; for the stoic Gore, it was impossible. The media reported daily on Gore's image manipulation. Most famously, the media reported that Gore had paid controversial and kooky feminist author Naomi Wolf $15,000 per month to advise him on transforming from a "beta male" to an "alpha male" and wearing "earth tones."

The Republican National Committee quickly issued a press release entitled "Al Gore and the Big Bad Wolf." The press release included a list: "10 signs of alpha male." One of the signs: "Real alpha males don't get rolled to the tune of $15,000 a month to learn how to be alpha males."[95] Bush, too, leapt on the story, joking at a white-tie dinner that he had met a woman exiting the elevator at the Waldorf. The woman—"I think her name is Naomi or something like that"—had told him he ought to wear more earth tones, Bush said. "Can you imagine a grown man, paying $15,000 for somebody to tell you what to wear?" he asked.[96]

Gore blew it in 2000—he should have won, and won big. Though Bush lost the popular vote, he won the presidency by the skin of his teeth. Real boots candidates do not need personal makeovers. Hiring the cast from *Queer Eye for the Straight Guy* to choose your wardrobe automatically makes you a suit in the eyes of most Americans—as Al Gore learned, to his everlasting shame.

★ ★ ★

IF BUSH'S BOOTS WON HIM THE 2000 ELECTION, they certainly reassured his reelection in 2004. Over the course of his first term, Bush strengthened his cowboy image; even his enemies labeled him a cowboy. But running against John Kerry, a notorious suit, Bush didn't even have to buy a new Stetson. He could wait for Kerry to implode all by himself.

And implode Kerry did. The Kerry campaign was full of gaffes. Kerry decided to look masculine by talking about hunting in Wisconsin. When asked what type of hunting he preferred, Kerry stated, "I'd have to say deer. I go out with my trusty 12-gauge double-barrel, crawl around on my stomach . . . That's hunting." There was only one problem: that's not hunting. No one hunts deer while crawling around on the ground. Columnist Mark Steyn wryly noted:

> This caused huge hilarity among my New Hampshire neighbors. None of us has ever heard of anybody deer hunting by crawling around on his stomach, even in Massachusetts. The trick is to blend in with the woods and, given that John Kerry already looks like a forlorn tree in late fall, it's hard to see why he'd give up his natural advantage in order to hunt horizontally . . . if you're a 14-point buck and get shot in the toe this autumn, you'll know who to sue.[97]

Kerry supplemented this fiasco by going goose hunting in Ohio later in the campaign, in full camouflage. The media was barred from the actual hunt, though they were allowed to photograph Kerry and his buddies returning from it. While Kerry claimed that everyone in his group got a bird, he showed up without one. When asked where his bird was, Kerry stated, "I'm too lazy . . . I'm still giddy over the Red Sox. It was hard to focus."[98] It also turned out that Kerry had borrowed the camouflage and the gun for the photo op.[99]

Bush painted Kerry as an effete northeastern suit at every opportunity during the 2004 campaign. Kerry handed him the paintbrush.

★ ★ ★

ON FEBRUARY 7, 2007, MSNBC's Chris Matthews appeared on Don Imus's morning show. "I'm so sick of the Southern guys with ranches running this country," Matthews raged. "I want a guy to run for president who doesn't have a f - - - ing ranch."[100]

Matthews is in the minority. Americans love cowboys, men in boots. We like our leaders tough, but warm. We like our leaders decisive, but deliberate. While suits often raise images of fast-talking city lawyers, boots remind us of pioneers building civilization in the wilderness. Though many liberals believe that the label "cowboy" is an insult, nothing could be further from the truth. Americans love John Wayne. We do not like the lawyer in *Jurassic Park*.

Suits cannot comprehend the attraction of boots. In 1840, Martin Van Buren's supporters couldn't understand the attraction of William Henry Harrison. "In what grave and important discussion are the Whig journals engaged?" they asked. "We speak of the divorce of bank and state; and the Whigs reply with a dissertation on the merits of hard cider. We defend the policy of the Administration; and the Whigs answer 'log cabin,' 'big canoes,' 'go it Tip, come it Ty.'

We urge the reelection of Van Buren because of his honesty, sagacity, statesmanship . . . and the Whigs answer that Harrison is a poor man and lives in a log cabin."[101] More than 160 years later, John Kerry mused about George W. Bush, "I can't believe I'm losing to this idiot."[102]

They cannot understand the allure of boots. That is why they lose.

Not all candidates must actually wear boots—but without the ideals that boots embody, candidates may be doomed to defeat. Boots are more than boots; boots are an attitude, an *authenticity*. Think Claude Rains (the suit) versus Jimmy Stewart (the boots) in *Mr. Smith Goes to Washington*. Whom would you vote for?

★ 2 ★
The Long and Short of It

ABRAHAM LINCOLN would have been terrible on television.

His face was quite unattractive; his opponents in the 1860 presidential campaign harped constantly on his homeliness. "A horrid looking wretch he is, sooty and scoundrelly in aspect, a cross between the nutmeg dealer, the horse swapper, and the night man, a creature 'fit evidently for petty reason, small stratagems and all sorts of spoils.' He is a lank-sided Yankee of the uncomeliest visage, and of the dirtiest complexion. Faugh! After him what decent white man would be President?" exclaimed the *Charleston Mercury*.[1] One detractor went so far as to state, "Barnum should buy and exhibit him as a zoological curiosity."[2]

Lincoln had a poor speaking voice, squeaky and uneven.[3] While campaigning for Zachary Taylor in the 1848 election, Lincoln spoke in Massachusetts, where certain papers derided his "awkward gesticulations, the ludicrous management of his voice, and the comical expression of his countenance."[4] At Lincoln's famous Cooper Union address in February 1860—the most important single speech of his 1860 campaign—his voice was described variously as "thin" and "squeaky," "pitched most uncomfortably high" with "a frequent tendency to dwindle into a sharp and unpleasant sound."[5]

So Lincoln wasn't exactly John Barrymore.

But Lincoln had one physical characteristic that helped him enormously in both the 1860 and 1864 elections—he was exceedingly tall.[6] And height, even in the pre-television era, was an asset.

By his own description, Lincoln was "in height, six-feet-four inches, nearly; lean in flesh, weighing, on an average, one hundred and eighty pounds; dark complexion, with coarse black hair, and grey eyes—no other marks, or brands, recollected."[7] By the standards of the time, he was enormous; the average Union soldier stood approximately five-feet-eight-inches.[8]

Lincoln used his height to his advantage while speaking. According to William Huntzicker, Lincoln would routinely "crouch down and then jump off the ground for emphasis." He wore a top hat, an affectation that had the double advantage of holding his notes and attracting attention in a crowd.[9]

His height was an especially strong advantage because of his wilderness background. "The Rail Splitter," as he became known, was supposed to be strong and rugged—and Lincoln looked the part. Cartoons of the time depict Lincoln as incredibly tall, quite robust, and usually in shirtsleeves.

Lincoln also had the good fortune to run against a particularly short man, Stephen Douglas. Douglas stood all of five-feet-four inches,[10] earning him the sobriquet "Little Giant." His stature also earned him a constant barrage of insults. While running for the presidency in 1856, Douglas garnered the scorn of Senator Thomas Howard Benton of Missouri, who caustically remarked, "His legs are too short. That part of his body, sir, which men wish to kick, is too near the ground."[11]

The Republicans made a fortune in political capital by contrasting the gargantuan Lincoln with the "Little Giant." One election cartoon shows Lincoln and Douglas in a footrace. Douglas is tiny. Lincoln is predictably huge; his legs stretch over Douglas's entire body. Both candidates are separated from the U.S. Capitol by a Lincolnesque rail fence—a fence Lincoln will clearly be able to hurdle. Douglas, however, will likely plow right into the fence.[12]

During the 1860 election, Douglas blundered tremendously while campaigning. At the time, active campaigning was considered degrading, and Douglas faced ridicule for engaging in it. So Douglas decided to disguise his New York campaign as a trip to visit his mother.

This was not the smartest political move. Newspapers immediately jumped on Douglas, using his small stature to paint him as a child in search of his mother. One handbill, circulated throughout the country, was entitled "Boy Lost." It stated,

> Left Washington, D.C., some time in July, to go home to his mother, in New York . . . He is about five feet nothing in height, and about the same in diameter the other way. He has a red face, short legs, and a large belly. Answers to the name of "Little Giant." Talks a great deal, and very loud; always about himself. He has an idea that he is a candidate for the presidency. Had on, when he left, drab pants, a white vest, and blue coat with brass buttons; the tail is very near the ground.[13]

Another cartoon entitled "Stephen Finding 'His Mother'" depicts a tiny Douglas being bent over the knee of "Mother" Columbia (a symbol of the United States) and paddled for his support of the Kansas-Nebraska Act.[14]

Lincoln emerged victorious in the 1860 election. During the next five years, he proved that his physical stature was representative of his moral stature.

★★★

SIZE MATTERS. It has become a well-known political adage that the taller candidate wins the presidency—and the adage has generally held true in the television era. The height factor in the TV era has become known as the "Presidential Height Index." Richard Nixon in 1972, Jimmy Carter in 1976, and George W. Bush in both 2000 and 2004 are the only shorter candidates to emerge victorious since 1952, giving taller candidates a 71.4 percent winning percentage in that period. So the odds certainly favor the taller candidate, if we take that factor in a vacuum.

And it didn't start with television. If we go back to 1900, we find that the taller man almost invariably wins. Only William Jennings Bryan in 1900, Alton B. Parker in 1904, and Wendell Willkie in 1940 lost to shorter opponents—and both Parker and Willkie lost to shorter Roosevelt juggernauts. The last shorter-than-average man to win the presidency was William McKinley (five-feet-seven-inches) in 1896 and 1900.[15]

But height is not always a predictor of victory. In the pre-1900 elections for which height information is available, height seems to matter very little. James Madison stood a mere five-feet-six-inches and served two terms as president, defeating DeWitt Clinton at six-feet-three-inches in the 1812 election; Franklin Pierce stood five-feet-ten-inches and defeated the massive Winfield Scott, six-feet-five-inches, in 1852.

The insignificance of height in the pre-1900 era can largely be attributed to the fact that candidates were rarely seen in public together. The first official presidential debate didn't occur until 1960. The fact that Lincoln's height was such a monumental advantage in 1860 partially reflects the fact that he debated Douglas repeatedly in 1858. By 1860, the contrasting heights had been imprinted on the public imagination.

Nonetheless, height certainly affects how we vote, if only because it shapes our perceptions in general. We tend to think of our leaders as tall; we like them that way. Jewish tradition says that Adam and Moses were uncommonly tall; many illustrations of Jesus depict him as tall and strong. Height denotes strength; physical strength denotes spiritual strength; spiritual strength denotes honesty and decision-making ability. The chain of inference isn't always accurate, and when we have evidence that shows it to be wrong in specific cases, we ignore the height factor—after all, we changed our minds about Jimmy Carter between 1976 and 1980. Nonetheless, our first instinct is to lean toward the taller man.

Taller men have a wide variety of advantages in fields including business and politics. Taller men make more money.[16] Scientists say that taller men are favored by evolutionary biology.[17] Why do taller men have such an advantage? Economists Nicola Persico, Andy Postlewaite, and Dan Silverman theorized that taller men are more successful in business and politics because they have higher self-esteem. As Steven E. Landsburg of Slate.com reported, "Tall high-school kids learn to think of themselves as leaders, and that habit of thought persists even when the kids stop growing."[18]

Do we favor taller men because they have more self-esteem? Or do taller men have more self-esteem because we favor them? When it comes to presidential politics, the question is irrelevant: in either case, there is little question that taller men have a few inches on the competition.

★★★

GEORGE WASHINGTON WAS NOT a particularly amiable man. He cultivated a "majestic, even forbidding, public persona."[19] And it paid off—his countrymen saw him as a godlike figure even while he was alive. Washington's birthday was celebrated annually as a national holiday, leading one anti-Washington paper to exclaim that Washington's birthday was treated like "'Political Christmas!' What is the idea of this expression, but ranking *Washington* with Jesus Christ?"[20]

Benjamin Franklin famously toasted the general in quasi-biblical terms. At a dinner at Versailles, after the British minister had toasted George III by comparing him to the sun, and the French minister had toasted Louis XVI by comparing him to the moon, Franklin allegedly toasted Washington thus: "George Washington, Commander of the American Armies, who, like Joshua of old, commanded the sun and the moon to stand still, and they obeyed him." After Washington's death, his legend only grew; Abraham Lincoln paid him glowing tribute in 1842 by stating, "To add brightness to the sun or glory to the name of Washington is alike impossible. Let none attempt it. In solemn awe pronounce the name, and in its naked deathless splendour leave it shining on."[21]

Washington's status as a living monument was aided in large part by his astonishing height. Washington repeatedly said during his lifetime that he was six feet tall, but historians estimate that he was at least six-feet-two-inches, and perhaps as much as six-feet-three-and-a-half inches.[22] This would make him a full head taller than the average American patriot.[23] As Libby Copeland of the *Washington Post* breathlessly reported, "Despite what he looks like on the dollar bill, it turns out George Washington may have been kind of hot."[24]

His contemporaries made much of his height. John Adams bitingly noted that Washington's political stature largely sprang from his physical stature. Washington, Adams said, was "like the Hebrew sovereign chosen because he was taller by the head than the other Jews."[25] Adams's wife, Abigail, was quite taken with him when first she met him. "You had prepared me to entertain a favorable impression of him," Abigail wrote John, "but I thought the one half was not told me." Benjamin Rush gushed, "There is not a monarch in Europe who would not look like a *valet de chambre* by his side."[26]

Washington's height became a subject of conversation at a dinner party attended by Washington, Speaker of the House Frederick Muhlenberg, and chubby Pennsylvania congressman Henry Wyn-Koop. At the party, Washington began discussing exactly how people should address the president.

"Well, General Muhlenberg," Washington remarked, "what do you think of the title of High Mightiness?"

"Why, General," Muhlenberg answered, "if we were certain that the office would always be held by men as large as yourself or my friend WynKoop, it would be appropriate enough; but if by chance a President as small as my opposite neighbor should be elected, it would be ridiculous."

Washington, sober as ever, didn't even crack a smile.[27] For our nation's father, height was hardly ever a laughing matter.

★★★

IF HEIGHT WASN'T A LAUGHING MATTER for Washington, it was a downright crying matter for John Adams. Adams had the unfortunate luck of ascending the presidential ladder between the stately Washington and tall, aristocratic Thomas Jefferson. While Washington was a giant in his own time, Adams described himself as resembling a "short, thick Archbishop of Canterbury."[28] By contrast, Jefferson was, by one description, "tall, and with a mild pleasing countenance, but whose mind and understanding are ample substitutes for every exterior grace."[29] One of Jefferson's slaves, Isaac, said that Jefferson was "a tall, straight-bodied man as ever you see, right square-shouldered. Nary a man in this town (Petersburg) walked so straight as my Old Master. Neat a built man as ever was seen in Vaginny . . . a straight-up man, long face, high nose."[30]

Jefferson's Federalist opponents attacked his Frenchified image, attempting to label him a radical and an atheist—a Jacobin. "Can serious and reflecting men look about them and doubt, that if Jefferson is elected, and the Jacobins get into authority, that those morals which protect our lives from the knife of the assassin—which guard the chastity of our wives and daughters from seduction and violence—defend our property from plunder and devastation, and shield our religion from contempt and profanation, will not be trampled upon and exploded," queried the pseudonymous "Christian Federalist" in *A Short Address to the Voters of Delaware*.[31]

That the Federalists were unsuccessful speaks partially to Jefferson's physical bearing. Jefferson did not look the part of the Jacobin radical. He was mild-mannered, willowy, aloof. He was no rabble-rouser. He lived on an estate in Virginia and tended to his books. He was more Reagan than Goldwater, more Clinton than McGovern. Any attempt to paint him as Robespierre was doomed to failure.

Republicans were more successful in attacking Adams's physical stature. They portrayed Adams as arrogant, monarchical, and mentally unstable. Adams, unlike Jefferson, couldn't shake the unfair depiction, particularly in the wake of the Alien and Sedition Acts. He was overweight and bald, attributes that emphasized his average height. If Adams had looked like Jefferson, he certainly would have been more successful in his bid for reelection.

★★★

THE ELECTION OF 1812 RANKS among the most interesting elections in American history. Democratic-Republican incumbent president James Madison had mired the country in an unpopular war with Britain—a war for which America was deeply unprepared. Federalist challenger DeWitt Clinton of New York had the support of many northeastern Democratic-Republicans; as mayor of New York City, Clinton presided over the construction of the Erie Canal.

DeWitt Clinton had another advantage: he was physically imposing. Standing six-feet-three-inches, Clinton was well built and rugged looking, "with brown hair combed back from his face to reveal the high, broad forehead that at the time was held to signify deep intelligence," according to biographer Evan Cornog. His lofty air and noble appearance led his political opponents to nickname him "Magnus Apollo."[32]

Madison was easily the least physically imposing president of all time. Madison was diminutive, standing five-feet-six-inches[33] (some historians put him as short as five-feet-two-inches[34]) and weighing less than one hundred pounds. John Quincy Adams's wife, Louisa, wrote that Madison was "a *very* small man in his person, with a *very* large head."[35] At his inauguration in 1808, Washington Irving described him as "but a withered little apple-John."[36] "I do not like his looks any better than I like his administration," sniped Daniel Webster.[37]

If ever a president was ripe for the picking based on his looks and his policies, it was James Madison. If Clinton wanted to run as a critic of the war, he could do so while portraying "Little Jimmy" as a little man bullied into war. If Clinton wanted to run as a proponent of stronger prosecution of the war, he could do so while chiding Madison as a wimp. Unfortunately for Clinton, he wanted it both ways. His coalition was based on northeastern antiwar voters and southern voters who believed Madison was not prosecuting the war against Britain strongly enough. Clinton tailored his message to each group.

Historian Norman K. Risjord wrote, "In trying to appeal to both war hawks and pacifists, Clinton earned the distrust of contemporaries and the scorn of historians. The irony is that he probably would have made a better war President than James Madison."[38] The strategy of running *against* a war while simultaneously running *for* more strenuous prosecution of a war has never and will never win a presidential election, no matter how tall the candidate is.

★★★

JOHN QUINCY ADAMS SUFFERED from the same physical shortcoming as his father: he was short. Standing a mere five-feet-seven-inches, Adams was, according to biographer Mary Hargreaves, "short and somewhat plump, with a high-pitched voice and tearing eyes, he had little physical presence by which to command attention."[39] Adams was bald, overweight, and tended to dress badly. He described himself in his diary as "a man of reserved, cold, austere, and forbidding manners: my political adversaries say, a gloomy misanthropist, and my personal enemies, an unsocial savage."[40]

Running against the six-feet-one-inch military hero Andrew Jackson, Adams's image molehills became mountains. Jackson was tall and rather striking looking. "Extremely slender and slightly round-shouldered," wrote biographer Robert Remini, "he stood six feet tall and had strong cheekbones, a lantern jaw, a long, straight nose, and a mouth which 'showed rocklike firmness.' His teeth were long and loose and gave an ugly ghastly expression to his nasal muscle."[41] Anne Royall, one of Jackson's contemporaries, described Jackson as "very tall and slender . . . His person is finely shaped, and his features not handsome, but strikingly bold and determined."[42]

Comics of the time capitalized on the height discrepancy between Jackson and Adams. One political print from 1824 depicts

Jackson, Adams, and Henry Clay in a footrace for the presidency. While Jackson is nattily decked out in his military uniform and shiny knee-length boots, Adams resembles Wallace Shawn circa *The Princess Bride*, bending forward at the waist to stretch for the finish line, wearing low-cut shoes that leave his ankles exposed.[43]

Adams's height probably didn't cost him the 1828 election; after all, he never debated Jackson. Nonetheless, Adams's short stature made it easier for Jackson to paint him as an aristocratic pantywaist.

★★★

POLITICIANS MAY COME AND GO, but height is forever, barring osteoporosis. Lincoln didn't just benefit from his height in the 1860 election; he benefited from his height four years later. Running against Union Army general George McClellan, Lincoln exploited his height again to the fullest.

George McClellan was an average-sized fellow. Dubbed "Little Napoleon" for his early Civil War successes and his five-feet-eight inches stature,[44] McClellan looked shorter than he was because of his unnaturally large upper body. "He was commenced for a tall man and built for one, as far down as the hips," wrote a journalist.[45]

McClellan had been made general of the Union armies in November 1861, and he had butted heads repeatedly with Lincoln. McClellan was exceptionally arrogant; he wrote upon his arrival in Washington, D.C., in 1861:

> I find myself in a new & strange position here—Presdt., Cabinet, Genl. Scott and all deferring to me—by some strange operation of magic I seem to have become the power of the land. I almost think that were I to win some small success now I could become Dictator or anything else that might please me—but nothing of

that kind would please me—there I won't be Dictator. Admirable self-denial![46]

In 1862, McClellan began mailing political advice to Lincoln—advice such as leaving slavery intact.[47]

McClellan wasn't merely arrogant. He was remarkably reluctant to enter battle. The Powell Doctrine states that you should not undertake military action unless you have and are prepared to use overwhelming force; the "McClellan Doctrine" (if there had been one) would have stated that even if you have overwhelming force, it would be better to wait until a few more guys show up. McClellan would have felt comfortable only if armed with nuclear weapons and facing an enemy army manned entirely by small, mewling kittens.

This, of course, led to some conflict with Lincoln, who preferred that the Union win sometime before the end of the nineteenth century. The conflict between Lincoln and McClellan led to one of the funniest exchanges in the history of warfare. After Lincoln told McClellan to keep him updated on proceedings in the field, an exasperated McClellan fired off this missive:

To President Abraham Lincoln
Washington DC
      Have just captured six cows. What shall we do with them?
          George B. McClellan

Lincoln fired back:

General George B. McClellan
Army of the Potomac
      Milk them.
          A. Lincoln[48]

Another exchange was more cutting. After McClellan claimed that his cavalry was fatigued, Lincoln responded, "Will you pardon me for asking what the horses of your army have done since the battle of Antietam that fatigue anything?"[49] At one war council, Lincoln remarked to a group of assorted generals that if McClellan was not going to use the army, he "would like to borrow it, provided he could see how it could be made to do something."[50] It was not much of a surprise when Lincoln fired McClellan in November 1863.

The election of 1864, then, was a grudge match. In this grudge match, McClellan had the early advantage. The 1862 midterm elections had been disastrous for Republicans, leaving them with a bare eighteen-vote majority in the House of Representatives.[51] The defeat at Fredericksburg in late 1862 added to the gloom. Richard Henry Dana wrote to Charles Francis Adams, "The most striking thing is the absence of personal loyalty to the President. It does not exist. He has no admirers, no enthusiastic supporters, none to bet on his head. If a Republican convention were to be held tomorrow, he would not get the vote of a State."[52]

The tide began to turn with the Union's victories at Gettysburg and Vicksburg. But battlefield reversals could always turn the tide; subterranean splits within the Republican Party threatened to shatter the surface. Horace Greeley wrote, "Who does not see that [McClellan's] fortunes rise as the country sinks, and that his chances would be brightened by his country's ruin?"[53]

McClellan ran as a war candidate, repudiating his own party's platform. By running as an advocate for the war, however, McClellan made enemies within his party. And they exploited his height. Henry Raymond of the *New York Times* ripped McClellan as "calculating, whiffling, mousing, hopping here a little way and there a little way, full of consequence and yet ever trying to hide in his own little shadow; all ambition and no courage, all desire and no decision."[54]

Raymond wasn't the only one rapping McClellan about his height. Cartoons universally depicted McClellan as an undersized, pugnacious little gentleman. One print compares the 1864 election to a game of bagatelle, a table game similar to billiards. Lincoln is tall; McClellan is dressed as a child, crying, "This Cue is too heavy! and the Platform's shakey!! O! O! I want to go back in the yard!!"[55]

A cartoon from *Harper's Weekly* on September 17, 1864, depicts Lincoln as huge, literally holding "Little Mac" in the palm of his hand.[56] Lincoln is about the size of his modern-day monument; McClellan looks like a GI Joe action figure. A December 1864 cover cartoon for a periodical called *Frank Leslie's Budget of Fun* depicts a chasm over which lie two planks: one Republican, one Democratic. The Democratic plank is two planks tied together; one is marked "War Democracy" and the other "Peace Democracy." Lincoln stands, strong and tall, next to the single Republican plank; McClellan, looking like Verne Troyer with a handlebar mustache, stands next to the Democrat plank. Lady Columbia, who must cross the chasm, leans toward the hardy Lincoln.[57]

Lincoln won his reelection handily over the undersized but feisty McClellan. *Harper's Weekly* celebrated with a cartoon of Lincoln stretched, like silly putty, from the top of the page to the bottom. The caption: "Long ABRAHAM LINCOLN a Little Longer."[58]

★★★

FOR ALMOST SIXTY YEARS, height mattered very little in presidential elections. It became an issue again with the election of Franklin Delano Roosevelt in 1932. It wasn't an issue because either candidate was undersized; Hoover stood five-feet-eleven-inches, and FDR stood six-feet-two-inches. Height became an issue because FDR was wheelchair-bound.

In 1921, at the age of thirty-nine, FDR was infected with either polio or Guillain-Barré Syndrome. Paralysis spread up both sides of Roosevelt's body from legs to chest;[59] only with physical therapy was he able to simulate walking using a cane.[60] FDR quickly realized that the nature of his condition would have to be hidden from the public. Jonathan Alter wrote, "Contracting a disease such as polio meant being excluded from normal life, if not shunted away in dark back bedrooms or dismal hospitals that looked like prisons and had names like the Home for Incurables and the New York Society for the Relief of the Ruptured and Crippled."[61]

FDR's people quickly informed the media that he was on his way to full recovery. The media was complicit in burying the story—in the seven years from 1921 to 1928, until his inauguration as governor of New York, the *New York Times* ran no more than six articles mentioning FDR's polio crisis.[62] During FDR's presidency, the press took no photos of FDR struggling to walk, sitting in a wheelchair, or being lifted into or out of his wheelchair.[63]

Alter counted FDR's polio as a political plus: "Polio wiped the residue of Harvard snobbery off FDR's public image."[64] But it wasn't the polio itself that aided FDR—it was his apparent recovery from it. A man with polio—through no fault of his own, of course—gives the impression of physical weakness. A man who has beaten polio gives the impression of renewed physical strength. FDR ally and 1928 Democratic presidential nominee Al Smith elucidated the traditional view: the presidency, he said, "requires a man of great vigor and bodily strength to stand the physical strain of it."[65] FDR also engaged in health baiting. During the 1932 campaign, his team undermined potential Democratic rival Newton Baker by raising questions about the health of his heart.[66]

So for the rest of his life, FDR would play the part of the mildly inconvenienced polio recoverer. In 1924, he introduced possible

Democratic presidential candidate Al Smith while supporting himself on the rostrum.[67] During his 1928 gubernatorial race, he fielded inquiries about his health by sarcastically stating, "Well, here's the helpless, hopeless invalid my opponents have been talking about. I've made 15 speeches today."[68] In 1931, FDR hired journalist Earle Looker to "challenge" him about his health; FDR then agreed to be examined by three doctors, all of whom would testify to his physical soundness. Though one doctor blanched at giving FDR a clean bill of health after examining him, the ruse went as planned. FDR's spokesman compared his disability to having a glass eye or going prematurely bald.[69]

To underline his physical health, FDR decided to fly to the Democratic National Convention in Chicago and make his acceptance speech there; he was the first president to make a formal acceptance speech. When asked about flying, a procedure that was still relatively dangerous, FDR jocularly pledged to bicycle from New York to Chicago.[70]

Notably, Hoover never made an issue out of FDR's health. In 1958, Hoover wrote a touching tribute to FDR's battle against polio: "I greatly admired the courage with which he fought his way back to active life and with which he overcame the handicap which had come to him. I considered that it was a great mistake that his friends insisted upon trying to hide his infirmity, as manifestly it had not affected his physical or mental abilities."[71]

Perceptions of FDR's height—and by extension, his health—carried forward through his election in 1944. FDR's personal physician informed the public that the president had "nothing wrong organically with him at all . . . He's perfectly OK . . . The stories that he is in bad health are understandable enough around election time, but they are not true."[72] FDR again stressed his physical health, delivering a speech at Soldier Field before one hundred thousand people, riding through New York City in an open car in a chilly rain.[73] Not surprisingly, his opponent, Governor Thomas Dewey of New York, declined to make FDR's health a campaign issue.[74]

Of course, Dewey had image problems of his own, especially with regard to his height. During the 1944 election cycle, Alice Roosevelt Longworth, TR's daughter, uttered the quip that would dog Dewey for the rest of his political career. Dewey, she said, "looks like the little man on the wedding cake."[75]

The remark was damaging because it was so apt. Dewey stood five-feet-eight-inches[76] and was perpetually insecure about his height. He would not allow photographers to take his picture if he was not posing, fearing that they would make him look short; he told aides to keep tall men away from him when photographers were near. Somehow, a photographer snapped a shot of Dewey sitting atop a telephone book at his desk.[77]

Dewey's problem cut deeper than his height. Like the little man on the wedding cake, he was aloof, cold, austere. As governor of New York, wrote Irving Stone, Dewey's legislature found him "cold, hard, dictatorial, unsympathetic, and unfriendly; they didn't like him as a person."[78] *Time* magazine criticized Dewey's "lack of humor, his unwillingness to pose for trick shots for the photographers, his narrow range of facial expressions, his tinge of Scoutmasterishness . . . his lack of warmth (he rarely visited newsmen in the lounge car) and his superefficiency (which sometimes leads him, in normal conversation to say 'period' at the end of a sentence, as if he were dictating)."[79]

In 1944, Dewey ended up the bridesmaid—off the wedding cake completely.

And he would never be the bride. In 1948, Dewey ran again as the Republican nominee. This time, he seemed assured of victory. Truman was massively unpopular; the war in Korea was massively unpopular. While FDR had been "larger than life, even in a wheelchair," wrote

David McCullough, Truman "would always be the 'little man from Missouri.'"[80] Truman stood five-feet-nine-inches tall.[81]

But Dewey's image problem would not go away. He was still cold. Mencken described Dewey's speeches as "essays sounding like the worst bombast of university professors . . . [Truman] made votes every time he gave a show, but Dewey lost them."[82]

And he was still relatively short. Truman himself never attacked Dewey's height during the campaign,[83] but no one had forgotten the Longworth line. Walt Kelly, a cartoonist for the *New York Star,* began drawing Dewey as the man on the wedding cake.[84] Journalist Pete Hamill, then a youngster, remembered his father observing of Dewey: *"One good shot of whiskey and he'd be on his face on the floor."*[85]

In the most shocking election result of the twentieth century, Truman defeated Dewey . . . by an inch or so.

★★★

JIMMY CARTER GOT LUCKY IN 1976. For the first time since William McKinley in 1896, Carter won the presidency as the shorter, nonincumbent candidate. Of course, he was running against Gerald Ford—and the legacy of Nixon and Watergate. Carter was still concerned about Ford's height (six feet). Before the debates, Carter's television advisor, Barry Jagoda, requested that Ford stand in a hole to offset his height advantage, a request immediately rejected by the Ford team.[86]

But for Ford, the potential image advantages usually attached to height had been worn away by years of jocularity about his perceived clumsiness. Tall men are often perceived as stately, determined, decisive; Ford, through little fault of his own, became known as a moronic bumbler. On June 1, 1975, Ford fell down the last few stairs of an airplane ramp while disembarking from a plane in Salzburg,

Austria. One network newscast showed the clip *eleven times*, including once in slo-mo.[87]

Chevy Chase imprinted the image of Ford as bumbler into the public consciousness on *Saturday Night Live*. First, he stated on "Weekend Update" that Ford's new campaign slogan would be "If He's So Dumb, How Come He's President?"[88] Chase also made clumsiness a staple of his Ford impersonation, including slapstick gags in which Chase stapled his ear to his head,[89] stabbed himself with pencils,[90] and stumbled into everything in sight. Once Chase stumbled into a lectern and hit himself in the crotch so hard that he had to miss two weeks of airtime.[91] Chase admitted that his impersonation was politically motivated, calling Ford a "terrible president" and shrugging, "Ford is so inept that the quickest laugh is the cheapest laugh, and the cheapest laugh is the physical joke."[92]

The irony is that Ford was likely one of the more athletic presidents in American history. In his college days, he played varsity football at the University of Michigan and received pro offers from the Detroit Lions and Green Bay Packers. Ford was an avid skier, swimmer, and golfer. Nonetheless, the American public thought he was a clumsy oaf. His size only mattered in that the American public saw him as a *big*, clumsy oaf.

Despite his image problems, Ford closed the electoral gap in the late days of the 1976 election. He didn't close it enough; Carter took the election by almost two million votes.

In 1980, Carter would not be so lucky. This time he faced a taller man without the baggage of Nixon or the perceived clumsiness of Ford. Ronald Reagan embodied a certain dignity; standing six-feet-one-inch, Reagan walked tall and handled himself with aplomb. His affability compensated for his stateliness—he never seemed out of touch with his audience. During the 1980 campaign, the *Washington Post* described Reagan as "tall and handsome."[93]

During a stop in Gilford, New Hampshire, a white-haired elderly woman read a poem about Reagan:

> He's a man
> And he stands
> Ten feet tall . . .[94]

The poem was printed nationally, thanks to the *Post*.

Meanwhile, Carter was "a modestly built man, fragile-looking and soft," a man who looked "vulnerable," according to Edward Walsh of the *Post* in 1980.[95] Like Thomas Dewey, Carter was uncomfortable about his height and manipulated photo ops so that he would be the tallest man in the picture.[96] Garrett Epps speculated that during the 1980 election Carter would use a presidential rostrum fixed with a "man-maker"—an aptly titled device designed to boost Carter's height.[97]

Carter's physical stature damaged him because of his reputation for general weakness and incompetence. He *looked* wimpy. The American public thought he was weak, and his personal appearance didn't convince them otherwise.

Reagan won the 1980 election easily. Executive recruiter Robert Half partially attributed Carter's loss to his size: "While there were, clearly, many reasons for the outcome of the 1980 presidential election, the fact that Ronald Reagan (six-feet-one-inch) is more than Jimmy Carter may be extremely relevant."[98] But Reagan could not have won on size alone; his stature was greater than Carter's in more ways than one.

★ ★ ★

THE 1988 PRESIDENTIAL ELECTION featured the largest height gap of the twentieth century. Republican vice president George H. W.

Bush stood six-feet-two-inches; Democratic nominee Michael Dukakis stood five-feet-eight-inches. Dukakis had to exaggerate his height throughout the campaign. At the Democratic National Convention in Atlanta, marketers created life-size cardboard cutouts of the Democratic candidates. The cutout of Dukakis wasn't exactly life-size, however—it was an inch taller than Dukakis himself. "If we had him his normal height," photo vendor James Lane explained, "people would think our cutouts aren't the real size."[99]

The Bush-Dukakis height differential loomed especially large on television—a situation with which Dukakis was not particularly comfortable. "[Height and other image perceptions] do matter to some extent," Dukakis admitted to commentator David Frost. "I think I'd be a lot more comfortable if they didn't matter quite so much, but the American people get a great deal of their information and a good deal of their sense of who one is from television."[100]

There was good reason for Dukakis's discomfort. Johnny Carson routinely made note of Dukakis's diminutive stature. "Dukakis . . . is pretty confident now," Carson cracked. "I understand he's already bought Phone Book 1 to sit on in the Oval Office." "Dukakis . . . took a break campaigning today," went another Carson jab. "He was in a seafood restaurant in Boston and he asked the waiter, 'Do you serve shrimps here?' And the waiter said, 'Sit down, we serve anybody.'"[101] "He may be the first president in history," Carson joked, "who will have to be lifted up to see his own inaugural parade."[102]

Before the debates, William Safire offered advice to Dukakis regarding his height:

Don't let them stand you on a box. Every photographer in the world wants the picture of you trying to close the six-inch stature gap; they'll be crawling behind the stage to shoot any hidden podium or elevated heels. Cross 'em up by lowering your lectern.

Quote James Madison, who was not too short to father the Constitution; confess to having exaggerated your height (I suspect that your claim of 5 feet 8 on your driver's license is a barefoot lie) and keep evoking David and Goliath with "slingshot parties" to watch TV.[103]

Dukakis ignored most of Safire's advice. The Dukakis campaign spent political capital debating with the Bush campaign about permissible methods of hiding Dukakis's height, leading Carson to suggest that the Dukakis campaign wanted the candidates to debate from crouches.[104] In the end, Dukakis stood on an "artfully constructed mound hidden underneath the red carpet"; the mound boosted Dukakis three inches. There was only one problem: when the debate ended, Dukakis would have to step off of the mound. When he did, reported Maureen Dowd, "the six-inch difference in height between the men looked suddenly dramatic."[105]

Bush's height also scuttled a rumored Dukakis debate tactic. If the debate was going poorly for Dukakis, rumor had it that Dukakis would challenge Bush to ignore the panel and debate him man-to-man. If Dukakis had done that, reported *Time* magazine, "Bush stood ready to exploit his most natural advantage: the 6-in. height gap separating him and the Democratic nominee. Bush would demand that Dukakis come out from behind his height-adjusted podium as a condition for attempting any reprise of Lincoln-Douglas pyrotechnics."[106]

The Bush campaign didn't shy from poking fun at Dukakis's height. "If you want to know who's on the side of the little guy," joked Ronald Reagan at a college rally the week before the election, "well, I'll tell you—it's the big guy, the big guy from Texas."[107] Reagan was referring to Dukakis's running mate, Lloyd Bentsen (six-feet-two-inches).[108] At the Republican National Convention, Senator John McCain (R-Arizona) used Dukakis's height to blast his defense policies: "Michael Dukakis seems to believe that the Trident is a chewing gum, that the B-1 is a vitamin pill and that the Midgetman is anyone shorter than he is."[109]

Asked early in the campaign whether he could beat Dukakis, Bush remarked, "I've got the height advantage."[110] Bush also told reporters at a press session during the RNC that Dukakis was "short on defense—short, get it?"[111] One Republican bumper sticker proclaimed, "Our Wimp Can Beat Your Shrimp." "Is short stature so great a weakness that it is to be equated with weakness of personality?" asked Marilyn Goldstein of New York *Newsday*. "I guess it is."[112]

Bush capitalized on the height differential for two reasons. First, Bush needed to counter charges that he was a wimp. "The Wimp Factor," as the cover of *Newsweek* bluntly put it,[113] dogged Bush throughout the campaign. Bush admitted that the perception of his wimpiness made people believe—wrongly—that he was "a little short guy."[114] If the Bush campaign could play up the height issue, they could counter perceptions of Bush as wimp.

Second, Bush could capitalize on Dukakis's height because the imagery fit. Shortness creates a presumption of weakness; that presumption fit Dukakis, who was weak on defense, weak on crime, and easily buttonholed on red meat issues like the Pledge of Allegiance. Ulysses S. Grant was five-feet-eight-inches, but he never had to battle his height—even in the age of television, his height would likely have been a relative nonfactor. But Dukakis was no Grant.

On Election Day 1988, George H. W. Bush demolished Dukakis. In the aftermath of the election, Bush team members stationed an adjustable height platform in their press office. The platform carried a label: "The Mike Dukakis Memorial Platform." "We like to keep it high," quipped a Bush aide.[115] So did the American people.

★★★

GEORGE W. BUSH, standing five-feet-eleven-inches, didn't inherit his father's height. He is, however, the most successful "shorter" presidential candidate since William McKinley (1896–1901). In 2000, he defeated slightly taller Vice President Al Gore; in 2004, he defeated a veritable giant in John Kerry. Bush has single-handedly proven that the presumption in favor of height is just that—a presumption only.

The slight height disparity made little difference in 2000. Gore was taller, but he was also more boring—a thickly built totem pole. Bush was shorter but had bigger personality. No one thought of Bush as substantially shorter than Gore. Part of that had to do with Gore's primary battle with Bill Bradley (six-feet-five-inches). During the primaries, Gore (six-feet-one-inch) dubbed himself "the candidate of the middle-height voter." "I promise to represent the interests of the vast majority of the American people—the reasonably statured," he joked.[116] Gore and Bush were "reasonably statured"—no more, no less.

Height became an issue again during the 2004 campaign. Democratic nominee Senator John Kerry stood a whopping six-feet-four-inches, five inches taller than President Bush. Kerry attempted to capitalize on his height. On one occasion, Kerry told the media that Americans shouldn't be afraid to switch horses in the middle of the stream. "When your horse is drowning, it's a good time to change horses in midstream," Kerry gibed. "May I also suggest that we need a taller horse? We could get through deeper waters that way."[117]

Kerry's height advantage, however, never translated into political advantage. Kerry learned the hard way that there is a difference between being tall and *standing* tall. Throughout the campaign he was labeled a flip-flopper, indecisive and weak on defense. Bush, by contrast, stood by his positions; his opponents attacked him for his Texas "swagger."

Counterintuitively, Kerry's height made him the butt of jokes. Kerry's long face, stiffness, deep voice, slow speech patterns, and hunched-over bearing gave his political enemies ample ammunition. Rush Limbaugh tagged Kerry with the nickname "Lurch," after the character from the *Addams Family*. *Saturday Night Live* noted his resemblance to the Scream mask from the eponymous movies. He was compared to Frankenstein's monster.[118]

And Kerry, like Frankenstein's monster, was exiled to the political Arctic.

How did Kerry's height become a detriment rather than a benefit? The answer is simple. Height isn't everything. First impressions can be overcome. Kerry had a decades-long reputation for waffling. He couldn't credibly pose as an advocate of strong defense, particularly after his statement that America's decisions about war should be subject to a "global test" for legitimacy. Kerry discarded his natural advantage by demonstrating that his height did not connote decisiveness or strength.

★★★

IN THE BIBLE, the children of Israel sought to establish a monarchy after their ascent to the land of Israel. Samuel, the prophet, saw that the king would be Saul, son of Kish, "an excellent young man; no one among the Israelites was handsomer than he; he was a head taller than any of the people."[119]

Samuel decided to announce Saul's anointing. When the people gathered to hear Samuel's announcement, however, Saul hid. The people "ran over and brought him . . . and when he took his place among the people, he stood a head taller than all the people." Samuel said, "Do you see the one whom the Lord has chosen? There is none like him among all the people." And the Bible says, "All the people acclaimed him, shouting, 'Long live the king!'"[120]

The political draw of height has a long and esteemed pedigree. Saul turned out to be an excellent general and a decent king. Height was an indicator of his toughness and his strength.

But height is not a universal indicator. It only establishes a presumption. Short candidates can be tough; tall candidates can be weak. Candidates, after all, are only people, and people are individuals. Winston Churchill clocked in at just under five-feet-seven-inches;[121] President James Buchanan, whose disastrously indecisive presidency hastened the outbreak of the Civil War, stood six feet. A tall wimp should not expect the public to overlook his wimpiness; a shorter powerhouse is often able to overcome his physical stature.

Nonetheless, taller candidates have that instant advantage. They don't have to overcome a presumption of weakness; they can build from a presumption of strength. They have an immediate aura of authority. Shorter candidates must build from the ground up; taller candidates build their images from the top down.

Our ideal presidents are still men like George Washington, Abraham Lincoln, FDR, and Ronald Reagan. None of them were members of the Lollipop Guild.

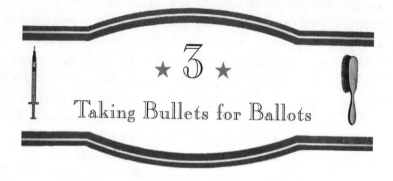

★ 3 ★

Taking Bullets for Ballots

GEORGE WASHINGTON LOOKED SPIFFY. It was June 1775, and the Second Continental Congress was meeting to discuss who would lead the Continental Army against the British. Washington, a delegate from Virginia, did not speak much during the proceedings.

He didn't have to.

His uniform spoke for him.

George Washington was the only member of the Second Continental Congress dressed in full military regalia.[1] Marvin Kitman wrote:

> He was wearing his old French and Indian War (1756–1763) uniform, which he had hung up in mothballs sixteen years previously—the blue coat with red facing of the first Virginia Regiment, which he led into battle . . . here was an ambitious young politician wearing his old army uniform to Congress among all those civilians. It was a most unusual occurrence, all political analysts would agree.[2]

Kitman also pointed out that Washington made sure to take his uniform out of storage for his first portrait in 1772—a portrait that included a conspicuously placed military rifle in the background.[3]

Washington stood out from the rest of the crowd, and not simply because of his enormous height. He was already a national figure, having fought valiantly, though somewhat unsuccessfully, in the French and Indian War. His early war experiences had demonstrated a certain incompetence. In one of his first military actions, Washington, then twenty-two, erected Fort Necessity. Unfortunately, Fort Necessity was about as successful as the Maginot Line. It stood at the bottom of a valley, open to enemy fire from surrounding heights on all sides. It became a muddy pond whenever it rained. All in all, it was a mess.[4]

But if Washington bungled at Fort Necessity, he excelled at public relations. After his first engagement with the French, he wrote to his half-brother, "I fortunately escaped without any wound, for the right wing, where I stood, was exposed to and received all the enemy's fire . . . I heard the bullets whistle, and, believe me, there is something charming in the sound." It was a felicitous turn of phrase—a turn of phrase that somehow made it into both colonial and British newspapers. Upon hearing the letter, King George III wryly remarked, "He would not say so, if he had been used to hear many."[5]

But Washington's PR wasn't all empty rhetoric—the man had personal courage. A year later, Washington, sick with dysentery, joined General Edward Braddock in a campaign to take Fort Duquesne. The British forces were outflanked and massacred; Washington had two horses shot out from under him. His coat carried the evidence of several bullet holes. Sent forty miles to British lines for reinforcements, Washington rode, walked, and crawled his way back. His exploits reinforced widespread perceptions of his military heroism.[6]

So Washington's reputation stood on his military background—

a background he trumpeted each time he insisted on being addressed as "Colonel Washington."[7] It was no wonder, then, that the Congress chose Washington to chair four military readiness committees. During the First Continental Congress, by contrast, Washington chaired zero committees.[8]

Washington's election as the general of the Continental Army was a foregone conclusion. He instantly became a colonial sensation. Dr. Solomon Drowne composed the following stanza after watching Washington ride by:

> With manly gait
> His faithful steed suspended by his side,
> Pass'd W—shi—gt-on along, Virginia's hero.[9]

With the victory over Great Britain, of course, Washington's star continued to rise. By the time he was forty-three years old, in 1776, his birthday was celebrated as a quasi-national holiday.[10] Washington had become a national institution.

Whom else would the country turn to as president? Washington's military service made him the obvious choice; he unified the country in war, and he would unify the country in peace. Washington's support for the Constitutional Convention had allowed the Convention to scrap the Articles of Confederation in favor of the new Constitution. His leadership would be necessary to legitimatize the system of government in its totality. "What will tend, perhaps, more than anything to the adoption of the new system will be an universal opinion of your being elected President of the United States and an expectation that you will accept it for a while," wrote Washington's friend, David Humphreys, in a letter to the general. Others were already busy labeling Washington "a second Cincinnatus," "the Saviour of America," and "Great Washington."[11]

Washington, needless to say, deserved all of his praise. He was not merely a general; he was a political giant. What he created in war he could have undone in peace; instead, he built a foundation upon which America has stood for more than two centuries. Upon his death, Henry Lee delivered the line most descriptive of Washington: "A citizen, first in war, first in peace, and first in the hearts of his countrymen."[12] Washington was first in war. But it was all that followed that made him truly great.

★★★

A STERLING MILITARY RECORD has never hurt a presidential candidate. Military men have proven their mettle on the battlefield; they have undergone severe hardship in defense of liberty. As president, men face similar, though more amorphous challenges. Americans have historically believed that he who stands up and leads under real fire can stand up and lead under political fire. The military image—the man scanning the horizon, on the lookout for potential enemies, prepared for action if action must be taken—shares a good deal with our image of the presidency.

The validity of military service has always been a sticking point in presidential elections. Every candidate who runs on his military record confronts political opponents willing to impugn that record. Andrew Jackson and William Henry Harrison had their detractors, just as John Kerry and George W. Bush do. Not everyone who serves is respected equally: Lincoln mocked his own service in the Black Hawk War, and Franklin Pierce's battlefield activity was viewed alternatively as cowardice or bravery.

With all of the hubbub about military service, however, one fact is certain: the so-called "chickenhawk" argument has never been politically successful. A *chickenhawk*, as defined by radical leftist

Michael Moore, is "a person enthusiastic about war, provided some-one else fights it; particularly when that enthusiasm is undimmed by personal experience with war; most emphatically when that lack of experience came in spite of ample opportunity in that person's youth."[13] Lack of military service, the argument goes, should dis-qualify any candidate for office who is not a complete pacifist.

Using Moore's definition, Americans have routinely elected chickenhawks. Think Lincoln, Wilson, and FDR—and that's just for starters. The simple truth is that military service is seen as a posi-tive for candidates—but not an absolute positive. His past military service will not aid an antimilitary candidate; a lack of military serv-ice rarely hampers a pro-military candidate. There are times when Americans prefer a military leader in power; there are times when Americans do not. But no military candidate has ever won office by assaulting a political opponent's civilianship. Americans respect mili-tary service—but taking enemy fire alone doesn't qualify you for the presidency. Benedict Arnold would not have been a candidate for president if he had returned to the United States after the Revo-lutionary War. He would have been hanged.

So military service counts. Nonetheless, during the last century, the luster of the military image has faded in political life. During the nineteenth century, Americans elected eight generals to the presidency. During the twentieth century, Americans elected only one. The twentieth century has seen only four genuine war heroes elected president: Truman, Eisenhower, Kennedy, and George H. W. Bush. Meanwhile, seven presidents without any military serv-ice have been elected.

This transition makes perfect sense. During countries' founding eras, they very often rely on famous generals to ensure national unity, guarantee the allegiance of the armed forces, and demonstrate the willpower to crush insurrection. Predictably, the most prolific period for U.S. president-generals came in the aftermath of the Civil War, when the country had to be reunified. After Lincoln's assassination, the next three elected presidents were Union generals; a fourth, Benjamin Harrison, took office between Grover Cleveland's two terms. Twentieth-century America was nowhere near as tenuous as nineteenth-century America; it did not need strongmen. Only Eisenhower, a politically adept national hero, was elected based on his military service—and even Eisenhower never experienced combat firsthand. And military leaders have been surprisingly unsuccessful in their most recent presidential bids; General Wesley Clark serves as a perfect example.

This isn't necessarily a bad thing. Electing presidents based on their governing philosophies makes government more politically responsive. After all, a war hero could turn out to be *Generalissimo* Francisco Franco. Safe and secure nations look first to leaders who campaign based on governing vision, not to leaders who campaign based on their ability to drill troops. In this sense, America has truly returned to her roots. After General Washington, America elected a string of philosophers: Adams, Jefferson, Madison, Monroe, Quincy Adams. Only the growing recognition that America faced military challenges within and without led to a string of military presidents.

Military service remains an asset. It demonstrates strength. It demonstrates willpower. For more than a century, however, it has not been the sole determinant of presidential qualification.

★★★

"SOME ACCOUNT OF SOME OF THE BLOODY DEEDS of *General Jackson*." So proclaimed the headline of a widely distributed handbill during the presidential election of 1828. The handbill featured the silhouettes of six coffins, meant to represent six militia-men Andrew Jackson had executed during the Creek War of 1813. The handbill accused Jackson of killing the men essentially for sport; their terms of service had allegedly expired, and they simply wanted to go home.

The executed men were described in glowing terms. "Harris was a Baptist preacher, with a large family," the handbill mourned. "Harris attempted to make some apology for his conduct, but while he spoke, he wept bitterly. The fear of death, the idea that he should never again behold his wife and little ones, and his son weeping near him, had taken such entire possession of his mind that it was impossible he should rally." Another militiaman was named Lewis. "Many a soldier has wept over his grave," stated the handbill. "He was a brave man and much beloved. He suffered twenty deaths." The handbill also carried a lengthy poem eulogizing the fallen militiamen, as well as a caricature depicting Jackson stabbing one Samuel Jackson "in the streets of Nashville."[14]

But Andrew Jackson was a genuine war hero. Dubbed "Old Hickory" for his toughness, Jackson commanded U.S. forces to victory during the Creek War. However, it was during the Battle of New Orleans that Jackson truly made a name for himself. That battle pitted British forces numbering eight thousand against an American force of only four thousand; the British were seeking control of the Mississippi River, a situation that could have doomed the United States to the ashbin of history.[15] But Jackson led the American forces to victory, inflicting more than two thousand casualties while sustaining just thirteen deaths, thirty-nine wounded, and nineteen missing in action.[16]

Jackson described the battle's end in magnificent detail. "I never had so grand and awful idea of the resurrection as on that day," he wrote. "After the smoke of the battle had cleared off somewhat, I saw in the distance more than five hundred Britons emerging from the heaps of their dead comrades, all over the plain, rising up, and still more distinctly as the field became clearer, coming forward and surrendering as prisoners of war to our soldiers. They had fallen at our first fire upon them, without having received so much as a scratch, and lay prostrate, as if dead, until the close of the action."[17]

The effect of the victory was electric. As Jackson biographer Robert Remini put it, "The Battle of New Orleans created the nation's first authentic military hero."[18]

Jackson would parlay that heroism into popular success in 1824 and 1828, and electoral success in 1828 and 1832. In an odd political maneuver, the Tennessee legislature adopted a resolution nominating Jackson for the presidency in 1824, heralding his status as "late major general in the armies of the United States . . . the soldier, the statesman, and the honest man; he deliberates, he decides, and he acts; he is calm in deliberation, cautious in decision, efficient in action . . . The welfare of a country may be safely intrusted [sic] to the hands of him who has experienced every privation, and encountered every danger, to promote its safety, its honor, and its glory . . ."[19] His national nomination by popular acclaim in 1824 relied almost solely on his military exploits.

Jackson's military stardom had not dimmed in 1828. Kathleen Hall Jamieson said, "Throughout the campaign of 1828, Jackson's supporters painted him as 'the Modern Cincinnatus,' 'The Farmer of Tennessee,' 'The Second Washington,' and 'The Hero of Two Wars.' Portraits of Jackson in general's uniform astride a horse were carried in processions alongside portraits of him in the clothing of a Tennessee farmer, hickory cane in hand."[20]

Supporters of John Quincy Adams relied on a two-pronged approach against the general. First, they sought to label him a dolt—a military man with no known ability as a statesman. One of their political handbooks labeled Jackson "no jurist, no statesman, no politician," explaining, "He is destitute of historical, political, or statistical knowledge; that he is unacquainted with the orthography, concord, and government of his language; you know that he is a man of no labor, no patience, no investigation; in short that his whole recommendation is animal fierceness and organic energy. He is wholly unqualified by education, habit and temper for the station of President."[21]

These qualms were not entirely without merit. Jackson was ambiguous on his politics. One particular Jacksonian ambiguity drove political opponent Henry Clay to distraction. After Jackson announced in an 1828 speech that he was for a "judicious tariff," Henry Clay sarcastically remarked, "Well, by - - -, I am in favor of an *in*judicious tariff!"[22]

But it wasn't just Jackson's ambiguity that frightened his political opponents. Senator Daniel Webster wrote before the 1824 election that he was "much alarmed at the prospect of seeing General Jackson President. He is one of the most unfit I know of for such a place. He has very little respect for laws or constitutions, and is, in fact, an able military chief. His passions are terrible."[23] Clay characterized Jackson as "ignorant, passionate, hypocritical, corrupt, and easily swayed by the basest men who surround him."[24]

Jackson's reputation for intellectual simplicity dogged him. One story had him accepting an honorary degree from Harvard University in 1833 (a ceremony boycotted by John Quincy Adams). After listening to a speech in Latin, Jackson rose to accept. His alleged speech sounds like a transcript from the Jesse Jackson Latin School for Public Speaking: "Ipso facto. Tempus fugit. Sine qua non. E pluribus unum."[25] Literal translation: "By the nature of the deed. Time flies. An essential condition. Out of many, one."

Of course, the strategy of attacking Jackson's personal ability was bound to fail. For the record, no candidate has ever won a presidential election by calling his opponent a simpleton. Though Jackson was not well-educated, he was a successful politician and an able administrator. He had served in the House of Representatives, the Senate, and on the Tennessee Supreme Court. He had served as the military governor of Florida. He was also the greatest military hero since Washington.

So Adams supporters were forced to attack Jackson's military record directly. They did this with gusto. Adams supporters distributed the coffin handbills far and wide; they had a "marked influence, especially in Ohio and Maryland, where they were the principal weapon of the Adams party. They were also widely circulated in western New York and in New Hampshire, and gave the Jacksonians in Kentucky a fright by the indignation they aroused there. In Philadelphia, where these handbills originated, an Adams parade was organized, in which the main feature was six black coffins for the militiamen."[26]

Such attacks were ultimately unsuccessful, however. Though Adams retained the presidency in 1824, Jackson won the popular vote and went on to claim the presidency in 1828. Jackson was immensely effective, both as a candidate and as a president. His effectiveness testified to his strength of personality—strength of personality that benefited him in Washington, D.C., as much as it had on the battlefield.

A story told by President Lyndon Baines Johnson in 1964 sums up the public view of Jackson. "I have heard it said that on the day he died," Johnson related, "the family pastor was talking with one of the President's closest friends. 'Do you think that the General will go to Heaven?' the pastor asked. The old man thought a moment and replied, 'Well, if he wants to go, who is going to stop him?' "[27]

★★★

LIKE JACKSON, 1840 WHIG presidential candidate William Henry Harrison ran on the strength of his military record. Unlike Jackson, Harrison's military record was more like Washington circa Fort Necessity than Washington circa Yorktown. Harrison's greatest military victory came at the 1811 Battle of Tippecanoe, against the inferior forces of Shawnee chief Tecumseh's "prophet" brother, Tenskwatawa. Harrison's forces were surrounded during the battle; he held the warriors at bay, but lost sixty-eight men. The Shawnee lost less than fifty. After the battle, the Shawnee abandoned their nearby base, Prophetstown, which Harrison torched.[28] As 1840 campaign biographer Robert Gray Gunderson stated, the victory was "rather dubious" at best.[29]

But that didn't stop Harrison supporters from turning Harrison into Julius Caesar. Harrison became "Old Tippecanoe." The rallying cry of the Harrison campaign became "Tippecanoe and Tyler, Too!" Campaign songs praised Harrison's victory at Tippecanoe; some of the songs included "Tippecanoe," "Old Tippecanoe," "The Soldier of Tippecanoe," "The Flag of Tippecanoe," "Tippecanoe and Jackets of Blue," and "A Tip-Top Song about Tippecanoe."[30] Harrison's supporters released a *Tippecanoe Text Book*, sold "Tippecanoe Shaving Soap or Log-Cabin Emollient," and smoked "Tippecanoe Tobacco" while dancing the "Tippecanoe Quick Step."[31] They joined Tippecanoe clubs.[32]

All that was missing was a declaration by Harrison that he was William Henry Harrison and he was reporting for duty. If Harrison had been able to land a jet on an aircraft carrier, he would have done it.

Meanwhile, Democratic incumbent president Martin Van Buren fumed. His supporters futilely attempted the same tactics Quincy Adams supporters had. Senator William Allen said that Harrison "does not rank among the successful and victorious generals of the late War." He also explained that Harrison, who was from Ohio, had been unpopular in Ohio during the war; Colonel George Croghan had been the popular fellow.

"While a sword was in preparation for the victorious Croghan," stated Allen, "a petticoat was contemplated . . . [for] Harrison."[33] For the rest of the campaign, Harrison endured the nickname "the Petticoat General."[34] General Jackson bashed Harrison's war record, averring that he "never admired Gen. Harrison as a military man or considered him as possessing the qualities which constitute the commander of an army."[35]

Democrats also pointed out Whiggish hypocrisy: Whigs were quite anti-general when Jackson was president, but Harrison's campaign had turned them into worshippers of the uniform. Henry Clay, a Harrison supporter, was suddenly a fan of military men turned presidential candidates; journalist Francis Blair rapped Clay for his inconsistency, sarcastically commenting that Clay was "as zealous for chieftains now, as he was against them a few years ago."[36]

Once again, military service trumped political know-how. This time, however, military service did not presage presidential stature. Harrison died a month after he took office.

★★★

EIGHT YEARS LATER, the Whigs successfully ran another general for the presidency: Zachary Taylor. The Democratic Party had split down the middle over the slavery issue, with former president Martin Van Buren drawing away a substantial number of Democrats to the Free Soil Party. They were not sunk, however. The Democratic candidate, General Lewis Cass, had been Andrew Jackson's secretary of war and had served valiantly in the War of 1812. And the Democrats could rightfully look with pride to the state of the country under James K. Polk. During the Polk Administration, America won the Mexican-American War, gaining "California, Nevada, Utah, most of Arizona and New Mexico, and parts of Colorado and Wyoming." Polk also ended the still-brewing Anglo-American conflict over the northern border of the United States.[37]

But the Whigs had something the Democrats did not have in 1848: a *recent* genuine war hero in the form of Zachary Taylor. As Bob Dole wrote, "The Whigs were desperately seeking a military hero in order to recapture the White House. Practically any soldier would do; convictions mattered far less than battlefield heroics."[38] Taylor was not "any old soldier." He was the victorious commander at Palo Alto, Resaca de la Palma, Monterrey, and Buena Vista. Taylor was not, however, a spectacular general. Taylor biographer K. Jack Bauer explained, "Taylor was a successful battlefield commander because he faced opponents whose tactical abilities and nerves were less than his and because his armies in early battles contained well-trained, self-confident subordinates."[39] Nonetheless he was a successful general, and a well-known general.

Taylor was also a political nonentity, an empty uniform. He had been a registered voter for forty years, but he had never voted. Taylor could not spell, "stuttered and squinted, lacked formal education, and was incapable of delivering a passable political speech." He was physically unattractive, standing a heavyset five-feet-eight-inches, with short stubby legs.[40]

Horace Greeley described Taylor as "a good old soul, but don't know himself from a side of sole leather in the way of statesmanship." Horace Mann was less benevolent in his assessment: Taylor was "a most simpleminded old man. He has the least show or pretension about him of any man I ever saw; talks as artlessly as a child about affairs of state, and does not seem to pretend to a knowledge of anything of which he is ignorant. He is a remarkable man in some respects; and it is remarkable that such a man should be president of the United States."[41]

"Old Rough and Ready," remarkable in his absolute vacuum of political credentials, captured the public imagination. Campaign songs enthusiastically lauded Taylor:

> Come fall in, boys, eyes right and steady
> And raise the shout for Rough and Ready,
> He licked Old Peg-leg with his Pass
> And now he'll use up Lewis Cass.
>
> (Chorus)
> Then go it, boys, strong and steady
> And raise the shout for Rough and Ready.[42]

Another song championed Taylor's candidacy by comparing him to George Washington, a doubtful comparison at best:

> Old Zack Taylor is the man,
> His countrymen select him,
> To fill the chair of Washington;
> And surely they'll elect him.[43]

All in all, campaign stops must have been a rollicking good time.

Cartoons of the time invariably depict Taylor in uniform, despite the fact that he did not like wearing his uniform, preferring to dress in "old clothes and huge tatterdemalion straw hats."[44] One campaign print shows Taylor uniformed, surrounded by framed scenes from his four major battle victories.[45] Even cartoons designed to target

Taylor reinforced his military image. One such cartoon, utilizing tried-and-true "military man as wholesale murderer" imagery, has Taylor in full military regalia, sitting atop a mountain of human skulls. The title: "An Available Candidate. The One Qualification of a Whig President."[46]

Taylor *was* available, and that was enough to lift him to victory in 1848. Taylor turned out to be a true nationalist, threatening the South with war if they made good on their threats to secede. Anyone "taken in rebellion against the Union, he would hang . . . with less reluctance than he had hanged deserters and spies in Mexico," Taylor said.[47] He never got the chance, dying two years into his term of office. His son, Richard, would end up fighting as a general during the Civil War—on the side of the Confederacy.[48]

★ ★ ★

THE 1852 ELECTION was the most martial election in American history. Both the Whigs and the Democrats ran major Mexican War heroes: General Winfield Scott for the Whigs, General Franklin Pierce for the Democrats. Scott, nicknamed "Old Fuss and Feathers" for his fancy wardrobe and high-falutin' airs, had served with distinction during the Mexican War. Scott was the nineteenth-century equivalent of General Douglas MacArthur. He served heroically during the War of 1812; he served even more heroically during the Mexican War, capturing Mexico City. He would go on to design the North's original Civil War strategy after his defeat in 1852—a strategy that was initially rejected in part, but adopted in whole over time, successfully, by Abraham Lincoln.

Franklin Pierce was far less of a hero than Scott during the course of his military career; he had been a brigadier general under Scott during the Mexican War. Pierce was an absolutely out-of-left-field nominee for president. The Democratic Party splintered during the convention; Pierce was chosen as the nominee on the forty-ninth ballot. He represented a split party by acting the part of a split candidate. Though Pierce hailed from New Hampshire, deep in antislavery territory, Pierce endorsed the morally indefensible Fugitive Slave Act.

Because the Whigs and Democrats were both split over the issue of slavery, the campaign focused almost exclusively on the military service of each candidate. It was an incredibly nasty campaign. Pierce supporters dragged out an episode from forty-three years earlier: Scott had been court-martialed for bad-mouthing a superior officer, convicted of "unofficer-like conduct," and sentenced to a year of suspension without pay.[49]

They also brought up an unfortunate spat with General Andrew Jackson. Scott bore no love for Jackson, whom Scott felt had grabbed all the War of 1812 glory for himself at the Battle of New Orleans. In 1817, Jackson bridled at a minor breach of military etiquette he received at the hands of Secretary of War George Graham. Jackson promptly upbraided Graham. Scott responded by castigating Jackson in public. When Jackson found out, he challenged Scott to a duel, calling Scott a "bully." Scott backed down, explaining, "I should think it would be very easy to console yourself under this refusal, by the application of a few epithets, such as coward, etc., to the object of your resentment, and I here promise to leave you until the next war to persuade yourself of their truth." Jackson was not placated by this high-handed response: he published the entire exchange.[50] It made for great fodder thirty-five years later. In 1852, it must have occurred to Scott that he would have been better off shooting Jackson.

Scott's political opponents also took the Quincy Adams tack— they attacked Scott as a brutal executioner of deserters. During the

Mexican War, several dozen Irish soldiers defected to the Mexican side and formed the San Patricios Brigade, convinced that they would be furthering the goals of Catholicism by doing so. It was a clear case of desertion, and Scott had no choice but to execute them. Pierce supporters "cynically used [the story] to infuriate those of Irish extraction."[51]

There was also the issue of Scott's widely reported complaints during the Mexican War. Scott had been called back to Washington to help President Polk come up with a plan to win the war. Eventually Polk settled on the idea of occupying large chunks of Mexico in an attempt to force the Mexicans to the negotiating table. Scott immediately began organizing the military effort that would be necessary for such a strategy.

Unfortunately for Scott, President Polk was undermining him. Polk was a Democrat; Scott was a Whig. Polk wanted Scott out of Washington, D.C., as fast as possible; Scott wanted to stay to finish organizing the effort. So Polk threatened to prevent Scott from taking up rank as general in chief. Scott responded by writing a miffed letter to Secretary of War William Marcy in which he penned the lines that would haunt him the rest of his career: he was, he wrote, "too old a soldier" to place himself in "the most perilous of all positions: A fire, upon my rear, from Washington, and a fire, in front, from the Mexicans."

Then, worse news for Scott: Zachary Taylor had won major victories at the Rio Grande. Scott would be denied his post as general in chief, Marcy informed Scott. Scott again fired off an ill-considered missive: "Your letter of this day, received at 6 PM, as I sat down to a hasty plate of soup . . ." Scott biographer John S. D. Eisenhower wrote, "That did it! Polk and Marcy published the letter in the *Congressional Globe* . . . The public laughed at the spectacle of a pompous general simpering at not getting what he wanted.

Trivial as the matter was, Scott never lived it down."[52] Political cartoons from the 1852 election routinely depicted a spoiled Scott sitting down to a nice bowl of soup.[53]

Most disgusting, Pierce supporters made an issue of a serious wound Scott received during the War of 1812. At the Battle of Lundy's Lane, Scott took a musket ball in the left shoulder, losing full use of his shoulder for the rest of his life.[54] Conflating Scott's "fire upon my rear" letter with his wound, political opponents suggested that Scott had been wounded "in the rear."[55]

If Scott suffered the slings and arrows of outrageous politics, Pierce fared no better. Pierce's military fame sprang from his gallant personal action at the Battle of Contreras during the Mexican War. Serving as a brigadier general under Scott, suffering from a serious ankle wound he had received the day before, Pierce insisted on returning to the battlefield, where he subsequently fainted.[56]

For the public of 1852, there was gallantry in battle and there was fainting in battle—and ne'er the twain should meet. Scott supporters pilloried Pierce for fainting, pasting him with the label "the fainting general."[57] One political cartoon of the time shows Pierce in two settings. In the first setting, he trains his troops in New Hampshire, bravely standing out front. In the second setting, he follows his troops into battle in Mexico, whining, "Oh! how bad I feel, and every Step I go forward, I feel worse. I got such a pain in the abdomen I must resign my Command and go home."[58]

Another cartoon depicts Pierce, chased up a tree by Democrats desperate for a candidate, complaining, "Gentlemen don't fire! If you please I cant [sic] stand the smell of Powder! It makes me feel faint even to think of it!!"[59]

In the end, Pierce triumphed. The Whig splits were simply too wide for Scott to bridge. Pierce was a nonentity, but a benevolent nonentity.

Unfortunately, Pierce was not quite so benevolent as president. He turned out to be one of the worst presidents in American history, presiding over the Kansas-Nebraska Act, ruling in favor of an illegitimate pro-slavery government in Kansas and essentially paving the way for the Civil War.

★★★

IN 1864, GENERAL GEORGE MCCLELLAN made his bid to oust President Abraham Lincoln. Lincoln had ousted McClellan from his post as general of the Union Army the year before. McClellan's run for president wasn't just politics—it was personal.

McClellan always had a low opinion of Lincoln. Lincoln was "an idiot," he said.[60] "I can't tell you how disgusted I am becoming with these wretched politicians—they are a most despicable set of men," he wrote to his wife in 1861. "I am becoming daily more disgusted with this imbecile administration . . . The presdt. is nothing more than a well-meaning baboon . . . 'the original gorilla' . . . It is sickening in the extreme . . . [to] see the weakness and unfitness of the poor beings who control the destinies of this great country."[61] Lincoln, then, was the first president to be called a smirking chimp.

McClellan supporters came in two stripes: Copperheads, who supported an immediate peace settlement and opposed abolition of slavery, and War Democrats, who wished to win the war. McClellan's Copperhead supporters were loudest and most obnoxious. They didn't back down from McClellan's assessment of Lincoln during the campaign of 1864. One particularly scurrilous, virulently racist piece entitled "The Lincoln Catechism" was released by New York Democrats:

I.

What is the Constitution?
A compact with hell—now obsolete.

II.

By whom hath the Constitution been made obsolete?
By Abraham Africanus the First . . .

Lesson the Fourth . . .
III.

What do loyal leagues call the masses of the people?
"A herd of cattle" – *vide* Secretary Stanton.

IV.

How many of this "Herd of cattle" have the abolitionists
caused to be maimed or slain in this war?
One million.

V.

How many widows have they made?
Five hundred thousand.

VI.

How many orphans?
Ten hundred thousand . . .

Lesson the Ninth . . .
VII.

Was Mr. Lincoln ever distinguished as a military officer?
He was—In the Black Hawk war.

VIII.

What high military position did he hold in that war?
He was a cook.

IX.

Was he distinguished for anything except his genius as a cook?
Yes—he often pretended to see Indians in the woods,
where it was afterwards proved that none existed.

XI.

Is there proof of this?
Yes—there are several men still living in Sangamon County, Illinois,
who were present in the brigade at the time.[62]

Lincoln, apparently, was the first "chickenhawk."

Democratic political cartoons blamed Lincoln for "whimsically" sacrificing hundreds of thousands of men. They relied specifically on an incident at Antietam. Lincoln visited the battlefield to check up on McClellan in September 1862. During his visit, Lincoln asked his bodyguard, Ward Lamon, to sing in order to lighten the mood; Hill sang a few songs, including a rather risqué piece entitled "Picayune Butler."[63] During the campaign of 1864, Democrats beefed up the anecdote, claiming that Lincoln had asked Lamon to sing him a "comic negro song" over the graves of Union dead. At anti-Lincoln rallies, Democrats carried banners reading "No More Vulgar Jokes."[64] Anti-Lincoln comics repeated the libel.[65]

Lincoln didn't like McClellan, either. During McClellan's generalship, Lincoln routinely slapped McClellan down with witty ripostes. While visiting Antietam, Lincoln remarked on McClellan's hesitancy to use his troops. Pointing out over the Union encampment, Lincoln asked one of his friends, O. M. Hatch, what the encampment was. "Why, Mr. Lincoln," replied Hatch, "this is the Army of the Potomac." Lincoln paused a moment, then caustically responded, "No, Hatch, no. This is *General McClellan's bodyguard.*"[66]

One of Lincoln's supporters, Senator Benjamin Wade of Ohio, openly blasted McClellan's military abilities. In one speech, Wade delivered one of the more scathing broadsides in the history of presidential politics. He told a story about his meeting with General McClellan: "We exhorted him, for God's sake, to at least push back the defiant traitors. Why can't you do it?

"'Oh, I have not men enough?' [Laughter]

"How many men have you? I know you have 160,000.

"'Well, you have got nearer the number than others have.'

"And more, I know that you have 190,000. How strong, pray tell, are the rebels?

"'Oh, they are at least 220,000 or more, and they are behind fortifications stronger than those of Sebastopol.'

"Well, I could not dispute with him on that point, because I had not been there to see, but I did not believe a word of it, neither does any Democrat in the United States believe it. [Laughter] I simply told him that to have got together such a number as that and to have supplied themselves with formidable armor, the rebels must possess some of the qualities of Christ in making bread. [Great laughter]

"'Believe it or not,' said McClellan, 'I have it on the best authority. A gentleman dined with me yesterday direct from Beauregard, and he reported that number.'

"Where is that gentleman now?

"'I don't know?'

"Well, I can guess, I think he is dining with Beauregard and telling him exactly how many men you have got. [Laughter and prolonged applause]"

After relating more stories regarding McClellan's incompetence, Wade went on to say that McClellan could be found at the front of his troops only in retreat. Wade professed confidence that no soldier would vote for McClellan. "No," he bellowed, "a true American soldier will vote neither for a coward nor a traitor." Then, to cap off the speech, Wade claimed that McClellan had not pursued and crushed the Confederates after the Battle of Antietam because McClellan wanted "to protect the war till both parties were tired, and settle all difficulties under a Democratic Administration."[67]

The election of 1864 *was* decided on the battlefield—by Generals Ulysses S. Grant and William Tecumseh Sherman. Timely Union successes drove Abraham Lincoln to reelection. Military service was no match for true military leadership.

★★★

THE ELECTION OF 1868 matched the most famous military hero of the Civil War, Ulysses S. Grant, against the controversial governor of New York, Horatio Seymour. As governor, Seymour had opposed the draft, the Emancipation Proclamation, and Lincoln's encroachment on civil liberties. Many had labeled Seymour a Copperhead, and his candidacy did nothing to diminish such indictments. His campaign was openly racist; one of his campaign songs was entitled "The White Man's Banner."[68] *Harper's Weekly* ran a cartoon depicting a confederate soldier wearing a hat reading "CSA" and carrying a confederate flag, side by side with a man wearing a hat reading "KKK" and carrying a Seymour-Blair banner. The title: "'Tis But A Change In Banners."[69]

The *New York Times* derided Seymour as "hollow and hypocritical in his position as governor during the war. While professing to aid the Government, he did all he could to embarrass it. Pretending to desire the preservation of the Union, he took the side of Vallandingham and the traitors at the North who were plotting for its destruction . . . His whole public course . . . Wears the aspect of treachery."[70]

Grant, meanwhile, campaigned solely on the basis of his military successes—that is, when he campaigned at all. Grant ran the tersest presidential campaign of all time, essentially uttering four words: "Let us have peace."[71] And it worked. *Harper's Weekly* labeled Grant "The Modern Gulliver Among the Lilliputians."[72]

When General Sherman balked at openly endorsing Grant, Grant cleverly arranged a tour of the western territories with Sherman and General Phil Sheridan. The *Times* declared the tour a historic gathering of "the Greatest generals of our nation, and the world." During the tour, Sheridan was far less neutral than Sherman. At one stop a member of a crowd shouted for Seymour. Sheridan responded by stating that if he were from the town, he would "duck that fellow in the Missouri River."[73]

Meanwhile, Seymour supporters labeled Grant a butcher, an ignoramus, and a drunkard. An anti-Grant parade in Nashville featured signs reading "Grant the Butcher," "Grant the Drunkard," and "Grant talks peace but makes war."[74] One anti-Grant song went like this:

> I am Captain Grant of the Black Marines,
> The stupidest man that ever was seen . . .
>
> I smoke my weed and drink my gin,
> Paying with the people's tin.[75]

The song may have been catchy, but it wasn't particularly effective. Grant won the 1868 election walking away. Four years later, he won a similarly lopsided matchup against newspaper editor Horace

Greeley. In the aftermath of the Civil War, Americans were not satisfied to leave the task of maintaining peace to anyone but the greatest military hero since George Washington.

★★★

THE CIVIL WAR REMAINED the backdrop for the next several elections, with several Union generals running for president. Generalship, in this setting, was less about leadership ability than about loyalty: the Reconstruction Era elections featured "waving the bloody shirt"—Republicans raising the issue of Democrats' wartime Confederate sympathies. Republicans routinely ran Union military leaders; Democrats occasionally responded by similarly running Union military leaders. In 1876, Republicans ran General Rutherford B. Hayes. In 1880, Republicans ran General James Garfield; Democrats responded with Gettysburg hero General Winfield Scott Hancock. In 1888 and 1892, Republicans ran General Benjamin Harrison.

But military service gradually dwindled in importance as the Civil War receded in immediacy. Teddy Roosevelt's service was a strong factor in his nomination for vice president in the election of 1900, but the next six presidents—Taft, Wilson, Harding, Coolidge, Hoover, and FDR—had no military service among them. Harry Truman's military service played little part in his 1948 campaign for president.

Then Dwight D. Eisenhower came along.

Eisenhower's claim to fame sprang entirely from his military career. After serving as Supreme Allied Commander in Europe during World War II, orchestrating the invasion of Europe, he took a position as president of Columbia University. He returned to the world stage in 1950, becoming Supreme Commander of the North Atlantic Treaty Organization.

Eisenhower's sterling record made him an attractive candidate for *both* major political parties in the aftermath of World War II. Thomas Dewey, the Republican presidential candidate in both 1944 and 1948, labeled Eisenhower a "very great world figure . . . one of the greatest soldiers of history . . . a man who really understands the problems of the world." Harry Truman told Eisenhower in 1945, "There is nothing that you may want that I won't try to help you get. That definitely and specifically includes the Presidency in 1948."[76]

Eisenhower didn't run in 1948, but he took the Republican nomination in 1952. He faced Governor Adlai Stevenson of Illinois, a dream opponent. Stevenson was bookish, uncomfortable on camera, and high-handed. Eisenhower was friendly, approachable, and the most popular American military figure since Grant. His appeal was universal. As political scientists Philip Converse and Georges Dupeux explained, "The past military splendor of the conquering hero diffuses through a wide variety of references which make up these images—patriotism, past record, leadership, capacities in dealing with foreign problems, etc."[77] All of that was particularly true for Ike. But Ike didn't have merely the military edge—he had the personality edge. Those two factors combined to swamp Stevenson in 1952.

Eisenhower's campaign focused, naturally, on his generalship during World War II. His campaign commercials touted his military leadership. One of Eisenhower's most hard-hitting ads was entitled "The Man from Abilene." It opens with the narrator discussing Eisenhower's upbringing in the "heartland of America." The narrator then touts Ike's World War II leadership, as film of Normandy and the liberation of France flashes across the screen: "Through the crucial hour of historic D-Day, he brought us to the triumph and peace of V-E Day." The narrator informs us, "Now, another crucial hour in our history—the big question . . ." And we cut to a younger man asking Ike directly, "General, if war comes, is this country really ready?" Ike, looking dead into the camera, sternly and indignantly growls, "It is not. The administration has spent many billions of dollars for national defense. Yet today we haven't enough tanks for the fighting in Korea. It is time for a change."

The ad shows footage from Korea as the narrator continues: "The nation, haunted by the stalemate in Korea, looks to Eisenhower." Cut to Eisenhower standing beside world leaders. "Eisenhower knows how to deal with the Russians. He has met Europe's leaders, has got them working with us. Elect the number one man for the number one job of our time. November 4th vote for peace. Vote for Eisenhower." It is a terrific ad, simultaneously attacking the Truman Administration for malfeasance on defense policy and stumping for Eisenhower as the answer to America's needs.

A lighter, animated Eisenhower ad, "Ike for President," subtly plays on Ike's military resumé. Animated figures, including Uncle Sam wearing an Ike button, march across the screen as a catchy marching tune by Irving Berlin plays. The bass line repeats, in straight martial quarter-time: "Ike for president, Ike for president, Ike for president . . ." The lyrics urge Americans to turn out for the general:

> We don't want John or Dean or Harry.
> Let's do that big job right.
> Let's get in step with the guy that's hep.
> Get in step with Ike.
> You like Ike, I like Ike, everybody likes Ike—for president.
> Bring out the banners, beat the drums,
> We'll take Ike to Washington.

Ike himself constantly invoked his service during World War II. In an October 1952 speech, Eisenhower indicted Truman's Korea policy:

> I know something of this totalitarian mind. Through the years of World War II, I carried a heavy burden of decision in the free world's crusade against the tyranny then threatening us all. Month after month, year after year, I had to search out and to weigh the strengths and weaknesses of an enemy driven by the lust to rule the great globe itself. World War II should have taught us all one lesson. The lesson is this: To vacillate, to hesitate—to appease even by merely betraying unsteady purpose—is to feed a dictator's appetite for conquest and to invite war itself.[78]

Stevenson, meanwhile, attempted a daring if misguided strategy: he attacked Eisenhower for his military background. One of his ads featured a woman standing before a piano, singing a song to the tune of "O Christmas Tree." The lyrics laud Stevenson, of course— but they attack Eisenhower for being militaristic. "A soldier-man is always bound / to think in terms of battleground," the singer warns. Then, striving desperately for a rhyme, the singer assures the audience that Stevenson is a "man-you-can-believe-in-son," a "civilian-son" who will not quit until "peace is won."

Unfortunately for Stevenson, Eisenhower was virtually impregnable on this score. Stevenson was forced to hearken back to Republican policies of 1931—a sure losing issue in an election where the Republicans ran Ike, a man Barry Goldwater later called "a dime store New Dealer."[79]

Eisenhower trampled Stevenson in 1952, and then did the same in 1956.

But Eisenhower was unique. Eisenhower was the last of the great generals; he was the last candidate for whom military service connoted leadership on a grand scale. In the post-Eisenhower era, military service connotes personal bravery, not leadership ability. And personal bravery as a political quality is often less valuable than leadership capability.

Certain candidates, however, still used military service successfully in their battle for the presidency. John F. Kennedy's military heroism demonstrated both physical strength and mental toughness. Kennedy famously served on *PT-109,* a swift boat in the Pacific. When a Japanese ship rammed his boat in the Solomon Islands, it sank; Kennedy and his crew swam to a tiny island. Kennedy dragged a wounded comrade during the swim, clenching a strap of the man's life jacket in his teeth. Eventually, his crew was rescued.[80] The *New Yorker* printed the story, and then in 1944 it appeared in *Reader's Digest;* the ensuing hubbub made JFK a national figure.[81]

During the 1960 presidential campaign, JFK brilliantly exploited the *PT-109* episode. The television show *Navy Log* chronicled JFK's heroism during his run for the Democratic nomination.[82] JFK's family sold *PT-109* insignia emblems for less than a dollar a piece. JFK utilized a letter from FDR's son that ripped Democratic rival Hubert Humphrey for not serving during World War II.[83] He used the *PT-109* incident to deflect questions about his Addison's Disease; he blamed his back pain on war wounds.[84] He used *PT-109* to deflect questions about his religious convictions—who would challenge the patriotism of a man who had risked all for his country?[85] Kennedy even ran television ads touting *PT-109.*[86]

But JFK was too smart to *admit* using *PT 109* for political gain. When the media asked JFK how he had become a war hero, Kennedy wryly remarked, "It was absolutely involuntary. They sank my boat."[87] Kennedy's boat sinking—that was certainly involuntary. The part about becoming a war hero—that was strictly orchestrated.

★★★

THE VALUE OF MILITARY SERVICE has dramatically declined in the post-Kennedy era. Though Johnson, Nixon, Ford, Carter, and Reagan served, their service had little impact on their respective elections. But it was the election of 1992 that clearly demonstrated how little military service has come to mean. Incumbent president George H. W. Bush ran against Arkansas governor Bill Clinton. H. W. Bush was a World War II hero; Clinton gamed the draft system in order to avoid serving in Vietnam.

The Bush campaign made hay out of Clinton's Vietnam malfeasance. They pounded Clinton on the question of trust. Could a man who had avoided the draft and refused to come clean about his draft avoidance be trusted to run the country?

But the Bush campaign didn't stay on message. While attacking Clinton on his trustworthiness, they also attacked his antiwar views—a foolish tactic with regard to a historically unpopular war. Bush campaign advisor Charles Black went after Clinton directly:

> We believe Bill Clinton is a patriotic American, but we question his values [in] going to demonstrate against his country. Listen, Governor Clinton had received, that very same year, a draft induction notice. Now, most Americans, when they receive a draft induction notice, report for duty. Governor Clinton, instead, pulled strings to avoid the draft notice and went to England to demonstrate against his country's policies, when his colleagues—people his age—were dying in Vietnam. It's bad judgment.[88]

Bush echoed Black's message during the first debate: "I just find it impossible to understand how an American can demonstrate against his own country in a foreign land—organizing demonstrations against it when young men are held prisoner in Hanoi or kids out of the ghetto were drafted."[89]

Those comments created a tremendous backlash. Democratic National Committee chairman Ronald Brown called the comments "despicable." Two-thirds of respondents to a *Newsweek* poll said that the comments were "unfair."[90]

So during the third presidential debate, Bush morphed his message to focus more narrowly on Clinton's trust issues. Bush reiterated that he had "expressed my heartfelt difference with Governor Clinton on organizing demonstrations while in a foreign land against your country, when young ghetto kids have been drafted and are dying." But Bush also explained that he was not questioning Clinton's antiwar activity, only his prevarication: "On April 17 [Clinton] said he'd bring out all the records on the draft. They have not been forthcoming. He got a deferment or he didn't. He got a notice or he didn't. And I think it's this pattern that troubles me, more than the draft. A lot of decent, honorable people felt as he did on the draft. But it's this pattern."[91]

Vice President Dan Quayle joined Bush in attacking Clinton. "The American people are beginning to see that Gov. Clinton lacks the integrity to be President of the United States," he stated. "He hasn't told the truth about avoiding military service. At first he said he didn't get a draft notice. Then it turns out that he did . . . That's my big difference with him on the draft. It wasn't failing to serve."[92]

Meanwhile, Clinton played the victim. "Here we are, on our way to a debate about the great issues facing this country and its future—and he descended to that level?" Clinton plaintively queried.[93] He dismissed Bush with a sigh: "I felt really sad for Mr. Bush."[94] And during the third debate, he compared himself to Lincoln: "I was opposed to the war. I couldn't help that. I felt very strongly about it, and I didn't want to go at the time. It's easy to say in retrospect I would have done something differently. President Lincoln opposed the war [presumably the Mexican War] and there were people who said maybe he shouldn't be president, but I think he made us a pretty good president in wartime."[95]

In the end, the draft issue did little damage to Clinton. It made it easier for him to pillory Bush as a mean-spirited attack dog; it made it easier for him to portray himself as a beleaguered man of principle. Clinton never posed as a military man—there was nothing there for the Bush campaign to debunk. His untruths about his Vietnam activity could have colored the public's perception of him; instead, the Bush campaign conflated his dishonesty with his antiwar activity, mooting both issues.

On Election Day, the alleged draft dodger defeated the war hero.

★★★

CLINTON NEVER CAMPAIGNED on the basis of his military service, so his opponents could never effectively attack his antiwar stance or draft manipulation. The same was not true of John Kerry during the 2004 election. Kerry based every facet of his campaign on his military service. Kerry had served on a swift boat—a la JFK, which was no coincidence—during the Vietnam War, and he had served heroically, receiving the Silver Star, the Bronze Star, and three Purple Hearts.

And he never let anyone forget it.

Subtlety was not Kerry's strong suit. Throughout the campaign, Kerry repeatedly hearkened back to his days on the swift boat, bringing his Vietnam buddies along on campaign stops, invoking his service continuously, annoying friends and foes alike. In what possibly constitutes the most egregious use of military imagery in campaign history, Kerry accepted his nomination for president by saluting, then infamously uttering the words that would damn him to a lifetime of mockery: "I'm John Kerry, and I'm reporting for duty."[96]

Sadly enough, the acceptance clunker was right in character. Kerry's obsession with touting his Vietnam service spawned a vast ocean of jokes. Conan O'Brien gibed, "Last night during the Democratic presidential debate, Howard Dean started off by apologizing to the crowd for having a cold. Then John Kerry apologized for once having a cold while serving his country in Vietnam."[97]

"As I'm sure you know, the White House begun [sic] airing their TV commercials to reelect the president and the John Kerry campaign is condemning his use of 9/11 in the ads," cracked Jay Leno. "He said, it is unconscionable to use the tragic memory of a war in order to get elected, unless of course, it's the Vietnam War."[98] Leno again: "I learned a piece of trivia about John Kerry at the convention: Did you know he was in Vietnam? Apparently, he was a soldier there."[99]

As with most presidential candidates who campaign on the basis of military service, Kerry's military record became a sticking point during the campaign. After returning from Vietnam, Kerry testified before Congress. He blasted the troops, stating that they had "raped, cut off ears, cut off heads, taped wires from portable telephones to human genitals and turned up the power, cut off limbs, blown up bodies, randomly shot at civilians, razed villages in fashion reminiscent of Genghis Khan, shot cattle and dogs for fun, poisoned food stocks, and generally ravaged the countryside of South Vietnam in addition to the normal ravage of war, and the normal and very particular ravaging which is done by the applied bombing power of this country." These war crimes, he said, were "not isolated incidents but crimes committed on a day-to-day basis with the full awareness of officers at all levels of command." Kerry's antiwar activism was uncompromising. He threw his ribbons (but not his medals) over the White House fence. He attended antiwar rallies with Jane Fonda.

None of this sat well with many Vietnam veterans, who thought it a tad disconcerting that Kerry was now campaigning on the basis of his bravery in a war he helped undermine. A group known as the Swift Boat Veterans for Truth, composed of Vietnam vets including some who served with Kerry, called Kerry's military heroism into question. They published a book entitled *Unfit for Command*, in which they claimed that Kerry lobbied for his Purple Hearts despite the fact that he had incurred only minor wounds, two of them self-inflicted; served a mere four months, as opposed to the usual year tour; and lied to receive his Silver Star and Bronze Star. They ripped what they saw as Kerry's post-tour political opportunism and treachery. The Swift Boat Vets ran television ads containing the same information.

The emergence of the Swift Boat Vets immediately sparked controversy and severely damaged Kerry's credibility, particularly in the aftermath of Kerry's tall tale about a secret trip to Cambodia during his tour of duty in Vietnam. On eight separate occasions in the Senate and to the media, Kerry explained that he had secretly and illegally been sent to Cambodia during Christmas of 1968. This turned out to be a blatant falsehood.[100]

During the course of the campaign, Kerry's military record became a detriment rather than an asset. He couldn't campaign as a strong military supporter—his Winter Soldier testimony excluded that possibility. He couldn't campaign on his courage under fire—the Swift Boat Vets undermined his claims, and his own Cambodia story undermined his credibility. David Letterman aptly summed up the situation: "Have you folks been following the controversy with John Kerry and his service in Vietnam and the Swift Boat campaign? It all took place in Vietnam, and now it just won't go away. I was thinking about this—if John Kerry had just ducked the war like everybody else, he wouldn't have this trouble."[101]

★ ★ ★

DURING THE CIVIL WAR, the Union faced an existential threat. Existential threats always increase the demand for men of military stature, and the situation in 1863 was no exception. Union General Joseph Hooker stated that he felt both the army and the government required a dictator. When Lincoln appointed Hooker the new commander of the Army of the Potomac, he cautioned Hooker about his comments: "Of course, it was not *for* this, but in spite of it, that I have given you the command . . . Only those generals who gain successes, can set up dictators. What I now ask of you is military success, and I will risk the dictatorship."[102]

America no longer has to risk dictatorships. The political value of military service has declined dramatically since George Washington wore his uniform into the national spotlight. Service is rarely seen as a dramatic reflection of leadership ability. Service is not considered an exclusive means of proving loyalty. Service can reflect bravery under fire, but that's about the extent of it.

As America has grown in strength and power, military service has become less and less important in presidential contests; it is certainly no longer the important qualifier it was in the aftermath of the Civil War.

This would have pleased the founders. "I must study politics and war that my sons may have liberty to study mathematics and philosophy," wrote John Adams. "My sons ought to study mathematics and philosophy, geography, natural history, naval architecture, navigation, commerce, and agriculture in order to give their children a right to study paintings, poetry, music, architecture, statuary, tapestry, and porcelain."[103] American leaders will always have to study politics and war, but America is not under the constant existential threat the founders faced. Countries in chaos often turn to great military figures; America is no longer in chaos. It makes perfect sense that as American security grows, a president's military record becomes less important than his philosophic and political positions.

★ 4 ★
Old School vs. New School

RONALD REAGAN TURNED SIXTY-NINE on February 6, 1980. If Reagan won the Republican nomination, his birthday would make him the oldest major party nominee in the history of the United States. It was a fact the media would not let him forget. Haynes Johnson of the *Washington Post* criticized Reagan's television appearance as well as his supposed touch of senility:

> Television, the instrument that catapulted Reagan into national political prominence years ago, is unkind to him today . . . in that pitiless eye of the TV camera closeups his age shows through—the lines around his eyes, the jowls, the so-called "turkey" neck of those approaching their 70s . . . There's a certain hesitancy, a stumble here and there, that one doesn't recall from other Reagan campaigns. He blows his lines now and then, says boycott when he means blockade, mentions turning over surplus funds to his gubernatorial predecessor instead of successor, refers to dismounting from an aircraft instead of disembarking, and displays at times an embarrassing unawareness of events.[1]

Newsweek seconded the motion, clucking, "Reagan and his staff still must reckon with the fact that he is no longer a young man. His continuing need for sufficient rest poses ticklish problems for aides trying to schedule his time during the twelve days he plans to spend in New Hampshire over the next three weeks . . . too many appearances might overtax the candidate; as one Reagan staffer has admitted: 'A tired Ronald Reagan is a bad Ronald Reagan.'"[2]

Reagan had never shied away from the age issue. After Reagan announced his candidacy for the 1980 presidency, Jack Kemp called Reagan "the oldest and the wisest candidate." Reagan latched on to the nickname, and for a time the media used the designation, shortening it to the "the O and the W."[3] Reagan also used a series of witty responses when asked about his age. After watching himself in *Knute Rockne—All-American* (1948), Reagan quipped, "It's like seeing a younger son I never knew I had." He labeled himself middle-aged, explaining, "Middle age is when you're faced with two temptations and you choose the one that will get you home at 9:30."[4]

But Reagan had never faced the age issue head-on, either. When asked about his age, Reagan was fond of replying, "It's better than the alternative."[5] It wasn't exactly a ringing endorsement of his physical and mental capabilities.

On February 6, 1980, Reagan turned the campaign around. He did it with flair, panache . . . and birthday cake.

Reagan celebrated his birthday repeatedly. The weekend before his birthday, he held a bash in Los Angeles which became a "Happy Birthday, Ronnie" party.[6] On February 6, Reagan held a birthday party in South Carolina, where he promptly fell into a giant birthday cake, emerging "with icing all over his coat."[7] That night he held another birthday party for 225 supporters and 50 media members in New Hampshire. During the party, Reagan blew out three candles on his birthday cake. Each candle, said

Reagan, represented a decade, since he was celebrating "the 30th anniversary of my 39th birthday."[8] In embracing his birthday, Reagan became a graceful model of aging.

But Reagan still had to prove that his age didn't hamper his faculties. As Roger Ailes, Reagan's 1984 campaign manager, put it, "People want to see a communicator have a range of emotions . . . There was some talk even then that he was too old to really hold down the job, that his mind wasn't sharp enough, and so on. Even his enemies said, 'You know, he's a nice fellow.' Tip O'Neill said, 'I like him.' But nobody really felt that he had a range of emotions."[9] Reagan's amiability left many with the impression that he was simply too old to be strong.

Reagan got the opportunity to prove them wrong during a February 23 Republican primary debate in New Hampshire. The *Nashua Telegraph* originally offered to sponsor a debate between Reagan and Bush. The other Republican candidates—Bob Dole, Howard Baker, John Anderson, and Phil Crane—cried foul, stating that excluding them from the debate was legally similar to a campaign donation to Bush and Reagan. The Federal Elections Commission agreed.

So Reagan offered to sponsor the debate himself. Except that he then invited Dole, Baker, Anderson, and Crane to show up.[10]

The other candidates showed up on the night of the debate. Understandably, Bush was miffed. His campaign manager, James Baker, refused to allow the debate to go forward if the other candidates were given slots. The crowd sat confused for half an hour as the candidates milled about the stage. Finally, Reagan decided to tell the audience what was going on. He picked up his microphone and began to speak.

Joe Breen, the editor of the *Nashua Telegraph*, ordered the soundman to cut off Reagan's microphone. Reagan looked stunned for a moment. He stood up from his chair, hesitated, and then picked up the microphone. He leaned forward. "Is this on?" he asked. The crowd responded that it was. Reagan sat down again. "Mr. Green," he said, mispronouncing Breen's name, "if I could—" Breen again ordered the microphone cut off.

Then, in one of the great campaign moments in American history, Reagan turned, glared, and angrily stated, "I am *paying* for this microphone, Mr. Green." The crowd and the other candidates went wild with applause, as Reagan sat, righteous fury still etched on his brow.[11]

It was a triumphant moment for Reagan. He had demonstrated his strength and power. He was still youthful enough to get mad as hell and not take it anymore. Ailes described the reaction: "Everybody jumped back and said, 'Holy cow, there's more to this guy than we thought. He's capable of getting tough. He's capable of being decisive.' That was the turning point of his campaign."[12]

Reagan later wrote, "Well, for some reason, my words hit the audience, whose emotions were already worked up, like a sledgehammer. The crowd roared and just went wild. I may have won the debate, the primary—and the nomination—right there. After the debate, our people told me the gymnasium parking lot was littered with Bush-for-President badges."[13]

Reagan won the nomination handily. He defeated Jimmy Carter in the election. On Election Day 1980, he became the oldest elected president in American history.

The age issue cropped up again four years later. By the 1984 election, Reagan was seventy-three years old, three years older than Dwight D. Eisenhower had been when he left office. His opponent, fifty-six-year-old Walter Mondale, again tried to use Reagan's age against him. This time it seemed to be working. Reagan fumbled during the first presidential debate; he looked and seemed unsure of himself, unclear in his grasp of the facts. Though

Reagan had been tough during his first term—surviving an assassination attempt, standing up to the Soviets, ending stagflation, even lifting weights and chopping wood at his ranch—Mondale's accusations began snowballing. Two days after the first debate, the *Wall Street Journal* headlined with the age issue: "New Question in Race: Is Oldest President Now Showing His Age?"[14]

The second debate would be the critical test. If Reagan could stand up to Mondale's pressure, he could be reelected. If he looked befuddled, Mondale would gain ground.

Sure enough, the issue of age reared its ugly head during the debate. One of the moderators, Henry Trewhitt of the *Baltimore Sun*, asked Reagan if he had any doubts whether he would be able to function on little sleep in an emergency. Reagan pounced on the question like a cat on a mouse: "Not at all, Mr. Trewhitt, and I want you to know that also I will not make age an issue of this campaign. I am not going to exploit, for political purposes, my opponent's youth and inexperience."[15] Even Mondale had to laugh. Reagan campaign consultant Ailes described it:

> It was not just the president's words. It was his timing, inflection, facial expression, and body language which made the moment powerful. As far as I was concerned, the debate was over. The news media had their lead quote for the next day, and everybody had a laugh. I watched Mondale's face. Even he broke into a smile, but I could see in his eyes that he knew it was over, too. I could almost hear him thinking, "Son-of-a-gun, the old man got away with it! He got a laugh on that line, and I can't top it." The public had the reassurance they were looking for, and Reagan had the election won.[16]

Age was an asset for Reagan because he was reassuring, fatherly. He didn't hide his age in his television appearances. He never acted as though he were forty-five. The public trusted Reagan for the very reason he cited in that crucial second debate with Mondale: "I might add that it was Seneca or it was Cicero, I don't know which, that said, 'If it was not for the elders correcting the mistakes of the young, there would be no state.'"[17]

★★★

AGE ISN'T JUST A NUMBER. It's a major factor in presidential elections, and it always has been. How the public perceives age, however, is largely up to the candidate. An older candidate may come off as stodgy, old-fashioned, stuck in his ways—a Bob Dole type—or he may come off as Ronald Reagan did: traditionally strong, fatherly, a solid figure guiding America through troubled waters. A younger candidate may seem wet behind the ears, green, too brash—William Jennings Bryan circa 1896—or he may seem confident, energetic, powerful—John F. Kennedy.

Most of our presidents are elderly gentlemen. Of course, part of this is the constitutional requirement that presidents be thirty-five years of age. The Constitution was framed in 1787; the average life expectancy in 1750 was about thirty-two years. Yet during the nineteenth century, when life expectancy ranged from forty years old (1815) to forty-four (1900),[18] the average president was elected at age fifty-six. The youngest elected president of the nineteenth century was Ulysses S. Grant, aged forty-six, and he was elected based almost entirely on his Civil War heroism. Politics was indeed an old man's game.

The twentieth century didn't change things much. The average life expectancy rose dramatically over the course of the century, but the average age of our elected presidents remained surprisingly stable, at fifty-six years old. And the television age didn't skew matters toward younger candidates: in elections from 1952 on, Americans elected presidents with an average age of fifty-eight.

The fact is that Americans trust men who look experienced. Not every younger face is JFK. During the nineteenth century, candidates under age fifty lost seven of the twelve elections in which they ran; candidates under age forty-eight lost seven of nine times. During the twentieth century, candidates under age fifty didn't fare much better: they lost six out of ten times. This isn't to say that men over fifty have fared well across the board, but they also compose the vast majority of presidential candidates. Age may not preclude defeat, but it can certainly pave the road to both the presidential nomination and the White House.

★ ★ ★

GEORGE WASHINGTON TURNED fifty-one years old on February 22, 1783. Seven months later, the Americans and British signed the Treaty of Paris, formally ending the War of Independence. And two months after that, General Washington rode for Annapolis, Maryland, to deliver his farewell address to Congress.

During that address, Washington played the part of the weathered man, aged by the burden of patriotic leadership.

"[T]here was hardly a member of Congress who did not drop tears," wrote founding figure James McHenry. "The General's hand which held the address shook as he read it. When he spoke of the officers who had composed his family, and recommended those who had continued in it to the present moment to the favorable notice of Congress he was obliged to support the paper with both hands. But when he commended the interests of his dearest country to almighty God, and those who had the superintendence of them to his holy keeping, his voice faultered and sunk, and the whole house felt his agitations."[19]

It was quite moving. But that was no surprise—Washington was a terrific actor. Washington's future vice president, John Adams, called Washington "the great actor," and suggested that Washington owed his success to "Shakespearian and Garrickal excellence in Dramatic Exhibitions."[20] This wasn't empty praise. Just hours before that display of frail nobility, Washington, who loved to dance, danced away the night with a long line of colonial ladies, all of whom longed "to get a touch of him," according to a witness.[21]

But perhaps that's unfair to Washington—perhaps the dancing tired him . . . or not. Washington gave the F. Murray Abraham-as-old-Salieri performance on at least one other occasion. At New-burgh, eight months before Washington's encore performance, Washington similarly played up his age while speaking to his troops. The troops were thinking of using the threat of military force to pressure Congress into paying their wages; Washington undercut them by playing his decrepitude to the hilt. While speaking before the troops, Washington pulled a pair of spectacles out of his pocket and gravely remarked, "Gentlemen, you will permit me to put on my spectacles, for I have not only grown gray, but almost blind, in the service of my country." Officers broke down in tears. The planned military coup dissipated. "On other occasions he had been supported by the exertions of the army and the countenance of his friends, but in this he stood single and alone," wrote Captain Samuel Shaw of the episode.[22] As Marvin Kitman put it, "It was a magnificent piece of theater and politics that could have won him an Emmy."[23]

Washington would live another fifteen years and survive eight years of presidency. He would go on to preside over the formation of the Constitution. He would only die at age sixty-six because he insisted on riding around his estate in freezing rain and snow.[24]

But at age fifty-one, Washington already realized the value of age. The father of our country campaigned as the *father* of our country.

★★★

JOHN ADAMS WAS LESS SUCCESSFUL on the age issue. Whereas Washington, as the symbol of Americanism generally, could safely proclaim that his age signified a lifelong love affair with America, Adams, a far more divisive politician, became the target of anti-Federalist wrath. Whereas Washington, a tall, stately figure, could rely on his powerful outward appearance to repel accusations of agedness, Adams, short and stout, could not. During the 1796 election, muckraking journalist Benjamin Franklin Bache labeled the fifty-nine-year-old vice president "old, bald, blind, querulous, toothless, crippled."[25]

And Adams, unlike Washington, felt old. Washington had the gift for acting; Adams did not. Adams was, as Benjamin Franklin described him, "always an honest man, often a great one"; Thomas Jefferson agreed, calling Adams "as disinterested as the being who made him."[26] That honesty carried over into his perceptions of his own decrepitude. It was "painful to the vanity of an old man to acknowledge the decays of nature," he wrote to his son, John Quincy, but he had to admit that with weak eyes and trembling hands, "a pen is as terrible to me as a sword to a coward."[27] By the election of 1800, the sixty-four-year-old Adams felt more than his age. "I am old, old, very old," he reported, "and I shall never be very well—certainly [not] while in this office, for the drudgery is too much for my years and strength."[28]

Adams's imperious manner, elderly appearance, and caustic honesty earned him the unremitting ire of his political enemies. They cashed in on his age, labeling him "quite mad."[29] Opponent Jefferson paid scurrilous journalistic hitman James Callender to spread libel about Adams.[30] In Callender's widely distributed, Jefferson-endorsed pamphlet, *The Prospect Before Us*, he went after Adams with both guns blazing: "The reign of Mr. Adams has been one continued tempest of malignant passions . . . Reader, dost thou envy that unfortunate old man with his twenty-five thousand dollars a year, with the petty parade of his birth-day, with the importance of his name sticking in every other page of the statute book. Alas! he is not an object of envy, but of compassion and of horror."[31] He added, for good measure, that Adams's writing style betrayed his senility. "Few other men," he wrote, "were capable of cramming so great a quantity of nonsense within so small a compass of words."[32]

Even Adams's supposed allies attacked him. In one of the greatest political back-stabbings in all of American history, leading Federalist and former secretary of the treasury Alexander Hamilton released a letter regarding Adams. In it, he accused Adams of less-than-impressive "intellectual endowment . . . he is a man of imagination sublimated and eccentric; propitious neither to the regular display of sound judgment, nor to steady perseverance in a systematic plan of conduct . . . to this defect are added the unfortunate foibles of a vanity without bounds, and a jealousy capable of discoloring every object . . . He has certain fixed points of character which tend naturally to the detriment of any cause of which he is the chief, of any administration of which he is the head."[33] Hamilton's letter likely turned the tide of the 1800 election in Jefferson's favor. It was no wonder that Adams hated Hamilton, whom he labeled "the bastard brat of a Scots peddler."[34] Hamilton's legendary ambition, said Adams, sprouted from "a superabundance of secretions which he could not find enough whores to draw off."[35]

In the election of 1800, old, cranky John Adams lost to the younger, taller, more aristocratic looking Thomas Jefferson. As David McCullough wrote, "To the victorious Republicans, and to generations of historians, the thought of the tall Jefferson, with his air of youth at fifty-seven, assuming the presidency in the new Capitol at the start of a new century, his eye on the future, would stand in vivid contrast to a downcast, bitter John Adams, old and 'toothless' at sixty-five, on his 'morning flight' to Baltimore."[36] Age isn't always a boon.

★★★

PERCEPTION OF AGE MATTERS far more than actual age. Never was that truism truer than during the election of 1840. General William Henry Harrison, at sixty-seven, was the oldest major party presidential candidate in American history, a title he would retain until the candidacy of Ronald Reagan 140 years later. Incumbent president Martin Van Buren was a decade younger than Harrison. In the end, however, it was "Old Tippecanoe" who monopolized the perception of youth, while Van Buren got stuck with the "old ninny" label.

The opposition press routinely attacked Harrison's age, calling him "Old Granny" Harrison[37] and suggesting that he was "failing, in body and mind from the approaches of old age."[38] Harrison was, said one newspaper, a "superannuated and pitiable dotard."[39] Representative Isaac Crary, a Democrat from Michigan, accused Harrison of senility.[40]

Harrison may have been old, but he was an old soldier—and as General MacArthur put it 111 years later, "old soldiers never die, they just fade away." Unless, that is, they choose not to fade away. And Harrison would not fade away. Like Reagan, Harrison confronted the age issue head-on, dissolving perceptions of decrepitude by campaigning vigorously. He had done the same thing in 1836 when he ran for president, taking to the campaign trail "to counteract the opinion, which has been industriously circulated, that *I was an old broken down feeble man.*"[41]

Harrison broke with tradition in actively campaigning, leading one newspaper to scornfully observe, "When was there ever before such a spectacle . . . as a candidate for the Presidency, traversing the country, . . . advocating his own claims for that high and responsible station? Never [!] . . . the precedent thus set by Harrison . . . appears to us a bad one."[42] But friendlier sources noticed that Harrison's campaigning did much to relieve him of the "Old Granny" stigma. "He is about 5 feet 9 inches in hight [sic]," wrote one onlooker, "very slender and thin in flesh, with a noble and benignant expression of countenance—a penetrating eye, expansive forehead and Roman nose. He is not bald but gray, and walks about very quick, and seems to be as active as a man of 45 . . . He appears better in the social circle than he does in public. —There is nothing of the 'Old Granny' about him, I assure you."[43] Harrison had a powerful voice and he didn't hesitate to use it, canvassing areas and speaking for hours on end.[44] And he was strong enough to handle a drink, swigging hard cider on the campaign stump.[45]

Meanwhile, Harrison capitalized on his old soldier image. He used it to explain his incoherent speaking style: "I am not a professional speaker, nor a studied orator, but I am an old soldier and a farmer."[46] He used it to mobilize his base of support, appealing to "the pioneers and old soldiers of the west." He characterized himself as "the oldest and most extensively known of the Veteran Pioneers."[47] He was not particularly modest. An abridged transcript of one of his speeches contained eighty-one "I"s. "What a prodigy of garrulous egotism!" one newspaper editor opined.[48]

One of Harrison's supporters, a young Whig named Abraham Lincoln, plagiarized Washington in making hay out of Harrison's age. "When an individual's hairs have grown grey, and his eyes dim in the service of his country, it seems to us, if his country-men are wise, and polite, they will so reward him, as to encourage the youth of that country to follow his example," Lincoln wrote for the *Sangamo Journal*.[49]

Harrison, like Andrew Jackson, united experience with a youthful vigor. Political prints of the time invariably make him look twenty years younger than he actually was. Harrison's youthful vigor lasted for a month after he took office. Then he died.

★★★

FRANKLIN PIERCE WAS a very handsome fellow. At forty-seven, Pierce had a nicely coifed head of hair, piercing dark eyes, and chiseled, movie star features. D. W. Bartlett, Pierce's campaign biographer, described him in predictably glowing terms:

> The personal appearance of General Pierce is elegant and commanding. He is within a few inches of six feet in height; is rather slight and thin than inclined to obesity; has a very pleasant and impressive address. His eyes are bright and piercing; his hair is greyish; his forehead, and indeed, face, very fine, open and frank in their expression. It is difficult to gain a fair idea of the man from a portrait. You need to see the gentleness of his manners, feel the kindliness of his nature, and witness the easy politeness of all of his actions. There is not a spice of aristocrat in the man; he is as polite to a beggar as to a prince, as free and generous to a farmer as to a Senator in the halls of Congress.[50]

If Pierce fit this description, it is a wonder that God did not choose him rather than Moses to receive biblical revelation.

Pierce was the predecessor to the TV candidate. He was young; at a time when the Democratic Party was split between sixty-something "Old Fogey" candidates and youngsters like thirty-eight-year-old Stephen Douglas, he seemed the reasonable choice.[51] He was pretty. As a New Hampshire man, he fit a particular electoral need. He was also a relative nobody, which is why it took the Democrats forty-nine ballots to nominate him for the presidency of the United States. When his wife heard about the nomination, she fainted.[52]

Pierce's Whig opponent was his former Mexican War superior officer, Winfield Scott. Scott, fondly known as "Old Fuss and Feathers," was already sixty-six years old by the time of the 1852 election. His campaign biographer, Edward Deering Mansfield, attempted the same Washington/Harrison "gray and blind in service of country" routine. He wrote:

> The old general, who has fought many battles and never known defeat, who has endured the hardships and toils of two wars, has been drawn from his retirement by the call of his fellow-citizens, and now appears on the political field to gather new laurels, and make a final dedication of all that remains of life to service of his country . . . May the genius of freedom, inspired by patriotism, throw her protecting mantle over the old soldier, and carry him in safety through this his last trial; may the tongue of slander for once be paralyzed; may party spirit stand rebuked before the illustrious soldier, now about to receive from the people their choicest meed of approbation.[53]

This is rather florid stuff. It reads more like a eulogy than a stump speech. Mansfield made it sound as though Americans owed the presidency to Scott as a sort of parting gift before Scott's imminent demise. Whereas Harrison gracefully combined the positives of age with a fiery campaign proving his vitality, Scott campaigned on his experience but never proved his vim. He campaigned ceaselessly on his past accomplishments, but rarely spoke of the future.[54] He lacked the common touch.

He even had an Edmund Muskie moment. At one campaign stop, Scott was greeted with a 21-gun salute. Unfortunately, one of the gunners overloaded his cannon; it blew up in his face, killing him. Scott was kept in the dark about the incident until a banquet for him that night. When he heard about the death, he broke down crying and had to be led from the room "like a child." "It is one thing to lose an arm in battle," he wept, "but, by God, no office in this world is worth a limb, let alone a life!"[55]

Franklin Pierce won the presidency, largely because of party divides, but at least in part because he was the most attractive candidate. He was not, however, a good president. Harry Truman summed it up well. "Pierce was a nincompoop," Truman stated. "He's got the best picture in the White House . . . but being president involves a little bit more than just winning a beauty contest, and he was another one that was a complete fizzle . . . Pierce didn't know what was going on, and even if he had, he wouldn't have known what to do about it."[56]

★★★

THERE HAVE BEEN MANY GREAT presidential nicknames. Lincoln was "Honest Abe." Reagan was "The Great Communicator" and "The Gipper." Jackson was "Old Hickory." Zachary Taylor was "Old Rough and Ready." TR, FDR, JFK, and LBJ needed only initials.

Then there was William Jennings Bryan. "The Boy Orator of the Platte."

It would be difficult to come up with a worse nickname for a presidential candidate. The nickname itself connotes immaturity and slickness. It says you're a big mouth. Better to be "Silent Cal," like Coolidge, than the "Boy Orator."

But the nickname fit.

William Jennings Bryan of Nebraska was the youngest presidential candidate in the history of American politics. During his knock-down, drag-out 1896 campaign fight against Republican nominee William McKinley, Bryan turned thirty-six. He was famous for his oratorical skill and his booming voice; he was a rabble-rouser, a class warrior, a direct predecessor to Louisiana's dictator-governor-senator Huey P. Long. He campaigned on a free silver platform—he wished for silver to join gold as the basis of the American monetary system, a development that likely would have created tremendous inflationary pressure and done great harm to the economy generally.

Most of all, Bryan was known for his youth. Early on, established Democrats snorted at the idea of a thirty-six-year-old presidential candidate. "Here was a young man barely thirty-six," wrote Senator C. S. Thomas of Colorado, "living in a comparatively unimportant Republican state west of the Mississippi River, audaciously announcing his probable candidacy for the presidential nomination. The very seriousness of the suggestion emphasized its absurdity."[57]

But Bryan refused to allow the age issue to hold him back. In seeking the nomination, Bryan relied on his legendary oratorical abilities. The free silver issue provided Bryan with fodder for one of the greatest campaign speeches of all time: the "Cross of Gold" speech, delivered at the Democratic National Convention. During the convention, Democrats debated whether to add a free silver plank to the party platform. Bryan represented the pro-free silver constituency.

"Cheer after cheer went up as Bryan of Nebraska, tall, smooth faced, youthful looking, leaped up the platform steps, two at a time," the *New York Tribune* reported. And Bryan didn't let down his audience. "Having behind us the producing masses of this nation and the world," Bryan thundered, "supported by the commercial interests, the laboring interests, and the toilers everywhere, we will answer their demand for a gold standard by saying to them: You shall not press down upon the brow of labor this crown of thorns, you shall not crucify mankind upon a cross of gold."[58] Bryan won the nomination on the fifth ballot.[59]

Now Bryan would have to sell himself to the general public. In doing so, Bryan embraced his age, making it a selling point. In a speech in Washington, D.C., Bryan stated that the young had the most stake in good government: "I see before me the faces of a great many who are young men, and I am glad to speak to the young, because we who are young, and who in the course of nature must live under our Government for many years, are especially interested in making that government good enough to live under."[60] At Yale: "If the syndicates and corporations rule this country, then no young man has a fair show unless he is the favorite of a corporation."[61]

Bryan wasn't the only one capitalizing on his youth. His opponents used his age to characterize him as a loudmouth radical, all style and no substance. "The Boy Orator makes only one speech—but he makes it twice a day," scoffed John Hay. "There is no fun in it. He simply reiterates the unquestioned truths that every man who has a clean shirt is a thief and ought to be hanged; that there is no goodness or wisdom except among the illiterate and criminal classes; that gold is vile; that silver is lovely and holy . . . he has succeeded in scaring the Goldbugs out of their wits."[62] The "Boy Orator of the Platte" was aptly named, remarked Republican senator Joseph Foraker. The Platte River in Nebraska, like Bryan, was "six inches deep and six miles wide at the mouth."[63]

The *Louisville Courier Journal* agreed. "He is a boy orator," the *Journal* editorialized. "He is a dishonest dodger. He is a daring adventurer. He is a political fakir. He is not of the material of which the people of the United States have ever made a President, nor is he even of the material of which any party has ever before made a candidate."[64]

Harper's Weekly routinely depicted Bryan as a child who knew not what he did. One cover cartoon was entitled "The Deadly Parallel." The cartoon was composed of two frames, side by side. The first frame depicted a young William McKinley in Union uniform. The caption read, "In 1861, William McKinley was upholding his country's honor,—and he's doing it yet!" That cartoon sat side by side with an illustration of Bryan as a baby shaking a rattle while sitting in a crib. The caption read, "In 1861, this is what William J. Bryan was doing,—and he's doing it yet!"[65]

Bryan lost the election. After the election, the *New York Tribune* published one of the most vitriolic indictments of a presidential candidate ever written:

> [The free silver cause] was conceived in iniquity and was brought forth in sin. It had its origin in a malicious conspiracy against the honor and integrity of the nation . . . It has been defeated and destroyed because right is right and God is God. Its nominal head was worthy of the cause. Nominal, because the wretched, rattle-pated boy, posing in vapid vanity and mouthing resounding rottenness, was not the real leader of that league of hell. He was only a puppet in the blood-imbued hands of Altgeld, the anarchist, and Debs, the revolutionist, and other desperadoes of that stripe.
>
> But he was a willing puppet, Bryan was, willing and eager. Not one of his masters was more apt than he at lies and forgeries and blasphemies and all the nameless iniquities of that campaign against the Ten Commandments. He had less provocation than Benedict

Arnold, less intellectual force than Aaron Burr, less manliness and courage than Jefferson Davis. He was the rival of them all in wickedness and treason to the Republic. His name belongs with theirs, neither the most brilliant nor the most hateful in the list.[66]

Bryan would run again in 1900, and lose again. He would run again in 1908, and lose again. But he would never shed his image as the Boy Orator; he remained a controversial figure for the rest of his life. His critics saw him as a perennial adolescent. Upon his death, H. L. Mencken caustically wrote, "He was born with a roaring voice, and it had the trick of inflaming half-wits. His whole career was devoted to raising those half-wits against their betters, that he himself might shine . . . He came into life a hero, a Galahad, in bright and shining armor. He [left it as] a poor mountebank."[67]

★★★

AT SIXTY-TWO, DWIGHT D. EISENHOWER looked nothing like John Adams. Eisenhower gave the impression of strength. He was determined looking but also genial looking; his eyes contained a stern hardness, but his smile was warm and friendly. Gerald Gardner wrote, "Ike's face was the most famous one of his day. His grin and his scowl became as much a part of the fifties as Roosevelt's cocky cigarette holder was part of the thirties."[68]

Eisenhower's good looks made up for his rather ambiguous politics; a journalist stated that "[when he] utters the most obvious platitude, [people] look at that serious face as if they had heard something that ought to be graven on stone and passed on to the third and fourth generation."[69] A Broadway musical capitalized on Eisenhower's famous good looks. In one scene, a violinist inspected the photographs on a conductor's piano:

MUSICIAN: Ah—Moiseiwitsch . . . Milsten . . . Piantigorsky . . . Solomon . . . (He picks up photograph and stares at it curiously.) And who is this?

CONDUCTOR: That's President Eisenhower.

MUSICIAN: Oh. Fine-looking man.[70]

Like Reagan, Eisenhower embodied the national ideal of politician-as-father-figure. And, like Reagan, Eisenhower was terrific on television. Campaign advertising historian Kathleen Hall Jamieson explained, "Eisenhower's televised appearances communicated that his image in World War II had been that of the 'GI General'—understanding, knowledgeable, sympathetic; in short, a wise father. Those who both saw Ike on television and voted for him would later claim that he was 'good-natured, sincere, honest, cheerful, and clear-headed.' "[71] But Eisenhower was careful not to come off as *too* paternal—he refused to wear glasses on television, necessitating the use of gigantic handheld cue cards.[72]

Eisenhower's opponent, Illinois governor Adlai Stevenson, was a decade younger than the general. Unfortunately for him, his nondescript appearance contrasted poorly with Ike's striking looks. "Let's face it," one of his aides said to a reporter, "people aren't thrilled when Adlai mounts a platform. He's too damn medium. He's medium height, has medium brown hair and not much of it, medium blue eyes . . . He could rob a bank. Nobody would be able to describe him."[73]

Claire Boothe Luce summed up the difference between the candidates nicely. Eisenhower, she said, was the universal candidate—"to older women, he was like a son; to middle-aged women, a husband; to young women, a father." Stevenson, by contrast, "seemed like a brother-in-law."[74]

The political brother-in-law loses to the father figure every time. Eisenhower swept the 1952 election.

By 1956, however, Stevenson's prospects looked less bleak. Ike was, after all, sixty-six years old; if he were to be elected again, he would serve as the oldest president in American history. And in 1955, Ike had a heart attack. He followed that with a bout of ileitis in 1956.

Stevenson's campaign seized on the age issue. But to exploit the issue, they would have to avoid looking mean-spirited. As the *New York Times* put it, "[M]any Democrats think the medical facts make the President's health a perfectly fair political issue—and their best hope for victory this year—but . . . have no idea how to use it without causing a backfire of sympathy for him."[75] Finally, they decided to run a print ad—an open letter signed by several political notables, urging Stevenson to make Ike's health and age issues in the campaign.

"Shall Vice-President Nixon assume presidential powers?" the ad queried. "Most men with heart trouble are not insurable," the ad warned. "Most healthy men over 65 retire from full-time work," the ad observed. "Most major corporations retire executives at age 65," the ad helpfully pointed out. "The army will not commission men with heart trouble or ileitis," stated the ad.[76]

The age issue had some traction. Polls showed that the public thought that men above sixty-five were too old for the presidency;[77] in October 1955, 62 percent of Americans thought Ike would not run again.[78] Fully 55 percent thought Ike shouldn't run again. Still, 56 percent said they would vote for Ike if he chose to run again.[79]

Ike countered the age issue by taking a page from William Henry Harrison's playbook—and writing a new page Ronald Reagan would utilize twenty-four years later. First, Ike actively campaigned to demonstrate his health and vigor. He utilized television, as he had four years earlier. But he went further. "The ruddy glow that is so characteristic of Ike simply did not come across in black and white," opined Allen Drury of the *New York Times*. "The only sure answer to this was fewer sermons from the White House and more face-to-face contact with the voters." Ike embraced the strategy with alacrity.[80]

Second, Ike embraced his age by hosting a nationally televised sixty-sixth birthday bash. Celebrities like Jimmy Stewart, Helen Hayes, and Irene Dunne showed up to honor Ike. The audience was given a guided tour of Eisenhower's life. As Jamieson described, "The audience was explicitly invited to see itself as part of Ike's extended family, particularly when the president's granddaughter introduces a cherubic little boy who carries a large piece of cake to the president. Hollywood stars sang the president's favorite songs and cut the cake, baked from Mamie's favorite recipe."[81]

The public was convinced. Once again, Eisenhower didn't need his glasses to see his gigantic victory margin.

★★★

AMERICA QUICKLY TRANSFERRED its affections from the oldest serving president to the youngest elected president. At forty-three, John F. Kennedy had already served six years in the House and eight years in the Senate; he had narrowly missed the vice presidential nomination in 1956. Loaded with charm, Kennedy was a media darling. "Kennedy's candidacy for the nomination . . . will prove a fascinating test . . . of the charm-school theory of high politics," observed Eric Sevareid of *CBS News* in 1959. "I do not mean to say that Senator Kennedy has no other qualities; but it remains quite true that his actual works, his practical experience, or his noteworthy utterances total, today, nothing like those of a Stevenson or a Nixon or a Symington or a Johnson or a Humphrey, or, for that matter, a Rockefeller." Kennedy's charm, posited Sevareid, "is inextricably connected with his youth . . ."[82]

Yet, as author Fletcher Knebel simultaneously noted, Kennedy's age might also act as a damper on his electoral hopes: "The very qualities, characteristics, and circumstances that attract national attention, and thus must be regarded as assets, are at the same time liabilities. People like his youth, freshness, and good looks, but are not sure they want that much youth, freshness, and good looks in the White House."[83]

Former president Harry Truman publicly and directly questioned Kennedy about his qualifications, stating at a press conference in July 1960, "I am deeply concerned and troubled about the situation we are up against in the world now and in the immediate future. That is why I would hope that someone with the greatest possible maturity and experience would be available at this time. May I urge you to be patient?"[84]

Kennedy responded by comparing himself to TR, William Pitt, Napoleon, and Alexander the Great.[85] He did not, however, compare himself to William Jennings Bryan or Thomas Dewey. Between them, Bryan and Dewey had lost a combined five presidential elections. Youth was no predictor of success.

But Kennedy had two advantages over Bryan and Dewey: television and Richard Nixon. "Kennedy's young looks are a big barrier to his path to the White House," wrote reporter Joe McCarthy. "Close up, he appears to be forty-three years old, but seen from a distance on the stage of an auditorium, his slim, boyish figure and his collegiate haircut make him seem like a lad of twenty-eight."[86] Fortunately, television was a close-up medium. Kennedy's television ads often featured extreme close-ups, focusing on his few wrinkles.

One of his ads explicitly touted his age. The ad quick-cut images of signs reading "Kennedy" with pictures of pro-Kennedy crowds as well as close-ups of the candidate. The soundtrack played a catchy song:

Kennedy, Kennedy, Kennedy, Kennedy, Kennedy, Kennedy,
Kennedy for me! (Kennedy, Kennedy, Kennedy, Kennedy, Kennedy)
Do you want a man for president who's seasoned through and through,
But not so doggoned seasoned that he won't try something new?
A man who's old enough to know, and young enough to do?
Well, it's up to you, it's up to you, it's strictly up to you!

Of course, the same could be said of Kennedy's opponent. Richard Nixon was hardly an old curmudgeon—he was only forty-seven years old. He and Kennedy had entered Congress in the same year. This took the age issue off the table for Nixon; certainly Eisenhower would have had an easier time with Kennedy, whom he could have dismissed as a young pup. The question of Kennedy's age was never posed during his four presidential debates with Nixon.

Nixon couldn't run on his experience, either. Though he had spent eight years as vice president and had been intimately involved in many matters of state, President Eisenhower completely undercut Nixon on the experience issue. When the press asked Eisenhower to name any major decisions in which Nixon had participated, Eisenhower snidely remarked, "If you give me a week, I might think of one."[87] Kennedy capitalized on the comment, using it in campaign commercials. During the first presidential debate, one of the moderators directly quoted Eisenhower's statement, and another asked Nixon what major ideas he had proposed to Eisenhower. The experience issue collapsed beneath Nixon.

Unlike Kennedy, Nixon looked bad on television. In his first debate with Kennedy, Nixon's upper lip and forehead were covered in a sheen of sweat. His lower teeth were carnivorously visible whenever he spoke. He had a slight five o'clock shadow. Whenever Kennedy spoke, Nixon stood there, favoring one leg, constantly fidgeting. When Nixon spoke, Kennedy appeared to be taking notes. Kennedy was the younger candidate, but he seemed the more mature candidate.

Kennedy won the 1960 election by one of the slimmest margins in electoral history. Lyndon Baines Johnson stated, "He never said a word of importance in the Senate and he never did a thing. But somehow he managed to create the image of himself as a shining intellectual, a youthful leader who would change the face of the country."[88] Tragically, Kennedy never had a chance to prove that his youth translated into political greatness. Kennedy changed the country more with his death than his presidency. Kennedy's murder released a torrent of social rebellion against authority. His youth—cut short as it was by an assassin's bullet—provided the center for a mass movement dedicated to remaking American morality. Kennedy's youth was the springboard for the 1960s.

★ ★ ★

WILLIAM JEFFERSON CLINTON saw himself as a Southern JFK. Young—Clinton turned forty-six during the 1992 campaign—soft-spoken, friendly looking, Clinton had a zestful charm about him. "Clinton was 'inauthentic' but there was a self-awareness, even transparency, with his ambition and skills," wrote campaign observers Allan Louden and Kristen McCauliff. "His appetites were part and parcel of the ambition, charm, compassion, and engagement that warranted voters' assent. *Clinton was Clinton*."[89] And Clinton was a kid—"the Comeback Kid," as he labeled himself.

In his television commercials, Clinton ran as the leader of a "new generation of Democrats." He repeatedly dragged out a photo of himself as a youngster meeting JFK. In his nomination acceptance speech, he made his theme the "New Covenant"; he used the word *new* a total of twenty-four times. He was a candidate for "change." During his first debate with sixty-eight-year-old incumbent president George H. W. Bush and sixty-two-year-old Ross Perot, Clinton aptly summed up his campaign platform: "We need a new approach. The same old experience is not relevant. We're living in a new world after the Cold War."[90]

Clinton echoed this theme throughout his campaign. "We don't need to elect the last president of the twentieth century," Clinton stated at a Florida State Democratic Convention. "We need to elect the first president of the twenty-first century."[91] He became the first presidential candidate to appear on MTV. During the appearance, he joked about his adolescent marijuana experimentation. "If you had to do it over again, would you inhale?" asked one particularly brainless audience member. "Sure, if I could," Clinton responded, grinning.[92] This highbrow witticism earned him the praise of the MTV generation. One UCLA student gushed, "Like many young Americans, I 'met' Bill Clinton on Tuesday night, sitting in my living room, on MTV, the music-video station better known for its coverage of pop icons than politicians. It was the highlight of the campaign so far."[93]

The media focused relentlessly on age, printing literally thousands of stories contrasting the elderly Bush with the younger and more vibrant Clinton. "The new president is nearly 23 years younger than the outgoing president, the biggest age difference by far since Dwight Eisenhower gave way to John Kennedy 32 years ago," pointed out Jeff Greenfield of *USA Today*. "[I]n electing 46-year-old Bill Clinton and 44-year-old Al Gore, America has put the baby-boom generation squarely in charge of our nation's affairs."[94] Opinion columnist William Schneider of the *Los Angeles Times* agreed: "What Democrats know about Clinton is that he is a smart, substantive, young, charming, experienced, attractive, moderate Southerner."[95]

"Clinton, the governor of Arkansas, is the youngest of the candidates at 45 and looks the fittest—for good reason," said the *Boston Globe*.

> As a Rhodes scholar, he rowed and played basketball, and as a candidate, he jogs, plays golf and softball, and when an injury slowed his running last year, he lifted weights . . . "The perception is we're being governed by a man of the World War II generation with no new ideas of where he wants to take us," said [William] Schneider. "All the Democrats are trying to say, 'We're fresh faces, we're young and vigorous and dynamic. George Bush is tired and old and not entirely well.'" [96]

The *New York Times* similarly drooled over Clinton:

> Addicted to card games of hearts, golf and crossword puzzles, a whiz on the tenor sax, Clinton has the look and loosey-goosey enthusiasm of a high school jock perched somewhere between eternal youth and paunchy middle age. But he also has the natural ease of a born politician—touching, hugging, making eye contact so deep that recipients sometimes seem mesmerized. Tabloid rumors aside, Clinton embodies the parallels between the seductions of politics and the seductions of sex. As one Clinton watcher said recently: "It's not that Clinton seduces women. It's that he seduces everyone."[97]

Still, there were many who doubted Clinton's ability to sway the public. He was, after all, a relative baby. "You wouldn't call Bill Clinton 'mister,' and you wouldn't call Bush 'George,'" explained Cokie Roberts of *ABC News*. And Fred Barnes, then of the *New Republic*, stated, "As much as a lot of reporters don't like George Bush, they find it hard to take Bill Clinton seriously as a president."[98]

But unlike Reagan, Eisenhower, and Harrison, Bush didn't seem lively. He didn't embrace his age. He was seasoned and experienced, but he had a reputation as a waffler. He also came off as a curmudgeon. When he was invited to appear on MTV, Bush responded that he was too old to become a "teeny-bopper."[99] As Clinton campaign pollster Stan Greenberg said, "I think they're looking for change. What's important about these two candidates is their energy and youth and ability to take on the kind of changes people are looking for . . . it's not that age is the issue, it's a lack of energy and a lack of vision and I think that will be the contrast."[100] Bush's age wasn't his big liability—it was his age combined with a perception of general political decrepitude.

Clinton won the 1992 election with 43 percent of the vote; Ross Perot captured 19 percent. Clinton didn't win because of his youth—he won because of Bush's agedness. Nonetheless, he ushered presidential politics into a new era: the era of the Baby Boomers.

That era continued with Clinton's reelection in 1996. Running against seventy-three-year-old Bob Dole, Clinton hardly had to raise the age issue. The media did it for him. "Bob Dole is so old he got Grecian Formula from the original Grecian," cracked Jay Leno.

"Of the candidates currently running for President, most lived through Vietnam and the Cold war," joked David Letterman. "A few even lived through the Second World War and the Great Depression. But only one candidate lived through the Civil War, the Declaration of Independence, and Columbus's Discovery of the New World. Elect Bob Dole. He's one thousand years old."

Leno again: "You know what the hot drink going around L.A. is? The cool new drink? These Metamucil cocktails. Who drinks orange Metamucil shooters? I mean, besides Bob Dole on spring break?"

And Letterman: "When Bob Dole first ran for office, of course it was easier. There were only thirteen colonies then."[101]

★★★

WHERE ARE WE WITH THE AGE ISSUE TODAY? Our last two presidents were first elected at ages forty-six and fifty-four. Youth may no longer be the barrier it once was.

Or is it? During the 2004 election, Senator John Edwards of North Carolina, fifty, ran for the Democratic nomination. Though he failed, he was granted a slot on the ticket with sixty-year-old nominee Senator John Kerry.

And with his fluffy hair and boyish smile, he proceeded to undermine the ticket's gravitas.

During the vice presidential debate with Dick Cheney, moderator Gwen Ifill pointed out: "Ten men and women have been nominees of their parties since 1976 to be vice president. Out of those ten, you have the least governmental experience of any of them."[102]

Jay Leno cracked, "The attacks have already started. John Edwards is too inexperienced to be president, he's too flashy, he's not up to the job. And those are just the things John Kerry said in the primary."[103]

Age mattered for Edwards. And age continues to matter because it is an indicator of experience—and experience will always matter. Baseball fans are constantly reminded that a team of talented youngsters won't cut it—veteran leadership is required. The same holds true in politics. Leadership by the not-yet-wise is a recipe for disaster.

★ 5 ★
The Beer Buddy Syndrome

W HO WOULDN'T WANT TO GRAB a beer with Bill Clinton? Homey, easygoing, one of the boys, 1992 Democratic presidential nominee Bill Clinton was the kind of fellow you'd want to invite to your barbecue. He was hang-loose and happy-go-lucky. He was funny. Clinton was the type of guy you'd hang out with at the local pub, swapping jokes about the ol' ball and chain. Even Republican Wisconsin governor Tommy Thompson, stumping hard for incumbent president George H. W. Bush, said that he'd "like to go out and have a beer with Bill Clinton."[1]

Clinton is actually allergic to beer.[2] But there is little doubt that during the 1992 election cycle, Clinton was the more likable candidate.

Much of Clinton's appeal sprang from his caustic sense of humor, which he tempered with laconic delivery. In November 1991, Vice President Dan Quayle announced that he would be a "pit bull" in attacking Democratic aspirants. "My," Clinton drawled, "that's got every fire hydrant in America worried."[3]

Clinton also recognized that he had to be careful not to come off as a wise guy. To that end, he repeatedly joked about his intelligence, turning himself from an Ivy League law student into just another boob. At one campaign event, Clinton was introduced as the smartest Democratic candidate. Clinton responded, "Isn't that like calling Moe the most intelligent of the Three Stooges?"[4]

He also joked about his staff, contrasting his own folksiness with their style. Well-coiffed communications director George Stephanopolous was "just a heartthrob away from the presidency," Clinton said. "I don't know what I'm going to do about Georgie . . . That sort of angelic funk look . . . He's going to be insufferable."[5] Of running mate Al Gore, Clinton wryly observed, "Al Gore is younger, better-looking and thinner than I am, and I resent it. But I'll get over it."[6]

Clinton particularly enjoyed directing his wit at President Bush. While speaking in Atlanta, Clinton drew on his Southern history to rip Bush's handling of the economy. Trusting the economy to Bush, Clinton joked, would be like "hiring General Sherman to be fire commissioner."[7] In Davenport, Iowa, on Halloween, Clinton handed out prizes to children with the best costumes. "The winner of the scariest is—George Bush," he announced.[8]

Clinton made sure to use down-home phraseology during the 1992 campaign to contrast with Bush's less-than-credible Texan style. In Tennessee, Clinton invoked some earthy imagery. The weather, Clinton stated, was "hotter than a pickup's windshield out here." The presidential race was "tight as a tick." The election wasn't about Democrats and Republicans—"That's a dog that won't hunt anymore."[9] Clinton bragged, "It's well known that I commune with [Elvis Presley's] spirit."[10] He challenged Bush to a good old-fashioned fistfight—a challenge that carried little risk for Clinton, who was twenty-two years Bush's junior.[11]

Perhaps most effectively, Clinton used humor to play the victim. President Bush had attacked Democratic nominee Michael Dukakis with gusto during his 1988 campaign, but he had never looked mean in doing it. Clinton saw that by playing the victim, he could paint Bush as a bitter old man. Clinton's wife, Hillary, was deeply involved in the campaign; when Bush criticized her, Clinton ruefully cracked, "If he wants to run against my wife, it's OK with me if he wants to be first lady—but I don't want to live with him."[12]

After the media reported that the Bush Administration State Department had unearthed files about Clinton's mother, Clinton went on the attack. "Now it turns out that the State Department was not only rifling through my files, but actually investigating my mother—a well-known subversive," Clinton told a crowd in Seattle. "[Leonid] Brezhnev was calling her to get tips on the third race at Oaklawn every night," Clinton joked. "She had a little shrine in the corner of our home to Joe Stalin."[13]

This strategy worked well for Clinton. Clinton's scandals worked to his advantage, gilding him in the public eye as a good ol' boy—a guy who had cheated, smoked, draft dodged, and lived to tell about it. In short, Clinton was a likable cad. Bush, on the other hand, had too sharp an edge. Bush campaigned vigorously against Clinton, ripping him on his draft dodging, his marijuana use, his personal morality. But it all backfired; the public began to see Bush as dour and mean-spirited.

Clinton, Bush said, was "leader of the Arkansas National Guard—the man who hopes to be commander-in-chief? Well, while I bit the bullet, he bit his nails."[14] "My dog Millie knows more about foreign affairs than these two bozos," Bush remarked, referring to Clinton and third-party contender Ross Perot.[15] Bush referred to Al Gore as "Mr. Ozone," and invoked Millie's intellectual prowess again, contending, "If I want foreign policy advice, I'd go to Millie before I'd go to Ozone and Governor Clinton."[16]

The media had a lot to do with the perception of Bush as mean.

They often called him "nasty" and referred to his comments as "sarcastic." When Bush questioned Clinton's decision to go to Moscow as a student at Oxford University during the Vietnam War, the media blasted him, labeling the criticism "not just patently desperate, but deplorably sordid," "not just nasty, but demagogic," "a new low in sly innuendo and overt mud-heaving."[17] As Bush groused, "I felt like one of those corn dogs at the fair, skewered by the Democratic opposition for nine months . . . He takes a little, gentle broadside and he starts to whine and complain."[18]

Bush simply did not have the good-natured humor of his predecessor, Ronald Reagan. Contrast Bush's acidic attacks with Reagan's warm jocularity during the 1992 contest. In 1988, Democratic vice presidential candidate Lloyd Bentsen had attacked Dan Quayle for comparing himself to JFK with regard to age: "Senator, I served with Jack Kennedy, I knew Jack Kennedy, Jack Kennedy was a friend of mine. Senator, you are no Jack Kennedy." During the 1992 campaign, Clinton's campaign compared him to Thomas Jefferson. Reagan pounced on the comparison, invoking Bentsen's comments. "I knew Thomas Jefferson," Reagan quipped. "He was a friend of mine, and Governor, you're no Thomas Jefferson."[19]

And Bush was no Reagan. When it came time for the election, Clinton trounced Bush, largely on the strength of his own folksy humor.

★★★

"PEOPLE NATURALLY LIKE TO BE in good spirits, to laugh, and feel uplifted—and are drawn to those who make them feel that way," wrote Drs. Ann Demaris and Valerie White in their book *First Impressions: What You Don't Know About How Others See You.* "You don't have to be a comedian. You can elevate others' moods in many ways, such as by smiling, being in the moment, acting playful or entertaining, and directing your attention to the positive and humorous elements in the situation."[20]

Simply put, we like people who are funny and engaging. We don't like people who are mean or boring. This holds true for both partygoers and presidential candidates.

It's the "beer buddy syndrome."

There's an episode of *The Simpsons,* Two Bad Neighbors, that aptly demonstrates the power of the "Beer Buddy Syndrome."

George H. W. Bush and Barbara move to Springfield, right across the street from the Simpsons. The Bushes get along famously with the uptight and religiously upright Flanders. They don't get along well with the Simpsons, however. Bart calls the former president and first lady by their first names, and accidentally shreds Bush's memoirs. "I'm going to do something your daddy should have done a long time ago," President Bush says, then puts Bart over his knee and spanks him. This touches off an episode-long feud between Bush and Homer, culminating in Bush's decision to move away from Springfield.

As soon as Bush leaves, another car pulls in. The license plate reads, "MR DUH." It is former president Gerald Ford.

"Say, Homer, do you like football?" Ford asks Homer.

"Do I ever!" answers Homer.

"Do you like nachos?" Ford asks Homer.

"Yes, Mr. Ford," answers Homer.

"Well, why don't you come over and watch the game, and we'll have nachos? And then, some beer," says Ford.

"Ooh!" exclaims Homer. As they walk into the house, they both trip, and simultaneously yell, "D'oh!" It is, presumably, the beginning of a beautiful friendship.

Now, this is obviously satire, and rather poor satire at that. But the episode certainly holds some truth. If Gerald Ford had not been Richard Nixon's vice president, he likely would have won the 1976 election. He was likable; H. W. Bush was not. Homer Simpson is a stereotypical caricature of the common man—he prefers a man who likes football, nachos, and beer to a man who insists on the particulars. If Bush were running against Ford in Springfield, there is little doubt who would win.

Presidential politics is Springfield writ large. The more engaging candidate typically wins. Al Gore campaigned like a tree stump and lost; Bill Clinton campaigned as a good old boy and won. Barry Goldwater campaigned as a rather ill-tempered and self-righteous fellow and lost; Ronald Reagan campaigned as a good-natured father figure and won. This isn't to say that sticks-in-the-mud don't become president—the nineteenth century was full of sticks-in-the-mud. But the best candidates—and the best presidents—use humor and a common touch to get things done.

★★★

HUMOR DIDN'T MATTER MUCH for the founders. The people were more concerned with statesmanship than friendliness; that was largely a function of the president's somewhat removed role with regard to the public. Washington displayed occasional wit, but mostly he acted the part of statue on a pedestal. Adams's wit was too sharp for his contemporaries—as Adams's secretary of war, James McHenry, put it, "Whether he is spiteful, playful, witty, kind, cold, drunk, sober, angry, easy, stiff, jealous, cautious, confident, close, open, it is always in the wrong place or to the wrong person."[21] One gets the sense that Adams would not have been fun to barhop with—he might have been a mean drunk.

Jefferson's image was one of farmer-philosopher; James Madison, wrote Bob Dole, "was [reputedly] a brilliant conversationalist, much addicted to punning and epigram. Maybe you had to be there; the written record, at least, provides little evidence to support the picture of a witty Madison."[22] James Monroe, John Quincy Adams, and Martin Van Buren were all somewhat humorless. Andrew Jackson wasn't just humorless—he could rightly be described as a mean old bastard. Jackson's humor ran along bloody lines. When asked on his deathbed if he had any regrets, Jackson quickly spat, "That I didn't shoot Henry Clay and hang John C. Calhoun."[23]

★★★

THE FIRST "BEER BUDDY" PRESIDENT was William Henry Harrison. If Harrison ran today, Budweiser would sponsor his campaign. Harrison, the first candidate to openly campaign for the presidency, ran largely on his love for hard cider during the 1840 campaign. The point of the hard cider imagery was that Harrison was a toughened old warrior who could drink with the best of them; incumbent president Martin Van Buren, by contrast, was a dandy who couldn't hold a shot of sarsaparilla.

Campaign songs focused on the contrast between the "Hard Cider Candidate"[24] and the frilly incumbent. One song went like this:

> Let Van from his coolers of silver drink wine,
> And lounge on his cushioned settee;
> Our man on his buckeye bench can recline
> Content with hard cider is he![25]

Such songs provided the backbone for Harrison's campaign. Horace Greeley, the Whig editor of the *Log Cabin*, wrote, "Our songs are doing more good than anything else . . . Really, I think every song is good for five hundred new subscribers."[26] The songs were sung between speeches at Whig rallies, creating an "electric" effect.[27]

Harrison referred to his proclivity for hard cider during his campaign speeches, and even guzzled some during one speech.[28] Whigs downed hard cider at all their events. "To honor their heroes," wrote 1840 campaign historian Robert Gray Gunderson, "high priests of Whiggery usually downed thirteen formal toasts, plus an indeterminate number of informal ones."[29] At one banquet, these thirteen toasts were announced:

1st.	The people.
2nd.	George Washington. (Drink standing and in solemn silence.)
3rd.	William Henry Harrison. (Nine cheers—music—Yankee Doodle—salute the artillery.)
4th.	John Tyler.
5th.	Virginia.
6th.	Maryland.
7th.	The District of Columbia—without a vote, she has a voice.
8th.	The President of the United States. ("That is to be," added several voices.)
9th.	The opposition party—union is strength.
10th.	The best Whig Senators from Virginia—Rives and Allen.
11th.	Log cabins and cider.
12th.	The opposition in Congress.
13th.	Our guests—the servants of the people, and the friends of the people.[30]

The best part was that there were no automobiles. No designated drivers necessary.

Harrison's campaign's utilization of hard cider created a word that still exists in common parlance—*booze*. Whigs took advantage of the market for log cabins and hard cider by creating pocket brandy and whiskey bottles shaped like log cabins. These were then filled with "Old Cabin Whisky." The manufacturer of Old Cabin Whisky? The E. C. Booz Distillery. To this day, *booze* remains slang for "alcohol."[31]

The hubbub over hard cider puzzled Democrats. One Democratic-leaning newspaper, the Albany *Rough-Hewer*, published the following dictionary:

PATRIOTISM—Guzzling sour cider.
CALUMNY—The truth.
ARGUMENT—Hurrah for Old Tip.
PERSONAL ABUSE—Telling facts.
LOG CABIN—A palace.
AN APPEAL TO THE JUDGEMENT—Hard cider *diluted* in whisky.[32]

Whig supporter George D. Prentice, columnist for the Louisville *Journal*, aptly summed up the Harrison campaign. "In what respect is hard cider an emblem of General Harrison?" a Democrat asked Prentice.

"All we know is that it runs well," Prentice retorted.[33]

It ran well enough. The ultimate beer buddy, William Henry Harrison, ousted Van Buren with ease.

★★★

ABRAHAM LINCOLN rightfully occupies perhaps the most honored place in the presidential pantheon. But that status obscures the fact that Lincoln was not merely a tremendous politician and a great man—he was funny as all get out. That was part of what made him our greatest president. "If I didn't laugh, I should die," Lincoln once explained to his cabinet.[34]

Lincoln's humor was homespun, folksy, and natural. He demonstrated his lighter side throughout his political career. During his first congressional race, Lincoln ran against Methodist minister Peter Cartwright, who routinely berated Lincoln about his sporadic church attendance. Lincoln decided to attend a religious meeting where Cartwright was speaking. At the end of Cartwright's speech, Cartwright asked the congregation to stand if they wanted to go to heaven. Most of the congregation stood. Then Cartwright yelled, "All those who do not wish to go to hell will stand!" By now, all the people were on their feet—except Lincoln.

Cartwright looked at Lincoln, then gravely intoned, "I observe that many of you accepted my invitation to give their hearts to God and go to heaven. I further observed that all but one of you indicated an aversion to going to hell. The sole exception is Mr. Lincoln, who failed to respond to either invitation. May I inquire of you, Mr. Lincoln, where you are going?"

"Brother Cartwright," answered Lincoln, "asks me directly where I am going. Well, I'll tell you: I am going to Congress."

Lincoln was elected.[35]

Lincoln's wit served him well in touchy situations. Once, during a debate, one of the audience members yelled at Lincoln, "You're a fool!" Lincoln stopped, turned, and lightly retorted, "Well, that makes two of us."[36]

Lincoln wasn't afraid to pillory his opponents. At one 1858 debate, Douglas referred to Lincoln's humble beginnings, stating that he had first met Lincoln when Lincoln was the liquor salesperson at a general goods store. "And Mr. Lincoln was a very good bartender, too," Douglas concluded.

"What Mr. Douglas has said is true enough," said Lincoln. "I did keep a grocery, and I did sell cotton, candles, and cigars, and sometimes whiskey. I remember in those days that Mr. Douglas was one of my best customers. Many a time have I stood on one side of the counter and sold whiskey to Mr. Douglas on the other side, but the difference between us now is this: I have left my side of the counter, but Mr. Douglas still sticks to his as tenaciously as ever."[37]

Lincoln used Reaganesque folk humor to trash Douglas. "When I was a boy," Lincoln explained at one debate, "I spent considerable time along the Sangamon River. An old steamboat plied on the river, the boiler of which was so small that when they blew the whistle, there wasn't enough steam to turn the paddle wheel. When the paddle wheel went around, they couldn't blow the whistle. My friend Douglas reminds me of that old steamboat for it is evident that when he talks he can't think, and when he thinks he can't talk."[38] Another time Lincoln stated that Douglas had a gift for "specious and fantastic arrangement of words, by which a man can prove a horse-chestnut to be a chestnut horse."[39]

Each joke, Douglas complained, "seems like a whack upon my back."[40] He wasn't far off. Before one debate, Lincoln handed his cloak to an assistant. "Hold this while I stone Stephen," he remarked.[41]

Lincoln used anecdotes to defuse volatile situations. Governor Charles Morehead of Kentucky confronted President Lincoln, insisting that Lincoln make concessions to the South. Lincoln proceeded to tell Morehead one of Aesop's fables about a lion who wanted to marry a princess. The princess's parents insisted that the lion file down his teeth and claws. He did so, and the parents bopped the lion on the head. Morehead gruffly replied that "it was an exceedingly interesting anecdote, and very *apropos*, but not altogether a satisfactory answer." Lincoln biographer David Herbert Donald wrote, "Lincoln used this technique throughout his presidency, to the bafflement of those who had no sense of humor and the rage of those who failed to get a straight answer from him."[42]

Lincoln became famous for his lively sense of humor and endless store of anecdotes. During the 1864 election, *Harper's Weekly* ran a cartoon summing up the public view of Lincoln. In it, a gigantic Lincoln holds Democratic nominee George McClellan in the palm of his hand. "This reminds me of a little joke," Lincoln drawls.[43] Lincoln's political enemies, too, recognized his penchant for joke telling. One Democratic song from 1864 was entitled "Hey! Uncle Abe, are you Joking yet?" It was sung to the tune of "Johnny Cope." The lyrics read:

> Hey! Uncle Abe, are you joking yet,
> Or have you taken a serious fit,
> And wisely set to pack up your kit,
> To be up and off in the morning?

> Honest Old Abe was a queer old coon,
> Joked with a n- - - - and play'd the buffoon,
> But now he shakes from his head to his shoon,
> All night unto the morning.[44]

Lincoln presided over the greatest crisis in national history. He retained power—and enough goodwill to govern—because he represented the people at large. His sense of humor was one of his strongest selling points. And Lincoln never lost his humor, even in the face of disaster. During the Civil War, Lincoln held a White House reception. Seeing Lincoln, a guest shouted, "Mr. President, I'm from up in New York State where we believe that God Almighty and Abraham Lincoln are going to save this country." Lincoln smiled. "My friend," he said, "you're half-right."[45]

★★★

TEDDY ROOSEVELT WAS ARROGANT. After his stint with the Rough Riders in Cuba during the Spanish-American War, TR wrote a somewhat self-congratulatory memoir entitled *The Rough Riders*; one wag suggested that it should have been entitled *Alone in Cuba*.[46] Roosevelt, Mark Twain wrote, was "the Tom Sawyer of the political world of the twentieth century; always showing off; always hunting for a chance to show off; in his frenzied imagination the Great Republic is a vast Barnum circus with him for a clown and the whole world for audience."[47]

But, like Tom Sawyer, Roosevelt was the kind of guy people would buy drinks for. His toothy grin became an ubiquitous symbol of his popularity, adorning editorial cartoons the country over. His trust-busting platform—and the alacrity with which he pursued it—ensured that the public viewed him as a crusader for honesty. "A man who has never gone to school may steal from a freight car," TR proclaimed, "but if he has a university education, he may steal the whole railroad."[48] He promised every American a "square deal."[49] TR recognized his broad appeal. "The most successful politician is he who says what the people are thinking most often in the loudest voice," TR stated.[50]

Just as Lincoln had, Roosevelt regaled audiences with folksy anecdotes. After a Russian pogrom in 1903, Roosevelt met with a group of Jewish leaders who wished Roosevelt to petition Tsar Nicholas II. His advisors informed him that it would be inadvisable to alienate the Russians; still, Roosevelt had to placate Jewish leaders. And so he told a story.

When I was myself in the army, one of the best colonels among the regular regiments who did so well on that day, who fought beside me, was a Jew! . . . You may possibly recall—I am certain some of my New York friends will recall—that during the time I was Police Commissioner, a man came from abroad—I am sorry to say, a clergyman—to start an anti-Jewish agitation in New York, and announced his intention of holding meetings to assail the Jews. The matter was brought to my attention. Of course I had no power to prevent these meetings. After a good deal of thought I detailed a Jewish sergeant and forty Jewish policemen to protect the agitator while he held his meetings. So he made his speeches denouncing the Jews, protected exclusively by Jews!

He continued telling such pithy anecdotes for the next hour. When the Jewish leaders left, they had secured no pledge from Roosevelt, but Edmund Morris reported that "the committee trooped out glowing with satisfaction."[51]

★ ★ ★

CONTEMPORARY LIBERAL HISTORIANS find it difficult to understand the allure of President Calvin Coolidge. When Ronald Reagan placed Coolidge's portrait in the Cabinet Room, the media stirred up a fuss. "Skeptics have abounded from the start," sneered *Time*. "Coolidge has never been heroic history. Arthur Schlesinger Jr. keeps reminding readers that Coolidge was noted for sleeping twelve hours a day. Schlesinger, who served John Kennedy, knew of no other President who spent that much time in bed sleeping."[52]

Newsweek similarly scoffed, "Fishing was more Coolidge's style than the horseback riding Reagan favors, and certainly he would have preferred a long afternoon snooze to Reagan's daily workout with the chain saw, but otherwise he would have approved thoroughly of this lazy, vacation-time Presidency—the rural setting, the phone calls few and far between, the luxury of sleeping through even an aerial encounter with a hostile country. He might have faulted Reagan for being a little too eager to get back to work, though: he himself knocked off for a minimum of two months every summer."[53]

Alan Brinkley of the *New York Times* was most brutal: "It has been a long time since anyone has had anything good to say about Calvin Coolidge, but President Reagan apparently is determined to set history right . . . Affable, charming Ronald Reagan clearly has not identified personally with the dour 'Silent Cal,' who had a sour, nasty sense of humor and a raging temper."[54]

This is revisionist history, pure and simple. For a more accurate description, turn to Coolidge critic H. L. Mencken: "The general burden of the Coolidge memoirs was that the right hon. Gentleman was a typical American, and some hinted that he was the most typical since Lincoln . . . He was revered simply because he was so plainly just folks—because what little he said was precisely what was heard in every garage and barbershop. He gave the plain people the kind of esthetic pleasure known as recognition, and in horse-doctor's doses."[55]

"Silent Cal," as he was known, explained, "I always figured the American public wanted a solemn ass for president, so I went along with them."[56] But Coolidge was far from solemn—he was famously hilarious in his taciturnity. He lived by the motto "I have never been hurt by what I have not said."[57] At one dinner, for example, a woman sitting next to Coolidge informed him that she had made a bet with one of her friends that she could get the president to say more than two words. Coolidge's answer: "You lose."[58]

After Coolidge returned from church one day, Mrs. Coolidge asked him what the sermon had been about. "Sin," Coolidge answered. "Well, what did he say?" she asked. "He was against it," said Coolidge.[59]

Another time Coolidge saw one of his political opponents, Senator William Edgar Borah, riding his horse through Rock Creek Park. The president turned to his driver and remarked, "Must bother him to be going the same direction as the horse."[60]

Coolidge, so another story goes, stood at a window, watching the rain. One visitor tried to engage the president in small talk. "I wonder if it will ever stop raining," the visitor sighed. "Well," said Coolidge, "it always has."[61] On another rainy occasion, a Secret Service agent bested Coolidge. The Secret Service agent observed that a storm was coming. "Well," asked Coolidge, "what are you going to do about it?" "Mr. President," answered the agent, "I'm only a Secret Service man. But you are President of the United States of America. What are *you* going to do about it?" The Secret Service agent immediately became one of Coolidge's favorites.[62]

Still, Coolidge didn't enjoy being shadowed by his Secret Service men. While fishing in the Black Hills, he and a guide managed to lose the Secret Service agents by canoeing downstream. A few minutes later, Coolidge and the guide heard splashes and cries upstream. After a few moments, a canoe paddle floated by. Then a pillow. Finally, a Secret Service agent's hat. "Been expecting that," remarked Coolidge.[63]

Coolidge was a great speechwriter, but he did not enjoy speaking. An audience member at one of Coolidge's speeches approached the president and said, "Mr. President, I was so anxious to hear your speech at the opening of Congress, I had to stand the *whole* forty-five minutes." "So did I," replied Coolidge.[64]

Another of Coolidge's speeches was much shorter. The chairman at an Amherst graduate dinner in Spain asked Coolidge, an alumnus, to send a message. He informed Coolidge that there would be no charges on the cable, so the cable had no length limits. Coolidge promptly sent a message. After the chairman announced

Coolidge's name at the dinner, to wild applause, he opened up the message and read it to the assemblage. The message: "Greetings. — Calvin Coolidge."[65]

Favor-seekers often left Coolidge's presence disappointed. One day a small bank president came to Coolidge, asking him if he would place a deposit of any size in the bank for publicity purposes. "Why don't you make me an honorary depositor?" asked Coolidge. As compensation for the joke, Coolidge later deposited some money with the bank.[66]

During his time as governor of Massachusetts, a state legislator whined to Coolidge that he had been told by another legislator to go to hell. Coolidge replied, "I've looked up the law. You don't have to go."[67]

Coolidge got away with such taciturnity because his thrift with words signaled an inner toughness while betraying a quick wit and vibrant humor. He was careful with words, and he was careful with taxpayer money. "Nothing is easier than spending the public money," he averred. "It does not appear to belong to anybody."[68] "More nearly than any other body of our citizens," said Coolidge, "the wage earners are the public."[69] Still, Coolidge was no worshiper of the simple dollar: "Prosperity is only an instrument to be used; not a deity to be worshiped."[70] Coolidge was one of the last presidents to believe fervently in the idea of a natural law: "Laws must be justified by something more than the will of the majority. They must rest on the eternal foundation of righteousness."[71]

These were not the words of a mere simpleton. But Coolidge carefully balanced his deeply American philosophy with a deeply American humor. He hated snobs. In an exchange everyone outside of Boston can enjoy, a rather imposing and snooty Massachusetts woman accosted Coolidge, a native Vermonter. "I come from Boston," she proclaimed. "Yes," Coolidge replied, "and you'll never get over it."[72]

Coolidge was immensely popular in his own time; his popular margin of victory in 1924 is the second largest in modern presidential history. His electoral landslide lends credence to another Coolidge anecdote. A man approached Coolidge and greeted him, sneering, "I didn't vote for you." Coolidge's response: "Somebody did."[73]

Millions did. Coolidge combined an air of removal with a quick wit and an earthy, if Puritan, ethos. He may not have been a typical "beer buddy" president, but the public treated him like one.

★★★

WHO WOULDN'T WANT TO BUY FDR A BEER? The man was garrulous, amiable, upbeat. While FDR's 1932 campaign theme song became "Happy Days Are Here Again," Republican incumbent president Herbert Hoover's campaign became linked with the Rudy Vallee hit song "Brother, Can You Spare a Dime?" FDR made himself the candidate of optimism.

FDR made a habit of smiling incessantly; Mencken labeled Roosevelt's grin a "Christian Science smile." But FDR's constant smile rubbed the American people the right way. As one reporter put it, "Roosevelt smiles and smiles and smiles and it doesn't get tiresome. He can smile more than any man in American politics without being insipid."[74] "He was the first president since his cousin Theodore to smile regularly and act as if he were enjoying himself," wrote Jonathan Alter.[75]

FDR also employed the most effective campaign prop since Lincoln's top hat: a cigarette holder. FDR employed a cigarette holder because he suffered from sensitive gums,[76] but the holder, constantly angled upward, signaled a jauntily pugnacious attitude that provided visual encouragement for Americans.

Roosevelt's optimism infected his speeches. In accepting the

Democratic nomination, FDR boxed Republicans' ears—but he also offered hope. There was a Hegelian light at the end of the tunnel; he said, "Out of every crisis, every tribulation, every disaster, mankind rises with some share of greater knowledge, of higher decency, of purer purpose." Then, in one of the most famous conclusions in all of American speechmaking, FDR promised that he would lead America out of the tunnel. "I pledge you, I pledge myself, to a new deal for the American people," he stated. "Let us all here assembled constitute ourselves prophets of a new order of competence and of courage. This is more than a political campaign; it is a call to arms. Give me your help, not to win votes alone, but to win in this crusade to restore America to its own people."[77]

FDR dismissed attacks with the sort of casual aplomb so effective in politics. When 1928 Democratic nominee Al Smith attacked Roosevelt for his class warfare, Roosevelt refused to address the criticism. "Attacking me?" he asked a reporter. "I haven't read the papers, not closely . . ." When another reporter insisted that FDR must have heard about the attack via radio, Roosevelt simply answered, "My radio isn't working now."[78]

This strategy served Roosevelt well throughout his political career. During the 1944 election, Republican nominee Thomas Dewey attacked Roosevelt for allegedly sending a destroyer to the Aleutian Islands to pick up Roosevelt's forgotten dog, Fala. FDR riotously engaged the allegation in a speech to the Teamsters Union:

> These Republican leaders have not been content with attacks on me, or on my wife, or on my sons—no, not content with that, they now include my little dog, Fala. Well, of course, I don't resent attacks and my family doesn't resent attacks, but Fala does resent them. You know, you know Fala's Scotch and, being a Scottie, as soon as he learned that the Republican fiction writers in Congress

and out had concocted a story that I had left him behind on an Aleutian island and had sent a destroyer back to find him—at a cost to the taxpayers of two or three or eight or twenty million dollars—his Scotch soul was furious. He has not been the same dog since. I am accustomed to hearing malicious falsehoods about myself—such as that old, worm-eaten chestnut that I have represented myself as indispensable. But I think I have a right to resent, to object to, libelous statements about my dog.[79]

Dogs have been indispensable political tools ever since.

It was all part and parcel of FDR's warm image. FDR's fireside chats revolutionized the art of politics, bringing presidents closer than ever to the people. His first fireside chat took place in 1933. Robert Trout of CBS introduced him: "The president wants to come into your home and sit at your fireside for a little fireside chat." Alter described the speech: "His speaking voice was a beautiful and relaxed tenor, not the contrived basso profundo of pompous politicians . . . A leader who began each radio speech by calling the people 'my friends' must be . . . friendly."[80] Of course, that voice was carefully prepared: before each fireside chat, Roosevelt had his nasal passages swabbed with ointment to improve that "beautiful and relaxed tenor." Roosevelt's aide, Tommy Corcoran, said that Roosevelt "looked upon a speech with the same care that a prima donna would take care of her voice before a singing appearance."[81]

Throughout his career, the press was exceedingly kind to FDR. Aside from protecting FDR's paralysis from the intrusive eye of the camera, the media also saw FDR as a savior of sorts. After his election in 1932, the *Cincinnati Free Press* praised FDR's optimism in glowing terms: "There is something contagious about the cheery smile and innate confidence." The *New York Daily News* went further, simultaneously labeling FDR an incipient American dictator but praising that dictatorship: "A lot of us have been asking for a dictator. Now we have one . . . Dictatorship in crises was ancient Rome's best era . . . The impression we get from various quarters is that practically everyone feels better already. Confidence seems to be coming back with a rush, along with courage."[82]

FDR was an aristocrat, but he was a "second-class aristocrat," in the words of a young lawyer of the time. He connected with the people on their level, with humor, good cheer, and a peppy bravura that would guide America through the Depression and World War II.

★★★

THE ELECTION OF 1960 pitted one of America's wittiest presidential candidates, John F. Kennedy, against one of its gloomiest, Richard M. Nixon. JFK's sparkling repartee contrasted sharply with Nixon's dogged issue pounding. After Kennedy was able to counter Nixon's "experience" advantage in the debates, his personality made him a stronger candidate than the darker, more foreboding Nixon.

Kennedy's humor was subtle and stylish. In 1958, Kennedy humorously twitted President Eisenhower's optimism about the economy. "As I interpret [President Eisenhower]," said Kennedy, "we're now at the end of the beginning of the upturn of the downturn. Every bright spot the White House finds in the economy is like the policeman bending over the body in the alley who says cheerfully, 'Two of his wounds are fatal—but the other one's not so bad.'"[83]

He was a master of disarming one-liners. JFK's father, Joseph, was an ultra-wealthy mover and shaker, an anti-Semite, and a pro-Nazi defeatist. He was also a brilliant politician. He informed Jack that if he wanted to be president, he would have to "get yourself plenty of laughs . . . keep smiling whenever you take a crack." And that's precisely what JFK did. During the 1958 Gridiron Dinner, JFK sat through a lampooning at the hands of a speaker who credited Joseph with attempting to buy the 1960 election for his son. When it came JFK's turn to speak, he pulled out a note from his "generous daddy" and read it aloud: "Dear Jack . . . Don't buy a single vote more than is necessary—I'll be damned if I'm going to pay for a landslide."[84]

JFK would use that same wit to great effect during his shortened presidency. Early in his presidency, Kennedy read answers to press inquiries from note cards. When asked why he did so, Kennedy quickly responded, "Because I'm not a textual deviant." After Kennedy appointed his brother attorney general, the media demanded an explanation. "I've been criticized by quite a few people for making my brother Bobby attorney general," he stated. "They didn't realize that I had a very good reason for that appointment. Bobby wants to practice law, and I thought he ought to get a little experience first."[85]

But JFK didn't solely rely on his own wit. During the 1960 campaign, JFK's tremendous speechwriters also pulled their weight. Before the Gridiron Dinner in 1958, JFK speechwriter Ted Sorenson called together the entire speechwriting staff to come up with humorous material. In one session, the team voted on 112 jokes and anecdotes.[86] It worked to perfection. During the speech, JFK told a joke written by speechwriter Clark Clifford targeting one of the 1960 frontrunners, Senate Majority Leader Lyndon Johnson.

"I dreamed about 1960 the other night," said Jack, "and I told [Missouri Senator] Stuart Symington and Lyndon Johnson about it yesterday. I told them how the Lord came into my bedroom, anointed my head, and said, 'John Kennedy, I hereby anoint you President of the United States.' Stu Symington said, 'That's strange, Jack, because I had a similar dream last night in which the Lord

anointed me President of the United States and outer space.' Then
Lyndon Johnson said, 'That's very interesting, gentlemen, because I,
too, had a similar dream last night—and I don't remember anointing either one of you.' "[87]

Many of JFK's jokes targeted Nixon's political opportunism—and
his image as a greasy, unshaven, evil manipulator. Throughout his
political life, Nixon was cast as Machiavellian. In 1959, journalist
Philip Potter described Nixon as "the scientific pitchman of politics,
who coldly tries to figure what will sell, packages his products neatly,
and then goes out to peddle them."[88] And Frank Holeman wrote,
"His own voting record, his speeches, 'fund,' jowls, heavy stubble of
beard, and ski-nose have been thoroughly exploited by enemy ora-
tors, cartoonists, and propagandists."[89]

JFK exploited Nixon's image to the fullest. During the 1960
campaign, JFK spoke at the Al Smith dinner in New York along
with Nixon. Earlier in the campaign, Nixon criticized Democratic
stump speakers for using profanity. JFK used the material to wonderful effect. A Republican supporter, said JFK, approached Nixon
about one of his speeches.

It was a "damn fine speech," the man stated.

"I appreciate the compliment, but not the language," Nixon
supposedly replied.

"Yes sir, I liked it so much I contributed one thousand dollars to
your campaign," said the man, undeterred.

"The hell you say," cried Nixon.[90]

JFK also made fun of Nixon's "Herblock" look. Herb Block, a
cartoonist for the *Washington Post*, routinely (and rather cruelly)
drew Nixon with heavy stubble, and a grimy look. When Nixon
accused JFK of telling a "barefaced lie," JFK seized on the Herblock
imagery: "Two days ago, Mr. Nixon, in that wonderful choice of
words which distinguishes him as a great national leader, asserted

that I told a barefaced lie. Having seen him four times close up in this campaign, and made up [in the TV debates], I would not accuse Mr. Nixon of being barefaced."[91]

Nixon, for his part, went relatively easy on JFK. He had two particular disadvantages. First, he did not want to look mean during the 1960 campaign. Paul Boller wrote, "In 1960 Nixon was criticized by some people for the 'kid-glove' campaign he was waging against Kennedy. 'I have to erase the Herblock image first,' he explained."[92] His mildly sinister look haunted him throughout the campaign, particularly after the disastrous first television debate with Kennedy. "People keep asking me, 'why can't you do something about your face?'" Nixon told an audience. "Well, if I grew a beard they'd say I was trying to look like Lincoln. A mustache might make me look like Dewey. And if I let my hair grow, they'd say I was trying to look like Bobby [Kennedy]."[93]

Nixon's second disadvantage was that he didn't have much of a sense of humor. One of his congressional contemporaries described him as "conscientious, intelligent and perceptive, but . . . too intense."[94] During the 1960 election cycle, Nixon did little to mitigate the public perception that he was somewhat of a killjoy. It was a mistake he would not repeat in 1968 and 1972, when his campaign deliberately attempted to create a "new Nixon," demonstrating Nixon's softer side with panel shows, humorous footage, and jolly photo ops.[95]

Why did JFK win the 1960 election? Personality had a lot to do with it. JFK's vice president, Lyndon Baines Johnson, opined that JFK "had a good sense of humor and . . . looked good on television, but his growing hold on the American people was simply a mystery to me."[96] JFK's hold shouldn't have been so mysterious—the two qualities LBJ mentioned were, and are, quite important to the voting public.

★★★

AS GOVERNOR OF CALIFORNIA (1967–1975), Ronald Reagan loved battling it out with student demonstrators. The student demonstrators posed a real threat to the functioning of state universities; they also provided Reagan with rich political material. During one rally, college antiwar demonstrators surrounded Reagan's car and held up a sign reading, "We are the future." Reagan grabbed a piece of paper and wrote something on it, then held the paper up to the window. The paper read, "I'll sell my bonds."[97]

When shaggy-haired students protested at another Reagan appearance holding signs like "Jane Wyman Was Right" and "Impeach Bonzo and His Co-Star," Reagan told the media, "Their signs say make love, not war. But they don't look like they could do much of either."[98] When similarly unkempt students informed Reagan that they would precipitate a "bloodbath," Reagan told them to take a bath.[99]

Reagan stood up to members of the younger generation who attempted to cite their age as authority for their radicalism. "You grew up in a different world," one student complained to Reagan. "Today we have television, jet planes, space travel, nuclear energy, computers." "You're right," Reagan quickly shot back. "It's true that we didn't have those things when we were young. We *invented* them."[100]

Reagan was a man of wit and class. His opponent in the 1980 election, incumbent President Jimmy Carter, had neither. While Carter campaigned in 1976 as a kindly Southern fellow with a toothy smile, the real Carter came to the fore during the 1980 election. Carter was essentially humorless; his tongue was acidic, and he used it to lash both political opponents and members of his own staff. Carter micromanaged constantly, and he read staffers the riot act if they failed to give him what he wanted.

"Sometimes his mean streak, which was undeniable, surfaced publicly," wrote Edward J. Walsh of the *Washington Post*. "Sometimes he seemed like Charlie Brown, the hapless hero of the *Peanuts* comic strip, who was forever being victimized by people and forces less virtuous than himself. At other times, he seemed more like Lucy van Pelt, the crabby little girl of the same comic strip, who angrily and defiantly shouted her philosophy of life: 'I love Mankind; it's people I can't stand.'"[101]

Throughout the 1980 campaign, Carter savaged Reagan, who simply rode above the fray. Carter accused Reagan of racism and warmongering; of "shooting from the hip" and threatening world peace. "Thus was born the issue of Jimmy Carter as a 'mean' mudslinger, as a 'ruthless and reckless' political opportunist,'" penned Richard Harwood of the *Post*.[102]

Though Carter pledged to excise viciousness from his campaign in the aftermath of a particularly virulent attack on Reagan,[103] he did no such thing. On October 7, Carter announced that Reagan was attempting to separate Americans, "Black from White, Jew from Christian, North from South, rural from urban."[104] Reagan sadly responded, "He's reaching a point of hysteria that's hard to understand."[105]

In the debate between Reagan and Carter, Carter reinforced the public perception that he was a loser. He went after Reagan hard and often—and Reagan responded with the most disarming debate tactic in presidential history. After one particularly strident attack on Reagan's past position on Medicare, Reagan shook his head and sighed, "There you go again." When the camera cut to Carter, Carter looked like he was "about to slug" Reagan, as one of Carter's aides put it.[106] Reagan later described the exchange: "The debate went well for me and may have turned on only four little words . . . *'There you go again'* . . . The audience loved it and I think Carter added to the impact of the words by looking a little sheepish on the television screen."[107]

Reagan's 1980 campaign featured him as warm, caring, and funny. His campaign commercials were homey, praising the virtues of family and small-town life. His campaign speeches invoked themes of renewal and strength.

Reagan also used his wit to dramatic effect, directing his ripostes at big government. "There's enough fat in the government in Washington that if it was rendered and made into soap it would wash the world," Reagan gibed.[108] It was a theme Reagan harped on throughout his career. Government was like a baby, went one cherished one-liner—"It is an alimentary canal with an appetite at one end and no sense of responsibility at the other." A government program, Reagan was fond of stating, "is the nearest thing to eternal life we'll ever see on this earth."[109]

Carter did not go unscathed. When Reagan called the economic recession of 1980 a "depression," Carter sneered, "That shows how little he knows." Reagan accepted the point, then turned his rapier on Carter. "A recession is when your neighbor loses his job," explained Reagan. "A depression is when you lose yours. And recovery is when Jimmy Carter loses his."[110]

Carter lost his job. Reagan took it. This time, the "beer buddy syndrome" steered America right—Reagan, one of the most effective presidents in American history, succeeded Carter, one of the worst.

★★★

GEORGE W. BUSH is a beneficiary of the "beer buddy syndrome." Of course, he also had the good fortune to run against Al Gore in 2000—a man who is approximately as much fun as a bucket of rocks. Then he got even luckier—in 2004 he ran against John Kerry, a man who is more likely to sip a fine snifter of brandy than a beer.

Bush had a party-boy reputation during his college years. Appearing on *The Tonight Show with Jay Leno*, Bush joked with Leno about his checkered past. "When you were out at a frat party, having a good time at Yale partying with the boys," asked Leno, "were you ever thinking, 'You know, I don't want to have that beer. I might be running for president.' Did that ever cross your mind?" Bush answered, "No."[111]

As the cowboy candidate, W's folksy manner and unassuming air made him a popular figure. Even though Bush gave up drinking at age forty, he still seemed like a fun guy to hang out with. Gore, by contrast, acted like a stiff. His deep but somewhat nasal monotone—and his repetition of key words like *lockbox*—made him tiresome. Everything about Gore seemed manipulated; everything about Bush seemed genuine. Gore proponent David Greising of the *Chicago Tribune* summed up Bush versus Gore:

> In terms of, if you want somebody who is friendly running the country, and somebody—as some of these polls indicate—whom you would like to have a beer with us, I think you could say that George Bush is the guy you would like to have a beer with, and you think would be friendly—you would rather spend an hour with him in the Oval Office. Al Gore would annoy the hell out of you.[112]

In 2004, Bush faced another all-boring-all-the-time candidate, Senator John Kerry. As Kerry supporter Ciro Scotti of *Business Week* put it, Kerry was a man for "whom constructing the public persona of a regular Joe is a daily challenge."[113] Kerry's frequent and expensive trips to the hairdresser, his elitist sporting choices, his history of marrying up in financial status—none of it played well with Americans. Neither did Kerry's reputation for treating normal people like commoners.

Boston radio host and *Boston Herald* columnist Howie Carr wrote:

> One of the surest ways to get the phones ringing on any Massachusetts talk-radio show is to ask people to call in and tell their John Kerry stories. The phone lines are soon filled, and most of the stories have a common theme: The junior senator pulling rank on one of his constituents, breaking in line, demanding to pay less (or nothing), or ducking out before the bill arrives. The tales often have one other common thread. Most end with Sen. Kerry inquiring of the lesser mortal: "Do you know who I am?"[114]

Once again, Bush triumphed.

Clearly, then, the "beer buddy syndrome" is still with us. The "beer buddy syndrome" doesn't always work to perfection; many incompetents are quite likable. Warren G. Harding was apparently a genial fellow. So was Franklin Pierce.

But the "beer buddy syndrome" remains important. It is shorthand for likability—and personal likability is often an indicator of presidential performance. Easygoing people are likable, and easygoing people are not easily rattled in emergency circumstances—just look at Ronald Reagan. Funny people are likable, and funny people can cope with hard times—just look at Lincoln. Witty people are likable, and witty people are often intelligent—just look at Clinton and Coolidge. Confident people are likable, and confidence often determines presidential strength—just look at FDR and TR.

We want America strong and confident rather than weak and vacillating—and we want the presidents who represent our country to have those same qualities. When it comes to choosing presidents, personality counts.

★ 6 ★
The Hair Makes the Man

WHO IN THE WORLD was Warren G. Harding?

That was the question on America's mind during the presidential campaign of 1920. Harding was a nobody; his political credentials were thin as carbon paper. He had owned a newspaper, had served in the Ohio state Senate, had been lieutenant governor, and had served in the United States Senate. During his time in the Senate, he had done nothing spectacular.

But he looked spectacularly good doing nothing.

Warren G. Harding had a face chiseled from granite. He may not have been a great man, but he *looked* like a great man. Joe Mitchell Chapple, one of Harding's contemporaries, described Harding as a Greek god: "He was to me the embodiment of manly strength and vigor, bronzed . . . with his premature gray hair, a diadem of full-orbed maturity resting on his brow—one of the handsomest men I ever looked upon."[1]

It was Harding's looks that launched his political career. Political strategist Harry Daugherty first met Harding in 1899; he immediately decided that he would make Harding president. Malcolm

Gladwell wrote, "Daugherty looked over at Harding and was instantly overwhelmed by what he saw."[2] Daugherty later explained that he pushed Harding's 1920 run for the White House because "he looked like a President."[3] H. L. Mencken scoffed shortly before Harding's nomination, "We move toward a lofty ideal. On some great and glorious day, the plain folks of the land will reach their heart's desire at last, and the White House will be adorned by a downright moron . . . [Harding is] a third-rate political wheelhorse, with the face of a moving-picture actor, the intelligence of a respectable agricultural-implements dealer, and the imagination of a lodge-joiner."[4]

Harding's 1920 campaign focused almost entirely on his personality—and, because it was his most obvious personal feature, his good looks. Though there were many crucial issues to discuss during the election cycle—the viability of the League of Nations, the pursuit of peace in Europe, domestic disturbances in the aftermath of World War I—Harding discussed none of them. He ran a front porch campaign; six hundred thousand people visited his home in Ohio. His slogans, "Back to Normalcy" and "Let's be done with wiggle and wobble," provided a vague sense of stability to an uneasy nation.[5]

He spoke in platitudes. William Gibbs McAdoo, Woodrow Wilson's son-in-law and an early contender for the Democratic presidential nomination, said, "His speeches leave the impression of an army of pompous phrases moving over the landscape in search of an idea. Sometimes these meandering words would actually capture a struggling thought and bear it triumphantly a prisoner in their midst until it died of servitude and overwork."[6]

Mencken, characteristically, was even more brutal:

I rise to pay my small tribute to Dr. Harding. Setting aside a college professor or two and half a dozen dipsomaniacal newspaper reporters, he takes the first place in my Valhalla of literati. That is, he writes the worst English that I have ever encountered. It reminds me of a string of wet sponges; it reminds me of tattered washing on the line; it reminds me of stale bean soup, of college yells, of dogs barking idiotically through endless nights. It is so bad that a sort of grandeur creeps into it. It drags itself out of the dark abysm of pish, and crawls insanely up the topmost pinnacle of posh. It is rumble and bumble. It is flap and doodle. It is balder and dash.[7]

Mencken did not overstate the case. In one speech, Harding invoked Christian imagery to say nothing in particular:

I tell you, my countrymen, the world needs more of the Christ; the world needs the spirit of the Man of Nazareth. If we could bring into the relationships of humanity among ourselves and among the nations of the world with the brotherhood that was taught by Christ, we would have a restored world; we would have little or none of war and we would have a new hope for humanity throughout the Earth. There never was a greater lesson taught than that of the Golden Rule.[8]

It is difficult to defeat this kind of rhetoric—no one is against the Golden Rule. To oppose such aphoristic niceties would be to assume, by definition, the role of an anti-Christ.

By preaching tautologies, Harding avoided taking a hard position on the issues of his day. As biographers Eugene P. Trani and David L. Wilson wrote, "The candidate concentrated on projecting an image to the electorate—he would provide decent, economical government in a dignified manner—rather than discussing the issues."[9]

Harding was "just plain folks," according to the *Morrow County Sentinel*.[10] Campaign manager Daugherty summed up the widespread public perception of Harding: "He was just a plain, honest American who meant what he said when he urged his policy of getting the country back to normalcy."[11]

But Harding was more than that. He brought a solemn-looking grandeur to his candidacy. Looking at Warren G. Harding's portrait through today's eyes, Harding bears a certain resemblance to an older Lionel Barrymore. If you saw Harding walking down the street, you would immediately think Wall Street executive, judge, or politician. Harry Daugherty thought "president." Harding rode his looks all the way to the White House, winning by the largest percentage margin to that time—where the "embodiment of manly strength" died, two years into his first term.

★★★

IF WARREN G. HARDING HAD BEEN BALD, he never would have been president. That silver thatch of hair set Harding apart and completed the picture of distinguished but powerful older gentleman. It set off his dark eyes and heavy eyebrows; it contrasted with his movie star tan. Harding's hair didn't make him president—but it didn't hurt either.

Hair is important to us. Out of our forty-three presidents, only five have been bald; one of those, Eisenhower, ran twice against the similarly bald Adlai Stevenson; another, Gerald Ford, succeeded to the presidency. This is an extraordinary statistic. The average age of winning presidential candidates is close to sixty, and more than half of American men begin balding by age fifty[12]—yet 88 percent of our presidents have had enough hair to comb over without looking silly. Clearly Americans do not like candidates who resemble Dr. Phil.

We judge people based on their looks; President Harding was the beneficiary of that tendency. Malcolm Gladwell called Harding's appeal "The Warren G. Harding Error." Gladwell wrote:

> Many people who looked at Warren G. Harding saw how extraordinarily handsome and distinguished-looking he was and jumped to the immediate—and entirely unwarranted—conclusion that he was a man of courage and intelligence and integrity. They didn't dig below the surface. The way he looked carried so many powerful connotations that it stopped the normal process of thinking dead in its tracks. The Warren G. Harding error is the downside of rapid cognition. It is at the root of a great deal of prejudice and discrimination. It's why picking the right candidate for a job is so difficult and why, on more occasions than we may care to admit, utter mediocrities sometimes end up in positions of enormous responsibility.[13]

Gladwell is correct; there are heavy downsides to rapid cognition. But there are also upsides. Hair can tell us a good deal about a candidate: it reflects age; it reflects money; it reflects general societal attitude. Hair, as other aspects of personal appearance, is subject to the dictates of fashion.

Hair is the reason that George McGovern didn't stand a chance in the 1972 election—though the issue wasn't McGovern's hair but his supporters' hair. Hair may be the reason that JFK won the 1960 election—and perhaps the reason men's hats went out of fashion. Reagan's Brylcreemed 'do satisfied voters that he was vigorous enough for the job. Lincoln's facial hair became an iconic inspiration for the next half-century of presidential candidates; Horace Greeley's bizarre neck beard and baldness made him easy fodder for caricaturists. John Kerry's expensive haircuts and well-coiffed running mate provoked guffaws; Ulysses S. Grant's close-cut beard accentuated his image of solidity. Andrew Jackson's wild mane reinforced his image as a wilderness man; John Quincy Adams's bald pate contributed to his reputation as an effete old man.

Brilliant political commentator and godfather of soul James Brown summed up the art of appearance. "Hair is the first thing," he wrote. "And teeth are the second. Hair and teeth. A man got those two things he's got it all."[14] Since John Adams, teeth have not been a campaign issue. Hair, on the other hand, remains a telling indicator of just who a candidate is.

★★★

GEORGE WASHINGTON DID NOT wear a wig. By the time he assumed the presidency, wigs had gone out of style. Instead, he frequently invoked his gray hair as evidence that he had served his country long and well. He needn't have done so; his reputation as the father of his country was already well secured.

For John Adams, however, hair was more of a problem. Adams, unlike Washington, was a controversial figure. He had a fiery temperament and an unbridled willingness to do what he thought was right, for good or ill. And Adams, unlike Washington, had a real political challenger in Thomas Jefferson.

Adams had beaten Jefferson in the 1796 election. By 1800, however, the incumbent was in poor shape. At sixty-five years old, Adams was short, bald, and ill-tempered; Jefferson, fifty-seven, was tall, well-coiffed, and aristocratic in temperament. Adams gave up wearing wigs as they went out of fashion, but wasn't above using wigs as physical weapons: after the 1796 election, Adams had foolishly retained President Washington's cabinet; the cabinet members irked him so much that he would periodically fling his wig at them during cabinet meetings.[15] Jefferson observed that Adams would specifically call meetings in order to indulge his temper, shouting obscenities at the cabinet members while "dashing and trampling his wig on the floor." "This only proves," Jefferson snidely concluded, "what you and I knew, that he had a better heart than head."[16]

Adams's wig-tossing exhibitions earned him the scorn of Jefferson's paid journalistic lackey, James Callendar. Callendar, who described Adams as a "hideous hermaphroditical character which has neither the force and firmness of a man, nor the gentleness and sensibility of a woman," used the alleged wig flinging to question Adams's "malignant passions." What "species of madness" had seduced Americans into voting for such a man?

"The historian will search for those *occult* causes that induced her to exalt an individual who has neither that innocence of sensibility which incites it to love, nor that omnipotence of intellect which commands to admire," Callendar poisonously penned. "He will ask why the United States degrades themselves to the choice of a wretch whose soul came blasted from the hand of nature, of a wretch that has neither the science of a magistrate, the politeness of a courtier, nor the courage of a man?"[17] Another journalistic rogue, Benjamin Franklin Bache, was more to the point: Adams, he wrote, was "old, bald, blind, querulous, toothless, crippled."[18]

Jefferson, by contrast, was the very picture of masculinity and health. In his youth, he had a tremendous head of red hair, a head of hair that drew the attention of his contemporaries. His hair whitened as he grew older, lending him a distinguished and handsome appearance; it was said that he grew more handsome as he grew older.[19] While Federalists tended to powder their hair or don wigs, Republicans wore their hair naturally,[20] lending a more democratic and less stilted look to the Democratic-Republican candidate.

A race between a short, bald, wig-heaving fire-breather and a tall, thick-haired, dignified, plantation Democrat is no race at all. Adams was no match for Jefferson in 1800.

★★★

ADAMS'S SON FACED THE SAME challenge in 1828. John Quincy Adams inherited his father's looks—and his shiny head. By the time of the 1828 election, Adams had lost all the hair on his head, though he compensated with a set of muttonchops that would put Elvis Presley to shame. The effect was rather off-putting, however; Adams looked upper crust and namby-pamby. Biographer John Torrey Morse described Adams's appearance:

> He was short, rotund, and bald; about the time when he entered Congress [after his presidency], complaints become frequent in his diary of weak and inflamed eyes, and soon these organs became so rheumy that the water would trickle down his cheeks; a shaking of the hand grew upon him to such an extent that in time he had to use artificial assistance to steady it for writing; his voice was high, shrill, liable to break, piercing enough to make itself heard, but not agreeable . . . He was irritable and quick to wrath; he himself constantly speaks of the infirmity of his temper, and in his many conflicts his principle concern was to keep it in control.[21]

Like father, like son.

Quincy Adams looked particularly bad when contrasted with his alpha male opponent, Andrew Jackson. Jackson's hair was thick, wavy, and wild. It stood straight up and back, granting him an electrified look—one of his contemporaries, Ann Rutherford, posited that Jackson slicked back his hair with bear's oil.[22] Though Jackson's hair whitened as he aged, he lost none of it; in a portrait painted two years before his death in 1837, Jackson retained a "shock of stiff white hair."[23] Jackson biographer John William Ward wrote, "One of the most distinctive of Jackson's physical characteristics was his bristling gray hair, which even until old age rose straight back from his high forehead."[24]

Jackson's hair wasn't the only hair at issue in 1828. Jackson had made his reputation by fighting Native Americans—and that raised images of scalping. During the Indian Wars, Jackson acquired the name "Sharp Knife" from Native American chieftans. He earned the nickname, once threatening that atrocity would be met with atrocity—"An Eye for an Eye, Toothe for Toothe and Scalp for Scalp."[25] When then Senator Jackson ran for president in 1824, fellow politicians supposed that Jackson would arrive at the Senate bearing "a scalping knife in one hand and a tomahawk in the other, allways [sic] ready to knock down, and scalp any and every person who differed with me in opinion." Jackson, instead, demonstrated remarkable fortitude and reasonableness.[26] Nonetheless, in 1828, Quincy Adams's supporters attempted to tar Jackson with his brutality during the Indian Wars; they distributed "coffin handbills" accusing Jackson of wholesale slaughter of Native American women and children.[27]

Jackson was able to counter charges of brutality easily—he simply portrayed Quincy Adams as a scheming aristocrat. Better a toughened military man than a short, bald, effete intellectual, Jackson's campaign said. Jackson biographer Robert Remini explained, "Adams's lordly and aristocratic manner was projected in the press to emboss their image of a President who was hostile to the aspirations of the majority of the American people."[28]

The 1828 election was bald snobbery versus rough-hewn democracy, said the Jacksonians. The American public believed them. Once again, an incumbent Adams was unceremoniously turned out of office—once again, hair conquered all.

★★★

ABRAHAM LINCOLN MADE A CRUCIAL DECISION in October 1860, just weeks before the most important election in American history—it was time to grow a beard. Lincoln's decision was the direct result of a letter he received from an eleven-year-old girl named Grace Bedell. "Dear Sir," Bedell wrote on October 15,

> My father has just come home from a fair and brought home your picture and Mr. Hamlin's. I am a little girl only eleven years old, but want you should be President of the United States very much so I hope you wont [sic] think me very bold to write such a great man as you are. Have you any little girls about as large as I am if so give them my love and tell her to write to me if you cannot answer this letter. I have got 4 brother's [sic] and part of them will vote for you any way and if you will let your whiskers grow I will try and get the rest of them to vote for you. you [sic] would look a great deal better for your face is so thin. All the ladies like whiskers and they would tease their husband's [sic] to vote for you to [sic] but I will try to get every one to vote for you that I can.

Lincoln replied four days later. "Your very agreeable letter of the 15th is received," he wrote. "I regret the necessity of saying I have no daughters. I have three sons—one seventeen, one nine, and one seven, years of age. They, with their mother, constitute my whole family. As to the whiskers, having never worn any, do you not think people would call it a piece of silly affection if I were to begin it now?" He signed it: "Your very sincere well-wisher, A. Lincoln."[29]

Lincoln put his protestations aside, however, and stopped shaving. The choice to do so sprang not merely from a desire to please a young girl but from political considerations. Lincoln was one of the ugliest men in politics. During the 1860 campaign, Lincoln's looks became a campaign issue. The *Houston Telegraph* stated that Lincoln was "the leanest, lankest, most ungainly mass of legs and arms and hatchet face ever strung on a single frame. He has most unwarrantably abused the privilege, which all politicians have, of being ugly."[30]

The Albany *Atlas and Argus* printed a joke about Lincoln. A uniquely ugly farmer approached Lincoln and leveled his musket at him, the paper reported. When Lincoln asked if the farmer truly intended to shoot him, the farmer replied, "Yes, sir . . . I've pledged myself if I ever saw a worse-looking man than myself, I would shoot him." "Well," Lincoln supposedly responded, "if I look worse than you do, fire away!"[31]

Democrats circulated a little ditty about Lincoln:

> Tell us he's a second Webster,
> Or if better, Henry Clay;
> That he's full of gentle humor,
> Placid as a summer's day.
>
> Tell again about the cord-wood;
> Seven cords or more per day;
> How each night he seeks his closet,
> There alone to kneel and pray.
>
> Tell us he resembles Jackson,
> Save he wears a larger boot,
> And is broader 'cross the shoulders,
> And is taller by a foot.
>
> Any lie you tell, we'll swallow—
> Swallow any kind of mixture;

But O don't, we beg and pray you—
Don't for land's sake, show his picture.[32]

With all that negative attention focused on his face, a beard couldn't hurt. It worked; the beard softened Lincoln's face and granted him a more distinguished look. It also brought the candidate in line with the latest fashions from Europe. In the 1850s, Britain adopted a beard-friendly attitude, largely because soldiers returning from the Crimean War came back bearded. Facial hair historian Allan Peterkin wrote, "Soldiers for most of the 19th century were the celebrated dandies, sex objects, and style setters, and were widely imitated . . . Not surprisingly, American presidents followed the fashion of the day despite its being set abroad. Even Uncle Sam had whiskers added to his clean-shaven face in about 1855."[33]

Lincoln won the election. On his way to the White House, he visited Grace Bedell's hometown, where he gave her a hug, smiled, and said, "You see, Grace, I let my whiskers grow for you."[34]

Before Lincoln, facial hair had been restricted mostly to the overgrown muttonchops of J. Q. Adams, Zachary Taylor, and Martin Van Buren. Lincoln changed all that, ushering America into the "Golden Age of Facial Hair." From Lincoln to William Howard Taft, a span of twelve presidents, only Andrew Johnson and William McKinley were clean-shaven. Of the electoral losers during that fifty-two-year span, only Samuel Tilden and William Jennings Bryan were clean-shaven. Clearly Lincoln had ended the reign of the razor.

★★★

DESPITE THE ADVENT of the Golden Age of Facial hair, not all facial hair was good facial hair. Horatio Seymour learned that lesson the hard way during the election of 1868. The 1868 Democratic presidential candidate and former governor of New York was bald on top, but wore his remaining hair up in curls. He also sported a well-developed pair of muttonchops, meeting beneath his chin in a bizarre neck beard. Seymour's strange appearance earned him the unremitting scorn of cartoonists.

Seymour had a checkered political past. As governor of New York, he had tolerated draft riots, leading to accusations that he was a Copperhead, or Southern sympathizer. Legendary political cartoonist Thomas Nast consistently depicted Seymour as the devil, his tufts of hair sticking up on either side of his head like horns.[35]

In one cartoon Nast drew the devil-haired Seymour in a dress as Lady Macbeth; his hand is covered not with blood but with the words "New York Draft Riots." "Out, damned spot!" Seymour cries, "Out, I say! . . . Here's the smell of the blood still: all the perfumes of Democracy will not sweeten this little hand. Oh! Oh! Oh!"[36]

In another cartoon, Seymour has sprouted a tail and hooves; to complete the satanic profile, he tempts the voters toward hell.[37] Continuing the references to *Macbeth*, one Nast cartoon depicted Seymour, vice presidential nominee Francis Blair, and former Confederate Wade Hampton surrounding a boiling pot, chanting:

> Double, double, toil and trouble,
> Fire burn and caldron bubble,
> Round about the hell-broth go,
> In the motley fragments throw;
>
> Hand of Treason, reeking red,
> Poison-fang of Copperhead . . .

Hampton's torch, Fred Douglass's fetter,
Booth's revolver, Blair's letter . . .

Seymour stirs the horrid broth —
Bound about his head a rag,
From the Alabama's flag . . .
Wand of witchery that bore
Treason's flag in '64;
With a weird and hissing sound
Rocks the caldron round and round,
And he cries, "'Tis very good!
Lo! The cup of brotherhood!"[38]

And they say today's campaigns are rough.

Seymour's opponent, General Ulysses S. Grant, wore a distinguished and closely shorn beard. One Union soldier at the crucial
battle of Vicksburg described Grant thus: "He stood solid, erect,
with square features, thin closed lips, brown hair, brown beard, both
cut short and neat. He weighed apparently about one hundred and
fifty pounds. He looked larger than Napoleon, and not so dumpy.
He looked like a man in earnest . . . ."[39]

An early biographer wrote, "His brow was straight and square,
but his head gave no indication of unusual capacity. His full beard,
cut close, partially concealed a square and heavy jaw and straight lips
which gave indication of his strong will and inflexible purpose . . .
His hair, which was worn short, was chestnut-brown in color."[40]

Grant's solid good looks, accentuated by his well-groomed but
undandified beard, helped him immensely during the 1868 campaign,
when accusations flew that he was a drunkard. He campaigned as a
tanner and a general, a determined and earthy fellow; he didn't look
the part of the disheveled wino.

And Grant crushed Seymour easily. *Harper's Weekly*, partisanly pro-Grant, ran an inflammatory cartoon depicting the president-elect holding aloft in one hand an American flag emblazoned with the words *Union* and *Equal Rights;* in the other hand, Grant held a sword. Grant was using the sword to stab Seymour through the neck beard.[41]

Four years later, Grant ran against another neck-beard devotee, New York publisher Horace Greeley. Greeley was perhaps the most unlikely presidential candidate in American history. As editor of the *New York Tribune*, Greeley vociferously supported Abraham Lincoln; he supported Grant in 1868. He then broke with Grant, critical of Grant's patronage policy, which he saw as corrupt. In 1872, he started the Liberal Republican Party, calling for cleaner government and an end to Reconstruction. The Democratic Party, his lifelong adversary, supported his presidential bid.

Greeley's strange political past was matched only by his strange physical appearance. Matthew Hale Smith described Greeley in 1869:

> His head is massive, fringed with flaxen hair around the base of the brain, till it blends with a loose, thin beard of the same color, which creeps out irregularly around the throat, and over a loosely-tied black silk neckerchief. In height he is a little below six feet. His eyes are of a grayish-blue. His eyebrows are so flaxen as to be almost unobservable. His dress has long been the subject of caricaturists . . . Physically, he is powerful but awkward. He stoops, droops his shoulders, swings his arms, and walks with a lounging, irregular gait.[42]

Thomas Nast once again did yeoman work for the Grant campaign. His cartoons pilloried Greeley. After Greeley accepted the Liberal Republican nomination by asking Americans to "clasp their hands across the bloody chasm,"[43] Nast went to work. One of his cartoons depicts the clownlike Greeley, tubby and sloppily attired, attempting to clasp hands with a Democrat over the infamous Andersonville prison.[44] Another shows Greeley, enormously rotund, ridiculously bald and heavily neck-bearded, clasping hands with a Confederate soldier who stands with one foot on the corpse of a murdered black man and the other on the American flag.[45] Further cartoons would show Greeley shaking hands with John Wilkes Booth over Lincoln's grave, handing a black man over to a KKK member who has murdered another black man, as well as a black mother and child.[46]

No one factor decides presidential elections. Except, that is, for the neck beard. Grant won a stunningly enormous reelection victory; Greeley did not win a single electoral vote.

★★★

THREE BEARDS (Rutherford B. Hayes, James Garfield, Benjamin Harrison), three mustaches (Grover Cleveland, TR, William Howard Taft), and one giant sideburns (Chester Arthur) later, the "Age of the Bankers" began. Woodrow Wilson's election victory in 1912 spelled the end of presidential facial hair; not a single president since has sported a mustache or beard. Part of the transition from hirsute presidents to clean-shaven ones can be explained by changes in technology and fashion. In 1895, the disposable razor blade was invented; in 1901, it was mass-produced; by 1906, hundreds of thousands were bought annually. When the United States entered World War I, the military ordered 3.5 million razors and thirty-six million blades for soldiers.[47]

Wilson was responsible for reinventing the image of the presidency and ushering in the Age of the Bankers. Sir Harry Lauder, Scotland's foremost entertainer during the first half of the twentieth century, painted a fascinating picture of Wilson:

Woodrow Wilson looked to me exactly what he was—a school-master. That long, clean-shaven face, the cold logic in his eyes, the lines about his mouth, in fact every outward aspect of the man savoured of the university classroom. If you had put on his head a mortar-cap, underneath his arm a couple of books, and in his right hand a cane you would have got the perfect dominie. I am told that few people ever warmed to him. He certainly over-awed me when I met him. When he shook hands with me I thought he did it coldly and perfunctorily but he allowed a genuine beam of enthusiasm to creep into his eyes as he thanked me for what I had done in the way of entertaining the American troops. While he spoke I thought what a remarkably well-groomed man he was. He was as neat and "kenspeckle" (Scots for dainty) as a new pin. He appeared to me to have devoted a good deal of attention to his personal adornment before leaving his bedroom that morning.[48]

Wilson was as punctilious with regard to policy as he was with regard to personal grooming. Politics, Wilson felt, could be separated from administration; groups of policy wonks could come up with the correct answers without engaging in political wrangling. To that end, Wilson demanded Congress authorize the creation of executive agencies charged with creating politics-free regulatory schemes, in contravention to the traditional constitutional separation of powers. The president, then, would become the chief administrative officer.

And Wilson looked like an administrator. So did his successors. Warren G. Harding was clean-shaven. A reporter for the *New York World* described the immaculately clean Calvin Coolidge as "outwardly neither impressive nor expressive, and looking at him therefore is rather wasting time. It will not inform you who it is who lives behind the cold mask of his lean and muscular face."[49] Herbert

Hoover, too, could have passed for an administrator, particularly since he had been one as head of the Food Administration during World War I and secretary of commerce under both Harding and Coolidge. FDR, too, had the clean-cut look of an administrator—and his policies enshrined Wilson's administrative state on the largest possible scale. The Age of the Bankers was truly the age of administrators and accountants.

★ ★ ★

DEMOCRATIC PRESIDENTIAL NOMINEE John F. Kennedy revolutionized the politics of hair. Where most of his contemporaries slicked back their hair—the "wet" look—Kennedy wore his hair dry, brushing it low across his forehead.[50] Sycophantic journalist Theodore White said in 1956 that JFK had a "boyish, open face, bronzed, hair almost golden with sun bleaching."[51]

His good looks and better hair made him a sex symbol before he ever ran for the presidency. By 1957, three years before his presidential run, Kennedy had become Washington's "hottest tourist attraction." *Life* magazine featured Kennedy in 1953, March 1957, and December 1957; the December article pitched Jack as a man who "has left panting politicians and swooning women across a large spread of the U.S."

According to JFK biographer Michael O'Brien, the December piece "received more letters and favorable comment than any feature story in the magazine's history."[52] JFK's media coverage irked his political rivals to no end. "I don't know how he does it," complained Senator Hubert Humphrey. "I get into *Photoplay* and he gets into *Life*."[53] Columnist William Shannon questioned whether JFK's hair should be enough to get him elected: "Month after month, from the glossy pages of *Life* to the multicolored cover of *Redbook*, Jack and

Jackie Kennedy smile out at millions of readers; he with his tousled hair and winning smile, she with her dark eyes and beautiful face . . . But what has all this to do with statesmanship?"[54]

It had nothing to do with statesmanship, and everything to do with image. His beautiful bouffant accentuated his youth and charisma. "You put a hat on Kennedy, you lose three-quarters of the head and all the charisma," observed campaign aide Dave Powers. "Kennedy's hair is almost a trademark,"[55] stated the *Charlotte Gazette-Mail*.

Before the 1960 election cycle, that trademark hair was long and "tousled." James Reston of the *New York Times* called the hair "a masterpiece of contrived casualness."[56] The Associated Press reported that "barbers get minute instructions on how to trim it . . . His aides admit that without the wistful forelock dangling over his right eyebrow . . . his appeal to women voters might suffer." Kennedy himself admitted that the hair was part of a strategy to broaden his base: "Two million more women than men are eligible to vote in this country."[57] He hired a stylist who would arrive at the Senate each morning to blow-dry his hair.[58]

But the longer hair had its drawbacks. As a forty-three-year-old candidate, he was already negatively associated with the younger generation; the overgrown coiffure made him look too counterculture. "As Kennedy's political image-making moved along with the popular culture of the 1950s, his long and unruly hair, his restless gestures, and his flashes of barely controlled fury all linked him to the young rebels who in the 1950s became heroes of the new youth subculture," explained John Hellman.[59]

Reporter Joe McCarthy posited that Kennedy's "collegiate haircut [makes] him seem like a lad of twenty-eight. An often-heard remark about Kennedy, credited to a New York political strategist, is: 'He'll never make it with that haircut.' Another politician in the

Midwest had said that Kennedy's youthful appearance is a bigger problem for him than his religion. 'It makes no difference how mature Kennedy may be,' this man says, 'if the bosses and the voters decide that he *looks* immature.'"[60]

And so in January 1960, the Kennedy hair changed drastically. It was trimmed down; the forelock met the scissors. "It must have been a tough decision," wrote the *Mansfield News Journal*. "That forelock has served Kennedy well as a political trademark. Still, as any advertiser knows, if a trademark becomes a liability the thing to do is to drop it. Kennedy does look a shade older now—though not quite as old as Vice President Nixon."[61]

The haircut didn't hurt Kennedy. "On the campaign trail, growing crowds roared their approval for Kennedy," JFK hair biographer Neil Steinberg said. "Women wept, fainted, crawled onto the hood of his car, or hopped up and down, trying to see Kennedy above the heads of crowds." One senator called Kennedy a cross between Elvis Presley and FDR.[62]

JFK had tremendous hair; he also had an opponent with boring hair. Richard Nixon wore a rather greasy widow's peak atop his high forehead. During the first televised presidential debate, Nixon's widow's peak did nothing to hide his sweaty forehead. Nixon also had to contend with his facial hair. For years, Herb Block of the *Washington Post* drew cartoons of Vice President Nixon with heavy stubble—and during the debate, Nixon lent credibility to those images by appearing with a five o'clock shadow.

"He has very translucent, almost blue-white skin," explained Ted Rogers, Nixon's campaign media advisor. "You can actually see the roots of his beard beneath his skin. TV is just an electronic development that goes beyond X-rays and radar. This X-ray quality of television made Nixon a bad visual candidate for television."[63] Kennedy, by contrast, looked cool, clean shaven, and collected—a man in control of both his facts and his bodily functions. Predictably, television viewers favored Kennedy, while radio listeners liked Nixon. "Snippets of behavior—such as Richard Nixon's . . . apparent five o'clock shadow during the 1960 presidential debates—can lead to trait impressions such as being shifty or unreliable without any explicit prompting," political scientist Carolyn L. Funk noted.[64]

Kennedy's slim victory over Nixon in the 1960 election did not spell the end of hats, as so many commentators have mistakenly reported. It is a myth that the hat industry died because Kennedy didn't wear a hat during his inauguration; in fact, he revived a tradition by wearing a silk top hat. As Steinberg pointed out, hats had been in fashion decline since 1903. It *is* true, however, that Kennedy rarely wore hats, a fact that irked manufacturers.[65]

Kennedy's election did, however, spell the dawn of a new day for hair. JFK's hairstyle legitimated bigger and longer hair. Steinberg theorized that JFK's hairdo paved the way for the Beatles' moptops: "An argument can be made that the Beatles hairdo is a descendant of Kennedy's style, which in 1963 was just a little shorter than the hairstyle John Lennon was wearing. The chain of influence is definitely there—after Kennedy's election, barbers in the United Kingdom said that young men were imitating Kennedy's mop of hair."[66]

And there is no doubt that Kennedy's haircut has continued to serve as an inspiration for Democratic politicians to this day. Jimmy Carter's crop of thick gray hair brushed across his forehead in a wave, just as JFK's did; Bill Clinton's hairdo closely followed the JFK pattern.

★★★

THERE'S LONG HAIR, and then there's *long* hair. JFK's haircut marked the outer limit of hair discretion; in 1972, Democratic presidential candidate George McGovern's followers crossed the line. Americans were already perturbed with the rise of the hippie generation, and McGovern's candidacy did nothing to alleviate those fears. McGovern's nomination followed on the heels of the catastrophic 1968 Democratic National Convention, in which long-haired college students had clashed with police, likely dooming Hubert Humphrey's candidacy. Now those same long-haired college students supported McGovern.

Columnist Jack McCallum, a McGovern supporter, fondly remembered the days when "with long hair and soiled T-shirts, we had clamored loudly for George McGovern."[67] "I also favored bell bottoms and long hair, and campaigned for George McGovern," agreed Dottie Ashley. "I was out one day handing out fliers promoting McGovern for President when a kid yelled, 'Mom, there's a Communist hippie at the door!' In spite of my chagrin and fury, I had to admit that the labels ran both ways. My clothes had given away my true image."[68] Then representative Tip O'Neill summed up the McGovern campaign in a nutshell. McGovern, he said, had been nominated "by the cast of *Hair.*"[69]

Where JFK distanced himself from the counterculture, McGovern embraced it. Though his hair was thinning on top, McGovern grew an imposing set of sideburns—columnist Mike Royko said that McGovern grew his sideburns "as lush as he could without impairing his hearing."[70] He shot his commercials using cinema verité, filming spontaneous statements with a handheld camera. He wore no jacket and a loosened tie, Howard Dean-style. The results were less than flattering. His off-the-cuff comments were often incoherent or tautological. "I would not pick McGovern in the first ten candidates that I've worked for to use that method [cinema verité]," said Charles Guggenheim, McGovern's ad-man. "McGovern would not be my first choice of a person to use on television period."[71]

It became clear as the campaign went on that McGovern would receive a historic drubbing at Nixon's hand. Desperate, McGovern ran the worst campaign commercial in the history of presidential politics. The ad shows a man in a voting booth, considering which candidate ought to get his vote. He speaks in a voiceover, as he stares at the ballot:

> Well, either way it won't be a disaster. What am I looking for? I mean—so I'll vote for Nixon. Why rock the boat? I'm not crazy about him. Never was. I've got to decide, though. I've got to make up my mind. I don't know about McGovern. I don't have that much time. I can't keep people waiting. The fellows are voting Nixon. They expect me to vote for him, too. Me vote for Nixon. My father'd roll over in his grave. The fellows say they are. Maybe they're not. Crime—I don't feel safe. Prices up. I've got a feeling— don't vote for Nixon. Why am I confused? Who am I measuring McGovern against? Gut feeling, my gut feeling. McGovern. This hand voted for Kennedy and it's just possible McGovern's straight. Maybe he can. That's the way.

Americans had a gut feeling that anyone who would run a commercial that bad would make a rotten president. Nixon swamped McGovern in a landslide of epic proportions. Long-haired hippies aren't much of a voting bloc.

★★★

"A LITTLE DAB'LL DO YA!" So runs the slogan for Brylcreem, the first mass marketed men's hair product in America. Brylcreem gives hair a high glossy sheen; it was a hallmark of the pre-JFK "wet" look. In the aftermath of JFK, sales of Brylcreem declined.

But there was one man who stuck with Brylcreem through thick and thin—1980 Republican presidential nominee Ronald Reagan. Reagan's rich head of dark hair puzzled his political opponents. Even some voters doubted whether Reagan's hair color was real. When reporter Peter Hart interviewed a schoolteacher in Missouri, she stated, "I want to know if he dyes his hair. If he does, I will not vote for him."[72] Reagan frequently received letters from supporters asking him whether he dyed his hair.[73]

He didn't. "I know for certain that no dye ever touched Reagan's hair," swore Michael Deaver, Reagan's White House deputy chief of staff. "For years, the Reagan haters had literally sifted through his barber's trash can, searching for a dyed gray lock that could serve as a tiny metaphor for a phony man and an even more phony presidency. They searched in vain. It was an old actor's trick—Brylcreem—that gave Reagan's hair that dark gloss, not Clairol for men."[74] When one reporter asked Reagan whether he dyed his hair, he leaned forward and told the reporter to grip his hair. It was natural and dry.[75]

Reagan's hair helped him immensely. As the oldest presidential candidate in American history, Reagan's dark coif eased fears that he was too decrepit to handle the presidency. "Crow's-feet may crinkle the corners of his eyes and a few strands of silver fleck his chestnut hair, but at 68, Ronald Reagan, lean, fast and fit as a ranch hand, seems to be the Republican to beat as he enters the Presidential campaign," stated *Newsweek* in October 1979.[76]

"For a man of 69, Mr. Reagan looks great," reported Lawrence Martin of the *Globe and Mail*. "The hair is almost jet black, the cheeks are as red as McIntosh apples, the shoulders are wide and strong, the smile is warm and friendly and his speech is effortless. Many expected the age question to become a big issue in the campaign but it hasn't."[77]

Reagan's opponent, incumbent president Jimmy Carter, wore whiter hair at age fifty-five than Reagan did at sixty-nine. "Carter must have a pretty fair stylist," observed Steve Martini, the presidential barber for Eisenhower, JFK, LBJ, and Nixon, "but he needs to get his hair a bit darker. He would come across as a stronger person. Now he has that tintype look, all white and washed out."[78] Carter's reputation as a weakling received another boost when he decided to reverse the part in his hair from right to left.[79]

A little dab did indeed do the job for Reagan. Reagan's Brylcreem look contributed to his carefully crafted image—old enough to know, but young enough to do. In the election of 1980, he trounced Carter.

★★★

HAIR REMAINS A PROMINENT FEATURE of today's presidential campaigns. The 2004 race pitted the Democratic "all-hair" team against incumbent President George W. Bush. Democratic nominee John "$1,000 Haircut" Kerry spent piles of money and oodles of time perfectly crafting his hair; his running mate, John Edwards, had such a beautiful hairdo that Rush Limbaugh dubbed him the "Breck Girl."

But the Democrats forgot something in 2004: hair is a means, not an end in itself. By focusing all their attention on their hair, the Kerry-Edwards ticket seemed lightweight and elitist. Kerry lent credibility to this idea when he explained the ticket's popular appeal. "This is the dream team," he said. "We have better ideas, better vision, a better sense of the difficulties in the lives of average Americans. And," he added, "we have better hair."[80] This didn't entirely mesh with the facts—President Bush's hair is quite underrated. In fact, in a poll commissioned by Wahl Clipper Corporation, Bush's hair defeated Kerry's by a broad 51–30 margin.[81] Nonetheless, the perception stuck: Kerry was more focused on hair than policy.

Edwards, too, had his hair troubles. Bald and tubby Vice President Dick Cheney slapped Edwards repeatedly, quipping, "People tell me that Senator Edwards got picked for his good looks, his sex appeal, and his great hair. I say to them: How do you think I got the job?"[82] Edwards's hairy situation has continued to dog him throughout the 2008 race. A YouTube video that shows Edwards primping his hair for a full two minutes and gazing at himself in a compact to "I Feel Pretty" from *West Side Story* has received hundreds of thousands of hits.

So hair matters—but it isn't all-important. Nixon, Reagan, and H. W. Bush campaign advisor Roger Ailes said:

> Sometimes we can make mistakes about others if, as we view them, we segment them and only get a partial picture. This person has good-looking hair; that person has no hair. This person should lose weight; that one should gain weight. We look at all these parts of people, but then we quickly perceive the person in totality. You can have the greatest head of hair in the world, or the greatest smile, or the greatest voice, or whatever, but after two minutes you're going to be looked at as a whole person. All of those impressions of your various parts will have been blended into one complete composite picture, and the other person will have a feeling about you based on that total impression. Enough of that image has to be working in your favor for you to be liked, accepted, and given what you want.[83]

Without hair, a candidate may be doomed, as John Quincy Adams was—or he may emerge triumphant, as Dwight D. Eisenhower did. With great hair, a candidate may win the White House, as JFK did—or he may go down in flames, as John Kerry did. With facial hair, a candidate may meet with disaster, as Horace

Greeley did—or he may meet with victory, as Ulysses S. Grant did. Hair, in isolation, does not define a candidate. It does, however, help shape candidates' images—and we use those images to pick our presidents. Who in the world would Warren G. Harding have been if he had been cursed with male pattern baldness? He certainly wouldn't have been president.

★ 7 ★
A Woman's Touch

T HE ELECTION OF 1884 WAS CLOSE—too close for President Grover Cleveland's comfort. The first Democrat to enter the White House since before the Civil War, Cleveland had been savaged during the election race. His Republican opponent, former secretary of state James G. Blaine, had a reputation as a corrupt bureaucrat; Edwin L. Godkin of the *Nation* claimed that Blaine had "wallowed in spoils like a rhinoceros in an African pool."[1] But Cleveland had a reputation as a boorish womanizer.

That reputation was not unfounded. On July 21, 1884, the Buffalo *Telegraph* had published a bombshell report, entitled:

A TERRIBLE TALE
A Dark Chapter in a Public Man's History

The Pitiful Story of Maria Halpin and Governor Cleveland's Son

The story reported that Cleveland had sired a child out of wedlock with Maria Halpin, that the child was now ten years old and named Oscar Halpin Cleveland. The story stated further that when Cleveland had lived in Buffalo, he had used his bachelor pad as a "harem."[2]

Cleveland responded to the story by making a clean breast of things. "Whatever you do, tell the truth," he wired to one of his campaign advisors. Cleveland admitted that he had engaged in an illicit relationship with Halpin, but refused to claim paternity, since Halpin had been around the block rather regularly.[3] Republicans leapt on the scandal, quickly distributing the most famous song in political history. It was entitled "Ma, Ma, Where's My Pa?" The chorus:

> Ma! Ma! Where is my Pa?
> Up in the White House, darling,
> Making up the laws, working the cause,
> Up in the White House, dear.[4]

Republicans took up the chant. At rallies, they would yell, "Ma, Ma, where's my pa?" Democrats soon came up with a retort: "He's gone to the White House, ha! ha! ha!"[5]

Fortunately for Cleveland, Blaine's personal background raised questions too. Political opponents charged that Blaine had impregnated his wife before the marriage—that they had been married, in fact, only three months before his wife gave birth. Everyone had heard that "James G. Blaine betrayed the girl whom he married . . . at the muzzle of a shotgun," puffed the *Indianapolis Sentinel*. "If, after despoiling her, he was craven to refuse her legal redress, giving legitimacy to her child, until a loaded shotgun stimulated his conscience—then there is a blot on his character more foul, if possible, than any of the countless stains on his political record." When confronted with the issue, Blaine sued the *Sentinel,* claiming that he had secretly married his wife before the impregnation.[6] His claim was unconvincing and did little to dispel questions about his moral virtue or his truthfulness.

Cleveland just squeaked by Blaine—his margin of victory was only twenty-three thousand votes.[7]

If he wished to repair his image, the forty-seven-year-old, three-hundred-plus pound Cleveland needed to take a wife. His choice was Frances Folsom, the daughter of his old law partner. Today, we would label the choice borderline perverse. Cleveland had been present at Frances's birth; he bought her first baby carriage. When Frances's father died in 1875, Cleveland became the eleven-year-old's de-facto guardian. Frances grew into a hot number, tall and well proportioned. When she turned twenty-one, Cleveland married her.[8]

Cleveland's supporters were thrilled. "Fair, fresh, genuine, in figure tall and graceful, with soft, brown hair and deep kindling eyes, she stood before all, the embodiment of all that is best, loveliest and sweetest in the womanhood of our nation," gushed an 1892 campaign biography. "She charmed everybody, and for a time even cast the President into the shade. No lady of the White House, not even Dolly [sic] Madison, was ever so popular."[9]

Cleveland's marriage did not silence his critics. During the 1888 election cycle, the incumbent president was accused of beating his young wife; the Democrats responded by placing Frances on campaign posters, the first use of the first lady in such a manner. Frances herself proclaimed the accusations "wicked and heartless lies. I can only wish the women of our country no better blessing than that their homes and their lives be as happy, and that their husbands may be as kind and attentive, as considerate and affectionate as mine."[10]

Cleveland won the popular vote but narrowly lost the 1888 election in the electoral college. Four years later, he returned to the presidency, Frances by his side. Where the 1884 election had focused primarily on Cleveland's personal life, the 1892 election virtually ignored it. Young and beautiful Frances Cleveland helped quash the personal attacks of elections past—she softened Cleveland's rough edges, making him seem warmer and more palatable to a broader audience.

Frances remained a controversial figure. Fiery columnist William Cowper Brann accused Frances of marrying Cleveland for his fame and money, caustically observing:

> Probably she has regretted a thousand times that she bartered her youth and beauty for life companionship with a tub of tallow, mistaken at that time for a god by a purblind public, but even though it be true, as often asserted, that the old boor gets drunk and beats her, a woman could scarce apply for a divorce from a man who has twice been president. Furthermore, association with such a man will lower the noblest woman to his level. Every physiognomist who saw Frances Folsom's bright face, its spirituelle beauty, and who looks at it now and notes it [sic] stolid, almost sodden expression must recall those lines of Tennyson's:

> As the husband is, the wife is; thou art mated with a clown,
> And the grossness of his nature will have weight to drag thee down.
> Cursed be the sickly forms that err from honest Nature's rule,
> Cursed be the gold that gilds the straighten'd forehead of the fool.[11]

And Hillary Clinton thought she had it tough.

★★★

CANDIDATES' WIVES RARELY MAKE or break a presidential campaign. For the first century of presidential politics, candidates' wives were rarely seen or heard—naturally, since presidential candidates did not openly campaign for much of that period. In many cases, the absence of wifely presence redounded to candidates' benefit. George Washington would have had difficulty coping with questions about his fortune hunting; he likely married Martha not out of love but out of desire for her sizable assets, since she was one of the richest women in Virginia at the time of the wedding. The good widow Martha had inherited seventeen thousand acres, thirty thousand pounds sterling, and 150 slaves from her recently deceased hubby.[12]

John Tyler never ran for reelection; if he had, he certainly would have faced questions about his marriage to Julia Gardiner, a statuesque woman thirty years his junior, just months after the death of his first wife.[13] Rumors circulated about Zachary Taylor's wife, Margaret—opponents falsely said that she smoked a corncob pipe. In fact, Margaret was simply reclusive and off-putting.[14] Lifelong bachelor James Buchanan's niece served as first lady.[15] Mary Todd Lincoln was mentally unstable.[16]

Occasionally, prospective first ladies served to flesh out the characters of their candidate husbands. That was certainly the case with Frances Cleveland. With the advent of television, candidates' wives have been forced into the spotlight more and more. Young and gorgeous Jacqueline Kennedy greatly aided her husband's political quest, contributing to his glamorous Camelot image. Rosalynn Carter's polish balanced Jimmy Carter's earnestness; Betty Ford's outspokenness only heightened perceptions that her husband was a bumbler. Hillary Clinton became a major campaign issue in 1992; she was simply too much of a harridan for many Americans. It was only after her famous hand-holding session with wayward husband Bill that Americans began to accept Hillary. Tipper Gore's job in the 2000 campaign was to demonstrate that her husband could be passionate—but that was too much of a stretch for the staid couple. Teresa Heinz Kerry may have had the broadest impact of any first lady candidate in American history.

First lady candidates, then, are just as important to today's presidential candidates as height or hair. It is no wonder that candidates' wives routinely take the stage to stump for their husbands.

★★★

THE ELECTION OF 1828 WAS EXCEPTIONAL in many ways, not least for its focus on the candidates' wives. Andrew Jackson's wife, Rachel, had a checkered history. At age seventeen, Rachel married Captain Lewis Robards, who turned out to be a philandering and jealous nut. Four years into the marriage, Rachel moved away from Robards to live with her family in Nashville. There she met Jackson. When Robards found out about Jackson, he quickly suspected that Rachel and Jackson were having an affair. He showed up in Nashville and dragged Rachel back to Kentucky with him. Two years later, in 1790, Jackson followed Rachel to Kentucky and sneaked her away to Mississippi.

But the saga wasn't over. Jackson heard in 1791 that Robards had given Rachel a divorce, and he immediately married her. There was one problem, however—Robards hadn't divorced Rachel. By law, the two were committing adultery. In 1793, Robards divorced Rachel on the grounds that Rachel "doth still live in adultery with another man." Rachel and Jackson legally married in 1794.[17]

By 1828, the sordid story should have been long forgotten. Unfortunately for both Andrew and Rachel Jackson, it wasn't. Supporters of incumbent president John Quincy Adams broke the story, asking, "Ought a convicted adultress and her paramour husband to be placed in the highest offices of this free and Christian land?"[18] Thomas Arnold, a congressional candidate from Tennessee and vocal Adams backer, distributed a handbill denouncing Jackson as a barbarian who had "spent the prime of his life in gambling, in cock-fighting, in horse-racing . . . and to cap all tore from a husband the wife of his bosom." Jackson, he stated, had been caught in *flagrante delicto,* "exchanging most delicious kisses." During Rachel's marriage to Robards, Jackson and Rachel had "slept under the same blanket," wrote Arnold.[19]

Jackson fought back hard, sending out newspapers and speakers to counter the charges. "The wife of his bosom has been wantonly attacked . . . to think that the affectionate partner . . . should be represented as faithless and worthless . . . is not such conduct abominable?"[20] Certain Jackson supporters attacked Adams's wife, spuriously claiming that the president and first lady had engaged in premarital sex. Jackson, however, refused to allow such charges to be leveled against Adams. "Female character should never be introduced or touched unless a continuation of attack should be made against Mrs. Jackson and then only by way of *Just retaliation* on the known guilty . . . I *never war against females* and it is only the base and cowardly that do."[21]

A month after Jackson's election, Rachel stumbled across a pamphlet defending her against the charges of bigamy and adultery. She was shocked by the charges the pamphlet responded to—so shocked that she "slumped to the floor and wept hysterically. From that moment on Rachel Jackson began a slow mental and physical decline."[22] On December 18, Rachel collapsed. Four days later, she died.[23]

Jackson never forgave Adams; for the rest of his life, he believed that Adams's supporters had driven Rachel to her grave.[24] Jackson placed a marker over Rachel's grave: "A being so gentle and so virtuous, slander might wound but not dishonor."[25]

★ ★ ★

FOR CLOSE TO TWO HUNDRED YEARS, the press gave enormous deference to presidents' White House sex lives. The elections of 1828 and 1884 concerned presidents' pre-White House indiscretions; their infidelities in the White House remained off-limits. During his 1920 presidential campaign, Warren G. Harding paid one of his former mistresses $20,000 to keep quiet; during his presidency, Harding engaged in a long-running affair with Nan Britton, a woman three decades his junior. Most notoriously, the two had sex in an anteroom next to the Oval Office, which is where their daughter was conceived.[26]

Harding's indiscretions were obscene; FDR's were no better. In 1918, Eleanor Roosevelt discovered that FDR was sleeping with Lucy Mercer, his secretary. Sara Roosevelt, FDR's mother, informed him that if he divorced Eleanor he would be disinherited; Roosevelt's closest political advisor, Louis Howe, told FDR that he could kiss his presidential aspirations good-bye if he dumped Eleanor.[27] By most accounts, Eleanor was shattered.

"The bottom dropped out of my own particular world," Eleanor wrote, "and I faced myself, my surroundings, my world, honestly for the first time."[28] It is difficult to buy Eleanor's shock and surprise; she was a uniquely unattractive woman, and she knew it. Eleanor had long worried that FDR was not in love with her—and FDR made no secret of his affair with Lucy, leaving letters from her all over his apartment. Eleanor, simply, was a political animal. Though she offered FDR a divorce, she knew he would not take it. "If you want to be President, Franklin," she told her husband, "you'll have to take me with you."[29] The Roosevelts' was now a power marriage, pure and simple.

Though FDR broke off his relationship with Mercer in 1918, he renewed it in 1941.[30] Bizarrely enough, FDR renewed the relationship with the help of his and Eleanor's daughter, Anna.[31] Lucy, not Eleanor, was with FDR when he died. John Kenneth Galbraith noted that Eleanor was hardly shattered by FDR's death.[32] Eleanor's bitter description of her marriage demonstrates the extent of the coolness that pervaded her relationship with Roosevelt: "He might have been happier with a wife who was completely uncritical. That I was never able to be, and he had to find it in some other people. Nevertheless, I think I sometimes acted as a spur, even though spurring was not always wanted or welcome. I was one of those who served his purposes."[33] And, she might have added, he served hers.

With the help of the media, FDR's wandering eye never met the public eye. In his diary, Raymond Clapper of the *Washington Post* stated that in 1933, the story of FDR's affair during World War I "buzzed around Washington." But, as Betty Winfield observed, "Clapper and others never mentioned it publicly." Just as they had with FDR's physical handicap, the press quietly tucked away information about FDR's infidelity.[34]

As a candidate for first lady in 1932, Eleanor contributed unending energy and organizational skill to FDR's campaign. She was so active that one Roosevelt critic complained that the country was receiving two presidents for the price of one.[35] With the help of suspected lesbian lover and journalist Lorena Hickok, Eleanor assumed a larger-than-life status: "The adroit reporter made sure Eleanor came across as modest and frugal, describing her as a woman who was 'embarrassed when she was recognized' and who lived 'a truly Spartan life'—wearing ten-dollar dresses, eschewing taxis for city buses, eating lunch at drug store soda fountains."[36] Eleanor flew to Chicago with FDR to help him accept the Democratic nomination; she became the leading figure in the Democratic Party's women's campaign. "Gracious, charming, patient, serene . . . and plainly the devoted helpmate," gushed one reporter.[37]

Most of all, Eleanor was ambitious. She later revised history, disingenuously claiming that entering the White House "deeply troubled" her.[38] The record disagrees. Eleanor took to the White House like a duck to water. "The spectacle of Eleanor Roosevelt always on the go became a national jest," explained historian Sol Barzman. "She was everywhere, watching, speaking, inspecting, writing, reporting back to the President . . . she was again the eyes and ears for her husband, and his legs as well." She lectured, spoke to the nation via radio, and wrote a newspaper column.[39]

For the rest of her life, Eleanor remained a towering figure—an icon of public service, involved in everything from visiting the troops during World War II to acting as chairman of the UN Commission on Human Rights.[40] She is considered by many the most influential woman in American history. Without FDR, Eleanor would not have been Eleanor. Then again, without Eleanor, FDR would not have been FDR.

★★★

THE ELECTION OF 1952 pitted the first divorced presidential candidate in American history, Democratic Illinois governor Adlai Stevenson, against a purported model of marital happiness, General Dwight D. Eisenhower. Stevenson had married Chicago socialite Ellen Borden in 1928, but the couple had divorced in 1949 at her behest.[41] This crippled Stevenson's 1952 candidacy; divorce was still stigmatized in 1952. "If a man can't run his family, he has no business trying to run the country," explained one Midwestern man. The sentiment was common.[42]

Whispers about Stevenson's personal life surrounded the 1952 campaign. With Adlai's sister, Buffie, appearing at women's functions rather than the traditional wife, rumors swirled that Adlai was a homosexual. The rumors became known around Washington as the "Stevenson innuendo." Stevenson biographer Jean H. Baker wrote, "In the rest of the United States, the gossip wove its way into telephone conversations and informal political discussions, barroom jokes and beauty shop frowns . . . Delegates in Chicago heard the smear even before the convention ended."[43]

J. Edgar Hoover's FBI purposefully disseminated the rumors. FBI agents were planted in major hotels and told to loudly discuss Stevenson's alleged homosexuality. Stevenson, they said, had been arrested in New York and Illinois for lewd acts; he frequented gay bars under the name "Adelaide"; he had a gay affair with the president of Bradley University; Hoover kept Stevenson's file in the "Sex Deviates" index in his office.[44]

The trumped-up scandal attached itself to Adlai, the bald intellectual who certainly seemed less masculine than his military-hero opponent. It was not hard to caricature a man who laughed that his slogan was "Eggheads of the World, Unite!" Republican congressman and vice presidential candidate Richard Nixon challenged Adlai's testosterone: "The idea of putting Adlai Stevenson in the ring with a man like Stalin petrifies me." Senator Everett Dirksen (R-Illinois) called Adlai one of the "lavender lads of the State Department." Columnist and radio commentator Walter Winchell announced over the national airwaves that "a vote for Adlai Stevenson is a vote for Christine Jorgenson and a woman in the White House." (Christine Jorgenson was the era's most famous transsexual.)[45]

The scandal gained more credence when Adlai's ex-wife announced that she would be writing a tell-all poetry book entitled *The Egghead and I.* In it, she said, she would "expose" Adlai. Though the book never appeared, Borden deeply damaged Stevenson's campaign.[46] For the rest of his life, Stevenson would be dogged by the "Stevenson innuendo." In 1965, while serving as ambassador to the United Nations, boorish LBJ referred to Stevenson as "the kind of man who squats like a woman when he pees."[47]

Eisenhower, by contrast, impressed the public as the archetypal family man. The rumors about Eisenhower and his wartime driver, Kay Summersby, were in all likelihood false;[48] Ike's relationship with his wife, Mamie, remained solid. "After thirty-six years of marriage," cooed *Newsweek*, "her face still lights up like a bobby-soxer's when she talks about Ike." *Newsweek* wasn't overstating the case. "The bigger the crowds, the more people I met, the happier I became," Mamie said. "Seeing thousands and thousands of people adoring Ike, believing in his leadership, kept me cloud-high all the time." This wasn't exaggeration, and it wasn't political posturing— by all accounts, Mamie was no political figure.[49]

Eisenhower wiped the floor with Stevenson in 1952.

In 1956, Stevenson's divorce continued to pursue him. "The divorce issue was brought up a lot in '56," explained William Wilson, Stevenson's live local television agent. "None of us knew what to do with it."[50] In response, the Stevenson campaign created a series of ads entitled "The Man from Libertyville." While carefully explaining his ideas to America, Stevenson was constantly surrounded by members of his family.[51]

It didn't help. Eisenhower trounced Stevenson again in 1956.

★★★

JACQUELINE BOUVIER was an extraordinarily beautiful woman. Dark-haired, tall, elegant, with classic good looks, Jacqueline was a real catch. She met Jack in 1951, when he was thirty-four and she was twenty-two; they dated at a distance for two years, then married in 1953.[52] In true Kennedy style, the wedding was enormous— Observers said that "the wedding festivities cost enough to start a fair-sized country bank."[53]

For the next several years, the attractive couple was a mainstay in all the glossy magazines. Both *McCall's* and *Redbook* wrote features on Jackie.[54] But the relationship between Jack and Jackie was strained. During the first year of the marriage, Jackie said, "I was alone almost every weekend." "Sometimes, when he is at home," Jackie told a reporter, "he is so wrapped up in his work that I might as well be in Alaska . . . He rushes to finish dinner so we can turn on TV or get to a movie on time."[55]

Jackie was the neglected housewife for a reason—Jack's busy sex life left little room for her. In 1956, he began an affair with Joan Lundberg, who graphically explained later that Jack "loved three-somes—himself and two girls. He was also a voyeur." Lundberg became pregnant by JFK; he paid for her abortion.[56] Lundberg wasn't Jack's only conquest. He caroused in Washington, D.C. He often engaged in orgies at the Carroll Arms Hotel, conveniently located across the street from the Senate Office Building.[57] JFK also pursued actresses Judy Garland, Jean Simmons, Lee Remick— and Sophia Loren, unsuccessfully.[58] During his presidency, the affairs only increased. He smoked pot and did cocaine in the White House; he might even have tried LSD.[59]

But the media never reported JFK's dalliances. Instead, they portrayed the Kennedy marriage as Camelot—innocent, clean-cut, all-American. Jackie contributed heavily to the image, claiming on the TV show *Home* that she pressed Jack's pants. "This must have been a campaign chore, for at home a maid, houseboy, cook, and nursemaid would seem to provide ample manpower to smooth out pants wrinkles," journalist Fletcher Knebel wryly observed.

But even Knebel was susceptible to the kind of media panting the Kennedys created:

> When the balance of Kennedy's presidential assets and liabilities is struck, it is uncertain in which column Jacqueline belongs. She is an obvious asset to the eyes and well-being of her husband, but an old political maxim says that the candidate's wife should not be too young or too attractive. Women tend to be jealous of both. A kind of middle-aged neutrality is preferred. Whether or not this is true, if Kennedy is elected President the First Lady will be 31 when she enters the White House and possessed of a supple grace and beauty. Admirers wager she will be able to go a full two terms without dieting.[60]

During the election of 1960, Jackie did not campaign particularly actively—except with regard to the Hispanic vote. She filmed what is surely the first foreign language commercial by a first lady candidate, speaking in Spanish to stump on her husband's behalf. She spoke in Spanish Harlem, addressing her *"amigos,"* then stating, in Spanish, "My Spanish is poor but my knowledge of your history, culture, and problems is better. I can assure you if my husband is elected president you will have a real friend in the White House." Republicans charged that Jackie was "pandering to foreign influences," but Jackie responded, "These people have contributed so much to our country's culture . . . It seems a proper courtesy to address them in their own tongue."[61]

After JFK's election, Jackie became a trendsetter, a fashion icon to millions. After JFK's assassination, she signified dignity in tragedy. To this day, Jackie is often seen as the prototypical first lady.

★★★

JFK WAS A SECRET BOOR; LBJ was an open one. Before male and female aides, the president stalked about naked, burped, broke wind, urinated, and defecated—all while talking politics.[62] When one of his friends visited the White House from Texas, LBJ promptly unzipped his pants, whipped out his genitals, and asked "Have you ever seen anything as big as this?"[63] Johnson was promiscuous and stocked the White House with good-looking women, hoping that others would think he was sleeping with all of them.[64] He engaged in sex in the Oval Office with at least six different women.[65] "Sex to Johnson was part of the spoils of victory," explained reporter George Reedy. "He once told me that women, booze, and sitting outside in the sun were the only three things in life worth living for."[66]

So Johnson was not exactly Mr. Suave. Fortunately for him, he had Lady Bird. Lady Bird loved LBJ, but she recognized that he was not capable of an all-encompassing marital relationship. "He never paid any attention to Lady Bird when she was around," said journalist John Chancellor. "The fact that she was fully aware and accepting of the terms of the relationship did not excuse him, but they both must be given credit for the truth that she was strong enough to have left him at any time. And he knew it."[67] Lady Bird knew of Johnson's affairs; by some accounts, she approved of them.

Marie Fehmer, LBJ's secretary, "remembered a trip to California with Mrs. Johnson shortly after she was hired. LBJ and Mary Margaret Wiley were already there, and when Lady Bird and Marie arrived, a woman's underwear was strewn all over the hotel room.

Instead of being angry, Lady Bird seemed to go out of her way to be nice to Mary Margaret." Similarly, Lady Bird once conveniently scheduled a trip so as to avoid an illicit weekend former congresswoman Helen Douglas was to spend with the president.[68]

Standing calmly by LBJ, Lady Bird provided the president's image with the stability and polish it lacked. She also provided valuable advice to Johnson. Johnson claimed that Lady Bird made up his mind about running for reelection in 1964.[69] Lady Bird attempted a brand new strategy during the campaign—in order to shield Johnson from direct Southern criticism of his civil rights program, Lady Bird campaigned in his stead in the South. She took a nineteen-car train called *The Lady Bird Special* across 1,682 miles and eight states, speaking forty-six times. One hundred and fifty reporters accompanied her.

Johnson aide George Reedy described Lady Bird's appeal: "She's very intuitive about people; she's not swept off her feet by flattery. She has a marvelous knack for saying the right thing at the right time. And she has extraordinary good sense."[70] During the whistle-stop tour, Southern whites relentlessly heckled Lady Bird, some holding "Goldwater for President" signs. Lady Bird's tour made LBJ look like a moderate; Goldwater was portrayed as the extremist.[71]

On Election Day, LBJ—with a helping hand from his wife—won a landslide reelection victory over Goldwater.

★★★

THE 1976 CAMPAIGN pitted dark horse Democratic candidate and former Georgia governor Jimmy Carter against President Nixon's successor, Gerald Ford. The candidates had much in common: both felt genial and trustworthy. The contrast between Betty Ford and Rosalynn Carter, however, was stark. Betty Ford was a garrulous controversialist; Carter was a steadfast, varnished politician. Betty Ford's positions on abortion, premarital sex, and marijuana use damaged her husband's credibility—both she *and* her husband seemed sort of goofy. Rosalynn Carter provided a more rational touch, balancing out Jimmy Carter's erratic presidential campaign.

Betty Ford was open to a fault. "When Ford said this will be an open presidency, we thought, 'O.K., let's let the first lady open up,'" explained Sheila Weidenfeld, the first lady's press secretary.[72] "She's the best kind of liberated woman," gushed radical feminist Betty Freidan. "I don't believe that being First Lady should prevent me from expressing my ideas," said First Lady Ford. "Why should my husband's ideas, or your husbands' prevent us from being ourselves?"[73]

That attitude did not pay off for President Ford. Betty was a strange combination of New Age openness and traditional housewife. During a shocking *60 Minutes* interview in 1975, Betty called *Roe v. Wade*, the decision creating a constitutional right to abortion, a "great, great decision"; she stated that she "wouldn't be surprised" if her eighteen-year-old unmarried daughter Susan were having sex; she bluntly asserted that young people living together was a fact of life; she admitted that if she were young, she would try marijuana. Though her comments were popular nationally, they were quite unpopular with conservatives. Dr. W. A. Criswell, the pastor of the largest Baptist congregation in the world, ripped Betty's "gutter type of mentality"; the LAPD seconded the motion.[74] "The immorality of Mrs. Ford's remarks is almost exceeded by their stupidity," the *Manchester Union Leader* angrily wrote.[75]

Still, that didn't stop Betty. She soon informed *McCall's* magazine that reporters had asked her every question under the sun, except for how often she slept with the president. If they had asked, she said, she would have told them "as often as possible."[76] As *Newsweek* observed, "while a Harris survey showed overwhelming approval for

Betty's plain speaking, the fine print pointed out that Southerners, rural conservatives, skilled workers and voters over 50 were not exactly beguiled."[77]

But Betty wasn't done yet. When the Equal Rights Amendment passed through Congress and required ratification at the state level, Betty threw her support behind the amendment. She called up state legislators to pressure them. "I realize you're under a lot of pressure from the voters today," she said to one female legislator from Missouri, "but I'm just calling to let you know that the President and I are considerably interested . . . I think the ERA is so important."[78]

Betty wasn't all controversy—she made public her fight against breast cancer, bringing attention to the disease. But all in all, she reinforced the perception of her husband as a well-intentioned oaf. After her husband's 1976 defeat, Betty became even more of an icon than she was during her tenure as first lady. The *New York Times* described her as "a product and a symbol of the cultural and political times—doing the Bump along the corridors of the White House, donning a mood ring, chatting on her CB radio with the handle First Mama—a housewife who argued passionately for equal rights for women, a mother of four who mused about drugs, abortion and premarital sex aloud and without regret."[79] During the election of 1976, however, Betty wasn't received with quite as much deference.

If Betty Ford personified irreverence, Rosalynn Carter personified polish. Rosalynn was an excellent speaker, and during the 1976 campaign, she put that skill to use. She and Jimmy campaigned separately, crisscrossing the country to reach as many people as possible. She worked eighteen hours per day. During the primaries, she spoke in thirty states; during the general election, she spoke in more than one hundred cities. She had her own personal Learjet. "It was like having two candidates," Carter's son Jack stated. "It meant we could travel twice as far and meet twice the number of people. I think that won it for us." And the media loved her, labeling her a "Steel Magnolia."[80]

Where President Ford had to put out Betty's fires, Jimmy Carter had Rosalynn to extinguish his own. When Jimmy told *Playboy* magazine that he had lusted in his heart after other women, Rosalynn wryly said, "Jimmy talks too much, but at least people know he's honest and doesn't mind answering questions."[81] Rosalynn was so convincing that Carter media advisor Gerald Rafshoon ran an ad allowing Rosalynn to address the *Playboy* controversy. "Jimmy's never had any hint of scandal in his personal or in his public life. I really believe he can restore that honesty and integrity, openness, competence in government that we so sorely need in our country today. I think he'll be a great president," Rosalynn informed the audience.[82]

Rosalynn's polish helped Jimmy more than Betty's forthrightness helped Ford. If voters didn't like her, Betty said, "they'll just have to throw me out."[83] They did. On Inauguration Day, Jimmy Carter became president.

★★★

HILLARY RODHAM CLINTON. The very name polarizes. Hillary Rodham Clinton was certainly the most ambitious first lady in the history of American politics. The 2008 presidential candidate and senator from New York splits the country right down the center. To liberals, Hillary is a goddess; to conservatives, she is a devil.

All of the controversy surrounding Hillary obscures the fact that during the 1992 election, she contributed mightily to Bill's success. Early on, Hillary acted the part of loyal wife standing stoically by her man through thick and thin. In late January 1992, Gennifer Flowers revealed that she had engaged in a long-standing extramarital affair with then Arkansas governor Bill Clinton. Hillary appeared with Bill on *60 Minutes* on January 26 to counter the charges. When host Steve Kroft pushed Bill on the adultery issue, Bill awkwardly stated, "You're looking at two people who love each other. This is not an arrangement or an understanding. This is a marriage. That's a very different thing."

Hillary quickly jumped in with the line that likely saved Bill Clinton's presidential campaign: "You know, I'm not sitting here like some little woman standing by my man like Tammy Wynette. I'm sitting here because I love him and I respect him and I honor what he's been through and what we've been through together. And, you know, if that's not enough for people, then, heck, don't vote for him."[84] The reaction was immediate and mostly positive. By January 27, *ABC News* was reporting that 80 percent of Americans wanted the media to drop the Flowers story, 70 percent approved of Clinton's appearance, and Clinton was actually *gaining* strength in New Hampshire.[85]

It was only later in the campaign that Hillary truly began her cringe-inducing behavior. In March, Hillary obliquely critiqued homemakers, stating, "I suppose I could have stayed home and baked cookies and had teas, but what I decided to do was to fulfill my profession, which I entered before my husband was in public life."[86]

At about the same time, she made several controversial statements about the reasoning capacity of children. "I don't believe in parental consent [for underage girls' abortions]," Hillary told NPR, "because I think that in many instances there's always—already been an irrevocable family breakdown. The parents are not going to be helpful and supportive. It's cruel to presume that any right answer is the one that should be imposed on everyone." She followed up that rather radical statement by opining that children should be able to sue their parents: "To assume that every child under a certain age, say 18 or 21, is incompetent is to treat a 17-year-old like a one-year-old and I don't think that's a very sensible proposal."[87]

Despite such gaffes, Hillary's favorable ratings continued to climb. By October, her favorable ratings were at 56 percent, as opposed to 25 percent unfavorable. Hillary never approached the popularity of Barbara Bush—Barbara's numbers in the same poll were 81 percent favorable and 12 percent unfavorable—but Hillary's clever political maneuvering with regard to her husband's penchant for promiscuity minimized the damage on that front.

Hillary's front-and-center campaign presence contributed in another important way: by making herself a target, she drew fire from Republicans including President George W. Bush. "Hillary Clinton in an apron is like Michael Dukakis in a tank," Bush campaign strategist Roger Ailes gibed.[88] "Of course, advising Bill Clinton on every move, is that champion of the family Hillary Clinton, who believes that kids should be able to sue their parents, rather than helping with the chores as they were asked to do. She's likened marriage and the family to slavery. She's referred to the family as a dependency relationship that deprives people of their rights," stated Republican National Committee chairman Richard Bond at the Republican National Convention.[89]

Pat Buchanan echoed those comments: "'Elect me, and you get two for the price of one,' Mr. Clinton says of his lawyer spouse, and what does Hillary believe? Well, Hillary believes that 12-year-olds should have the right to sue their parents, and Hillary has compared marriage and the family as institutions to slavery and life on an Indian reservation."[90] Bush defended criticism of Hillary, averring, "If you're out there on issues . . . and you have an activist past, that is a little different than if you're not taking positions."[91]

Attacking Hillary actually backfired on Bush—he began to be perceived as mean, a perception reinforced by Bill's defense of his "victimized" wife. "They're running against Hillary, basically trying to make it a Willie Horton-like issue. And it's not really about Hillary, but they've had to grossly distort and outright falsify her views in order to attack her. What they . . . what they're trying to do is make it kind of a Willie Horton kind of thing against all independent working women," Bill complained.[92] As for Bush, Clinton joked, "You'd think he was running for First Lady."[93] Bush's National Convention bump soon wore off, his support among women eroded,[94] and he never recovered.

During the next eight years, Hillary's profile continued to rise—and her politics continued to divide. She was most popular when she played the part of loyal wife; she did the worst when she took an active part in politics. Her "Hillarycare" proposal contributed to the landmark Republican congressional take-back in 1994; her support of Bill during the Lewinsky scandal bolstered his popularity and made her an object of sympathy. On the whole—and certainly in 1992—Hillary as first lady was a net positive for her husband.

★★★

FOR EIGHT YEARS, Al Gore stood in the shadow of Bill Clinton. In 2000, he tried to escape that shadow, making particular use of his wife, Tipper. If Hillary was a more militant and radical Eleanor Roosevelt, Tipper was more along the lines of Lady Bird Johnson or Rosalynn Carter—a family woman concerned with family causes. In 1985, Tipper cofounded the Parents Music Resource Center, a group dedicated to informing parents about the potentially toxic content of rock and rap music. Tipper specifically stated that Americans would not receive a "two for one" if they elected her husband; she refused to be labeled a political advisor to Gore.

"The point is, we always shared," Tipper said. "We've always asked each other for advice. And now, suddenly, it's being, you know, microscoped and analyzed out. Like I'm a political adviser. No. I'm his wife. Yes, we talk. My opinion counts, and his opinion counts with me. That's it. We talk about everything. We always have."[95] Unlike Bill's relationship with Hillary, Gore's relationship with Tipper was not subject to speculation. Tipper campaigned hard for her husband, speaking routinely on his behalf.[96]

But Tipper was also an actor in perhaps the strangest moment of the 2000 campaign: the Tongue Lock. At the Democratic National Convention, Gore "spontaneously" grabbed Tipper, bent her over, and laid a long kiss on her. "The sheer carnality of the kiss—the can't-wait-to-get-back-to-the-hotel-room urgency, the sexual electricity flowing south—was riveting," gushed columnist Lance Morrow.[97]

The kiss was a rather obvious attempt to shake the public perception that Al Gore was a block of wood. "The Kiss sent an obvious political message—here's a man still passionately, faithfully in love with his wife, unlike the president he hopes to succeed—that was ultimately far less important than the total openness and surrender it implied," wrote Nick Gillespie. "Yes, Gore will let us watch, if that's what it takes to woo us."[98]

Naturally Gore denied the accusation that the Tongue Lock was staged: "I didn't map out some strategy. I was really overcome by the emotions in the hall. It's hard to describe what it's like to stand up in front of that many thousands of people who were not only clapping and cheering, but really feeling an outpouring of emotion . . . We've been married 30 years . . . I think anybody who watches that can tell that it was not scripted."[99] From a man who scripted everything including his "alpha male" wardrobe, this was less than convincing.

The Tongue Lock set tongues wagging. "I don't know if you saw this or if you heard about it, but this is really strange," cracked Conan O'Brien. "Last night, when Al Gore finally took the stage at the Democratic National Convention, he grabbed Tipper Gore and gave her a huge open-mouthed kiss on the lips. Did you see this? It's amazing. Yeah, apparently, Tipper hadn't been kissed like that since Monday night, when President Clinton took the stage."[100]

"Al Gore walked onstage at the Democratic National Convention and gave a deep, passionate kiss to his wife. It only served as another reminder that he's no Bill Clinton," joked Argus Hamilton.[101]

"The Democrats are doing very well now. Apparently, the convention did a lot for them," said Bill Maher. "It was a good convention. In fact, the LAPD bragged today that they kept things in very good order. They said they only had to turn the fire hoses on once, and that was to separate Al and Tipper Gore."[102]

The Tongue Lock served its purpose. "The kiss might not have turned political analysts on, but it apparently tugged more than a few heartstrings," reported the *Greensboro News & Record*. "After months of trailing Bush, Gore experienced a big post-convention bounce in the polls. He even won over some independent and undecided voters. His biggest boost, however, was among women voters. A CNN/*USA Today*/Gallup poll found that Gore has a 22-point lead among women voters. Bush has a 19-point lead among male voters. In focus groups, women applauded the kiss while some men booed it."[103]

The election was too close to call in the last days of the race. In late October, in need of a last-second push, Gore reverted again to smooching his wife.[104] It wasn't enough; though Gore won the popular vote, Bush won the presidency.

★★★

TIPPER'S PRESENCE in the 2000 campaign was a boon for Al Gore. Teresa Heinz's presence in Democratic presidential nominee John Kerry's 2004 campaign was a disaster. Kerry suffered from perceptions that he was an elitist and a UN type. He suffered from the widespread perception that throughout his career, he had been a man on the make. Heinz spoke with a thick foreign accent. She had worked for the UN, was aggressive, had used botox, and her marriage to Kerry looked suspiciously like a marriage of mutual convenience. She was, in short, the worst first lady candidate in American history.

Maria Teresa Thierstein Simões-Ferreira was born in Mozambique and immigrated to the United States to work as an interpreter for the United Nations. There she married billionaire John Heinz III, heir to the Heinz ketchup fortune. Heinz III served several terms in Congress and then entered the Senate. He was killed in a small aircraft collision in 1991. A year later, Teresa began dating Senator John Kerry of Massachusetts.

"It's an attraction that's different because, you know, I was still wounded. And you are lonely still, also, you know. So at that age, I think, what you look for is some comfort, some friendship, some understanding," Teresa explained. They married three years later, in 1995. They signed a prenuptial agreement. For eight years, she remained Teresa Heinz; only when Kerry began campaigning for president did she adopt his last name.[105]

This checkered history dogged Kerry throughout his campaign. He had divorced a woman, Julia Thorne, whose family was worth $300 million; though the couple separated in 1982, Kerry waited until 1988 to have the marriage annulled. During the separation, Kerry dated Morgan Fairchild, Cornelia Guest, and Patti Davis. The divorce was a good career move for Kerry, who hooked up with

Heinz, worth $500 million and the overseer of the $1.2 billion Heinz Foundation.[106]

Kerry's penchant for marrying up in wealth created a severe public relations problem for him. The situation was rich ground for comics. "John Kerry's wife Teresa Heinz is on the cover of *Newsweek* magazine this week and they said that if he is elected president, she will be the oldest first lady in American history. But that doesn't bother John Kerry, he said, 'To me, she looks like a million bucks,'" cracked Jay Leno on April 29, 2004.[107] "Teresa Heinz is on the cover of *Newsweek* magazine," Leno joked a day later. "John Kerry said he first noticed her when she was on the cover of another magazine, *Fortune*."[108]

"There was an embarrassing moment at a recent Democratic fundraiser," stated Craig Kilborn. "When John Kerry was handed a $10 million dollar check, he said, 'I do.'"[109] Kilborn wasn't done. "Today, John Kerry announced a fool-proof plan to wipe out the $500B deficit. John Kerry has a plan, he's going to put it on his wife's Gold Card."[110] Conan O'Brien got in on the act: "*Shrek 2* made over $120 million during its first week. In a related story, John Kerry asked Shrek to marry him."[111]

This kind of attention does not help presidential candidates. The public began to wonder whether Kerry would attempt to divorce Teresa and marry Bill Gates under Massachusetts's gay marriage regime.

Heinz's wealth wasn't Kerry's only problem. Heinz had a tendency to say the wrong thing at the wrong time. In a June 2002 *Washington Post* feature story, Heinz made a fool of herself. "Teresa Heinz is getting up a full head of rage while her husband, Sen. John Kerry, fidgets," wrote reporter Mark Leibovich. "Every time Heinz raises her voice, Kerry tries to play down his wife's agitation, which only inflames her more." In the article, Heinz made light of Kerry's

Vietnam dreams and interrupted him repeatedly. The piece discussed Heinz's past psychiatric issues, her tendency to refer to her deceased husband as "my husband," and an incident in which Heinz told Kerry that he was living in her house.

Leibovich concluded:

> Over two long interviews, Teresa Heinz is by turns effusive and harsh, warm and slightly bitter, solemn and melodramatic. And she is always, unfailingly, smart, original and provocative. She hits on the following things: the excessive drinking of a Massachusetts politician, the miscarriage suffered by one senator's wife, her own miscarriage, and the Boston TV reporter who is an "unhappy, lonely man." She speaks of how her oldest son, John IV, started "hating her" two years ago, when his daughter was born. (He declined to comment.) She also talks about how shy she is.[112]

In other words, Heinz was a bit nutty. That nuttiness shone through during the campaign. She informed Dr. Phil's shocked wife that she had been a "witch" with her children, and that she called her miscarriages "pinkies."[113] She stated at an Arizona fundraiser that she wouldn't be surprised if the Bush Administration somehow produced Osama bin Laden before the 2004 election.[114] She told one reporter from a Pittsburgh newspaper to "shove it." She informed a crowd that those who wanted President Bush for four more years wanted "four more years of hell."[115] She questioned whether Laura Bush, who had been a librarian and schoolteacher, had ever held a "real job."[116]

Then there was Teresa's accent. It made her seem foreign; it was vaguely unsettling. She foolishly opened her Democratic National Convention speech by speaking in five languages, accentuating rather than diminishing the perception that she was not quite American.[117]

Heinz helped cripple Kerry's bid for the White House. It was not much of a surprise when Teresa dropped the Kerry from her name again after the 2004 campaign.[118]

★★★

NOT EVERY FIRST LADY CANDIDATE is a disaster on the order of Teresa Heinz Kerry or a success on the order of Eleanor Roosevelt. Most fall somewhere in between. Laura Bush and Nancy Reagan are both typical first ladies—women who support their husbands to the hilt and mainly remain in the background. Such women may provide the most important aid to their husbands—support behind the scenes. They do not create fires that must be extinguished. Their ambitions are the same as their husbands'.

This is not to say that all presidential contenders' wives ought to remain silent. Many wives can add sparkle to their husbands' campaigns. But the danger inherent in creating a second politician—a politician whose views are often directly ascribed to their spouses—may be greater than the potential reward.

If potential first ladies are features of a presidential candidate's image, perhaps we should dismiss the stigma associated with attacking a nominee's spouse. We attack a politician's hair, height, weight, humor, military service, bookishness, age—in short, everything, both relevant and irrelevant. Should first ladies be immune? After all, no matter what politicians say, we are getting a "two for one" deal.

★ 8 ★

The Magic Formula

$\mathcal{S}$ORRY, FOLKS. There is no magic formula that can unerringly predict winners and losers in presidential elections. A haircut may cause a sensation in one election (JFK, 1960) and fall flat in another (John Kerry, 2004). Height may be a boon to one candidate (Lincoln, 1860 and 1864) but a bust for another (Winfield Scott, 1852). Age may demonstrate seasoned experience (Dwight D. Eisenhower, 1952 and 1956) or decrepitude (Bob Dole, 1996).

Acting like a cowboy may thrill voters (George W. Bush, 2000 and 2004) or it may alienate them (Barry Goldwater, 1964). Acting aloof may cripple one candidate (Al Gore, 2000) but boost another (Woodrow Wilson, 1912 and 1916). Military experience may ensure victory (Ulysses S. Grant, 1868 and 1872), or it may spell defeat (George McClellan, 1864). An outspoken wife may hurt a candidate (Gerald Ford, 1976) or aid him (Bill Clinton, 1992).

Still, we can spot trends. Americans generally like boots rather than suits; tall men rather than short men; candidates above age fifty; nominees with good but inexpensive haircuts; people we wouldn't mind sitting next to at a bar; men with military experience, if that military experience is important enough; and men with wives who aren't catty or loud.

And we can form educated opinions about each of these factors for each candidate. For some candidates, certain factors never become an issue: the first lady issue, for instance, played no part in any election until the mid-twentieth century, except for Andrew Jackson (1824 and 1828) and Grover Cleveland (1888 and 1892). But by measuring the impact, pro or con, of each image issue, we can quickly determine which presidential candidate has the image advantage.

Here, then, are the top ten image candidates of all time. Each applicable factor has been ranked on a scale from -5 (worst) to 5 (best). After adding together the applicable factors, we determine a percentage grade for each candidate by dividing the number of points by the number of points possible. Every election is different, so we can't assume that just because Bill Clinton's draft dodging didn't hurt him in 1992, it wouldn't have hurt him against Dwight D. Eisenhower. To that end, we have added an adjusted score—how would these candidates fare in today's political climate? It is worth noting that every one of these politicians was a master of image. There is no doubt that each would have adapted to changing times, so our adjusted scores are not necessarily the final word.

1. WARREN G. HARDING, 1920

Warren G. Harding was the purest image politician in American history. Nominated for his good looks, Harding died in office after his administration subjected the country to a series of devastating corruption scandals. Rarely has image contrasted so sharply with ability.

Height: 5. At six feet tall, Harding was solidly built and powerful looking. He looked fit as a fiddle (and he was apparently ready for love—at least according to Nan Britton).

Age: 5. At fifty-five, Harding was the perfect age. He seemed healthful, tanned, vital. He radiated an air of solemnity and gravitas.

Hair: 5. His thick silvery hair was an aesthetically pleasing addition to his bronzed, chiseled face.

Beer Buddy: 5. Everyone liked Warren G. Harding—even those who thought him an intellectual midget. "His home people declare him as sincere as Roosevelt; affable as McKinley, and with Blaine's capacity for inspiring friendships," wrote campaign biographer Joe Mitchell Chapple.[1] Harding's penchant for making friends served him ill in office—his "friends" betrayed him repeatedly. "I have no trouble with my enemies," Harding once declared. "I can take care of my enemies all right. It's my friends that keep me up at night."[2]

FINAL SCORE: 100%

Woodrow Wilson successfully put to rest the suits versus boots debate, and Harding was the beneficiary. He had no military experience, but he didn't need any. His wife, while helpful, had no impact on his image.

ADJUSTED SCORE: 68%

Harding could easily be elected today. His affable image, combined with his impressive personal appearance, would remain a powerful asset. Harding was lucky to run in 1920 in one respect: the media did not investigate his sexual exploits. Harding was quite promiscuous—during the 1920 election, he paid off a former mistress to keep her mouth shut. This would certainly become a major campaign issue today (-3).

2. GEORGE WASHINGTON, 1788 AND 1792

General Washington ran unopposed—twice. Potential opponents were smart to stay out of his way.

Suits vs. Boots: 4. Washington was a boots candidate, all the way, a rich and cultured wilderness man. Experience in the French and Indian War lent him an air of adventure; marrying Martha Washington didn't hurt his bank account. Washington loved his plantation and lavished his attention on it. Here was a true American Cincinnatus.

Height: 5. Standing somewhere between six-feet-two-inches and six-feet-three-and-a half-inches, Washington towered over his compatriots. John Adams suspected that Washington's height lent him an amorphous leadership quality. Washington was, literally and figuratively, a giant among men.

Age: 5. The "Father of Our Country" didn't take his title lightly. Washington often relied on his age to garner support, citing his graying hair and weakened eyes as evidence of his lifelong commitment to his country. It worked to perfection. Marvin Kitman wrote, "He did it the way Ronald Reagan would have done it."[3]

Military: 5. The man was George Washington. Need we say more?

FINAL SCORE: 95%

Washington's hair didn't matter very much, though he wore his own and powdered it. Martha didn't matter much either—which is fortunate for George, since George married her for her money. As for Washington's personality, it too was ignored. The man was a demigod in his own time, and no one expected a demigod to pal around with mere mortals.

ADJUSTED SCORE: 37%

Today's media would have savaged Washington. The Father of Our Country would have faced scrutiny over his lavish, un-bootslike spending habits (2), questionable military tactics (4), gold-digging (-3), and his cold austerity (-3), though he would have gained points for keeping his hair (3).

3. ABRAHAM LINCOLN, 1864

Lincoln benefited from political divisions and his strong wartime leadership. Also, the South couldn't vote. Nonetheless, it pays to remember that Honest Abe wasn't just a great man—he was a terrific politician.

Suits vs. Boots: 5. Abe Lincoln revivified log cabin imagery, spoke often of his wilderness upbringing, and became known far and wide as "the Rail Splitter." He was folksy, witty, and wise. In short, Abe was a paramount boots candidate.

Height: 5. Lincoln stood a full six-feet-four-inches. Lincoln's impressive height had been perhaps his most recognizable feature since 1858, when Lincoln debated "Little Giant" Stephen Douglas, who stood a mere five-feet-four-inches. Next Lincoln faced "Little Napoleon," General George McClellan, five-feet-eight-inches. No contest.

Hair: 5. Lincoln's beard was already iconic. When Lincoln grew out his beard to please an eleven-year-old girl, he created a political image that shaped the next fifty years of presidential facial hair.

Lincoln's beard helped round out his gaunt, rather ugly face, giving him an appearance of melancholy wisdom. McClellan's handlebar mustache was stylish, but it contributed to his image as a dandy.

Beer Buddy: 5. Lincoln's modern image overshadows the fact that he had an arch wit, a folksy sense of humor, and a gentle disposition. Lincoln's storytelling prowess was legendary. Plus, he had once been a bartender.

Military: 3. Lincoln had very little military experience, but his Civil War leadership paid electoral dividends, particularly after major battle victories by Generals Sherman and Grant in the lead-up to the 1864 election. It didn't hurt that Lincoln had already repudiated McClellan's military leadership by firing him in 1863.

FINAL SCORE: 92%

Lincoln's age made little difference in the 1864 election; fortunately for him, neither did his wife's nuttiness and Confederate relatives.

ADJUSTED SCORE: 25%

Lincoln's beard worked for three reasons: beards were popular, Lincoln was ugly, and Lincoln's beard had already been emblazoned in the public mind. If Lincoln ran today, none of those factors would apply. His beard would seem like a shoddy cover-up for his unappealing mug. Being a practical politician, Lincoln would remain clean-shaven—and a clean-shaven Lincoln was not a pretty sight (-2). Lincoln's height would have helped less than it did in 1864; he was gawky and awkward looking, particularly since his size contrasted sharply with his high-pitched voice (2). Mary Todd would have hurt Lincoln's candidacy—her mental problems and three Confederate brothers would have damaged the president (-4).

4. TEDDY ROOSEVELT, 1904

War hero. Trust-buster. Big-game hunter. Politician extraordinaire. The candidate with the infectious grin and heavy mustache was one of the most popular presidents in American history. After all, who could dislike the man who inspired the teddy bear?

Suits vs. Boots: 5. "Now look!" Senator Mark Hanna of Ohio exclaimed upon hearing of TR's election. "That damned cowboy is President of the United States."[4] Heavily image conscious, Teddy hunted regularly, rode horses—and made sure never to get caught by the press while playing golf. His early cowboy days in the Dakota territories left an indelible mark on TR, who later claimed, "I never would have been president if it had not been for my experiences in North Dakota."

Age Score: 4. At forty-six, TR was young and vital. He was also experienced—he was the incumbent president of the United States.

Beer Buddy: 4. Though TR was reputedly arrogant, he was also "more fun than a goat," according to Secretary of State John Hay.[5] We'll take Hay's word for it.

Military: 4. TR wasn't a general, but he was a self-promoting Spanish-American War hero. That was good enough for his supporters, who championed his stint in Cuba as a Rough Rider.

FINAL SCORE: 85%

Teddy's hair wasn't an issue, since his opponent also sported a mustache. His wife, too, remained out of the spotlight.

ADJUSTED SCORE: 60%

TR was a master of publicity. He was also a handsome fellow, if somewhat on the short side at five-feet-eight-inches (-1). His wife was cultured and, by all accounts, delightful (2). His mustache might have to go, but his thick thatch of brown hair would accentuate his youth (3). All in all, TR's maverick image remains as vibrant today as it did in 1904.

5. ULYSSES S. GRANT, 1868 AND 1872

General Grant followed in the political footsteps of Abraham Lincoln and the military footsteps of George Washington and Andrew Jackson. Chosen to carry the Republican banner after Lincoln's death, Grant became as successful on the political battlefield as he was on the actual battlefield. He ran roughshod over his opponents, Horatio Seymour and Horace Greeley.

Suits vs. Boots: 5. Though Grant was unsuccessful at every non-military career he tried, his supporters harped on his pre-Civil War tenure as a tanner. A lifelong horseman and farmer, Grant's boots credentials were well earned.

Hair: 3. Grant likely didn't mean to make his beard the focus of caricaturists. Nonetheless, his close-shorn beard and hardy looks closely paralleled Lincoln's, emphasizing the fact that Grant would fill Lincoln's shoes.

Beer Buddy: 3. Grant was often solemn, but he also struck those around him as honest and friendly. "I found this great man affable and just in his remarks, courteous in his demeanor, and the mode in which he shakes hands told me at once of his sincerity and honesty," wrote a European visitor.[6] His opponents called him a drunk, but the charges did not stick.

Military: 5. The victor of Shiloh and Vicksburg, the former general in chief of all the armies of the Union, the recipient of General Robert E. Lee's surrender, Grant could safely rest on his substantial military accomplishments.

FINAL SCORE: 80%

Grant's age, height, and wife played no role in the two campaigns.

ADJUSTED SCORE: 50%

Grant's facial hair would not be an asset today; it was an asset at the time because beards were popular, and because Grant effectually succeeded the bearded Lincoln as the standard-bearer for the Union cause (2). Grant's military accomplishments are awe-inspiring, but he would surely be criticized for his heavy expenditure of Union troops (4). His height, five-feet-eight-inches, would be a detriment rather than an asset (-1). His wife would provide slight benefit (2). Without hard evidence of drunkenness, Grant's alleged alcoholism would likely meet with the same criticism and defense it did in 1868.

6. ANDREW JACKSON, 1828

Old Hickory whupped the tar out of John Quincy Adams. He was a rough, tough, mean son-of-a-gun. He was also an enormously effective image politician.

Suits vs. Boots: 5. Jackson, said paradigmatic suit John Quincy Adams, was "a barbarian who could not write a sentence of grammar and hardly could spell his own name."[7] In 1806, lawyer Charles

Dickinson impugned Rachel Jackson's honor. Jackson challenged Dickinson to a duel. Dickinson fired first; the bullet struck Jackson directly in the chest. Jackson didn't move an inch. He stood, "his feet sloshing in blood that had drained from his chest," and then coldly shot Dickinson through the abdomen. Dickinson died. Jackson carried Dickinson's bullet in his chest all the way to the grave.[8] It doesn't get more boots than that.

Height: 5. Jackson's reedy build contrasted sharply with John Quincy Adams's short tubbiness. Cartoons of the time capitalized on the contrast.

Hair: 5. Jackson's wiry, wild shock of hair was as iconic in its time as Lincoln's beard was during the Civil War. It reinforced his wilderness image—and again, contrasted sharply with Quincy Adams's baldness.

Beer Buddy: 4. Jackson wasn't the typical beer buddy. He wasn't the type of fellow you'd want to hang out with on a regular basis, unless you were a loyal lackey—you might say the wrong thing and end up on the wrong side of a duel. He was, however, the type of fellow you'd want on your side in a bar fight. John Derbyshire of *National Review* said that if we made a list of presidential SOBs, Old Hickory would top the list.[9] Nonetheless, Jackson had the common touch—for the first time in presidential history, a "commoner" occupied the White House.

Military: 5. As the greatest American military hero since Washington, Jackson's only hardship was deflecting accusations that he had pursued his foes too vigorously and treated his troops too brutally.

Spouse: -2. Jackson was one of the few early presidential candidates for whom his wife was an issue. Jackson's mishandling of his marriage led to charges that his wife was an adulteress and bigamist.

FINAL SCORE: 73%

Jackson's age had no impact on the 1828 election—J. Q. Adams was precisely the same age.

ADJUSTED SCORE: 60%

Jackson was one of the rare early politicians who would succeed now. Populist, hardy, heroic, Jackson could appeal to the masses. His beer buddy rating would likely be lower than it was at the time, since he wasn't Mr. Friendly (3). His marital woes would follow him (-3). He would have to tone down the hair (4). His military record would come under fire for excessive savagery (4). Even at sixty-one, Jackson was still chock full of piss and vinegar. He would remain a formidable electoral foe today.

7. FRANKLIN PIERCE, 1852

Yes, Franklin Pierce. Pierce was easily the most handsome man to occupy the White House. "Pierce was a nincompoop," proclaimed Harry Truman. "He's got the best picture in the White House . . . but being president involves a little bit more than just winning a beauty contest, and he was another one that was a complete fizzle . . . Pierce didn't know what was going on, and even if he had, he wouldn't have known what to do about it."[10] Pierce may have been a nincompoop, but he was a particularly effective image politician.

Suits vs. Boots: 2. Pierce was born in a log cabin, but he received a classical education and became a lawyer. His supporters focused on his humble beginnings. Nathaniel Hawthorne, one of Pierce's best friends, penned a campaign biography: "In 1785, being employed as agent to explore a tract of wild land, [General Benjamin Pierce] purchased a lot of fifty acres in what is now the town of Hillsborough. In the spring of the succeeding year, he built himself a log hut, and began the clearing and cultivation of his tract . . . In 1789, he married Anna Kendrick, with whom he lived about half a century, and who bore him eight children, of whom Franklin was the sixth."[11] Pierce's own refusal to embrace sectional loyalties (Pierce was a pro-slavery candidate from New Hampshire) contributed to his image as a man of the land rather than a northern city boy.

Height: 1. Pierce stood a compact five-feet-ten-inches; his proportionality and good looks compared favorably with Winfield Scott's aged enormity (six-feet-five-inches).

Age: 3. At forty-seven, Pierce seemed hearty and healthy; Scott, at sixty-six, did not.

Hair: 5. Pierce had fantastic hair before fantastic hair was fashionable. His thick, curly black hair hung down loosely over the left side of his forehead, giving him a studied, disheveled appearance. He had a few gray hairs at the temples, adding a distinguished touch.

Beer Buddy: 5. Nobody seemed to dislike Pierce personally. Pierce, said biographer James Rawley, was "a boon barroom companion, possessing both personal magnetism and a desire to please others."[12]

Military: 4. Brigadier General Pierce became a Mexican War hero, despite fainting spells brought on by wounds incurred in battle. Though his military record did not come close to matching that of his opponent and former superior officer, Pierce was able to capitalize on his military service.

FINAL SCORE: 67%

Pierce's wife, Jane, did not contribute to the campaign. In fact, Jane opposed Pierce's run for the presidency.

ADJUSTED SCORE: 68.5%

As Warren G. Harding's image did, Pierce's image profile largely stands the test of time. Pierce's military record came under heavy scrutiny in 1852—nothing would change today. Today's political climate would heighten Pierce's appeal; his wife, Jane, would receive tremendous sympathy for the tragic death of their son, Benny, during the campaign (4).

8: FRANKLIN DELANO ROOSEVELT, 1944

After twelve years as president of the United States, FDR was an American institution. His victory in the 1944 election was a foregone conclusion. Upbeat, brilliant, warm, FDR was the first man to take full advantage of mass media—his use of radio revolutionized the art of politics.

Height: 4. FDR's height worked to his advantage in 1944. When he stood, FDR was six-feet-two-inches; his opponent, Republican nominee Thomas Dewey, was five-feet-eight-inches. FDR was a veritable giant; his opponent was "the little man on the wedding cake." The media helped FDR minimize the political effects of his polio.

Age: -1. FDR's doctors reported that the president was healthy. Nonetheless, Dewey charged that FDR was a "tired old man."[13] FDR was reelected, then died five months later.

Hair: 2. The still-well-coiffed FDR looked younger than his health.

Beer Buddy: 5. FDR's jauntily angled cigarette holder and winning grin helped millions through hard times. It would be difficult to find a more popular beer buddy than FDR.

Military: 4. As Lincoln did, FDR receives points for leading the nation during a time of war.

Spouse: 5. Eleanor Roosevelt remains the prototypical first lady.

FINAL SCORE: 63%

FDR's suit image didn't hurt him during the Age of the Bankers.

ADJUSTED SCORE: 43%

FDR's image would never survive mass media scrutiny today. His polio would not have been buried—it would have become a front-page issue (2). His age would have been connected more strongly with his health (-2). His military leadership would have been attacked, particularly in the aftermath of allegations about the Roosevelt Administration's failure to prevent the attack on Pearl Harbor (3). Eleanor would have been a far more controversial figure today than she was in 1944. Her suspected lesbianism, far-left political activism, and open power marriage would remind voters more of Hillary Clinton than Lady Bird Johnson (2). FDR would have overcome all of this for two reasons: Dewey was an especially weak image politician, and FDR was already an icon.

9: RONALD REAGAN, 1980

The Great Communicator was a consummate image politician. A former actor, Reagan knew the value and art of image framing— and he used it productively in his campaign against incumbent Jimmy Carter.

Suits vs. Boots: 4. Reagan focused on his midwestern upbringing, his modest roots, his love for the countryside, and his ranch in Santa Monica. He chopped wood, rode horses, and wore a cowboy hat.

Height: 3. Reagan stood six feet one inch; Carter stood five-feet-nine-inches. During the presidential debates, Reagan looked taller than the incumbent; he also stood ramrod straight, demonstrating dignity and pride.

Age: 3. Reagan turned sixty-nine in 1980, making his age a hot-button issue throughout the campaign. Reagan not only defused the issue by emphasizing his age, he turned his age to his advantage by talking about his experience and calling America back to a better way of life. Reagan was, he said, the oldest and the wisest. Americans believed him.

Hair: 4. Reagan's pitch-black hair reinforced perceptions of youthfulness—this was no gray old man.

Beer Buddy: 4. As FDR did before him, Reagan constantly wore a smile. He reassured Americans that the best was yet to come. As the campaign wore on, Carter began to look desperate, mean, and petty; Reagan continued to radiate kindness and optimism.

Military: 1. Though Reagan could not serve overseas during World War II because of poor eyesight, he served as a captain in the Army Air Force in Hollywood, making training films for the troops. That experience popped up in his campaign commercials.

Spouse: 2. Nancy Reagan modeled adoration throughout the 1980 campaign, irritating Reagan's opponents. She helped Reagan project the image of ideal family man.

FINAL SCORE: 60%

ADJUSTED SCORE:

No adjusted score is necessary for such a recent candidate.

10: JOHN F. KENNEDY, 1960

When we think image politics, we think John F. Kennedy. The hair, the smile, the charm—Kennedy was . . . well . . . Kennedy.

Suits vs. Boots: 0. Kennedy hit the precise midpoint between suit and boots. He wasn't rough-hewn enough to be a boots candidate; he wasn't stiff enough to be a suit.

Height: 1. Kennedy was six feet, an ideal height; Nixon, however, was five-feet-eleven-inches, so JFK didn't see much of an advantage here, although he derived an advantage from Nixon favoring his bad knee during the first presidential debate.

Age: 3. Kennedy's age could have been a problem for him—at forty-three, Kennedy was the youngest presidential candidate since Thomas Dewey in 1944. With his youth and energy, he was able to capture the heart of the nation without losing on the experience issue; Nixon was only four years older than JFK.

Hair: 5. No comment necessary.

Beer Buddy: 4. Kennedy was witty, loved sports (Jackie broke her ankle shortly after marrying JFK during one of those famous Kennedy touch football games), and knew how to have a good time. Of course, the public didn't know just how much JFK loved to carouse. If they had, they wouldn't have approved.

Military: 4. As Teddy Roosevelt did, JFK knew how to market. His heroism in World War II became a national story—a story reprinted again and again at the behest of his powerful father, Joseph.

Spouse: 4. Jackie Kennedy epitomized class and glamour. She campaigned in Spanish for her husband, became a fashion icon, and enchanted Americans from coast to coast.

FINAL SCORE: 60%

ADJUSTED SCORE: 40%

Kennedy's military experience would have come under scrutiny (3). So would his nightlife and, by extension, his marriage (-2).

What do these scores tell us? They show us how much image matters . . . and how much politics matter. Take, for example, the 1960 election. We have already seen that JFK's final image score in 1960 was 60 percent. Here is Richard Nixon's:

RICHARD NIXON, 1960

Suits vs. Boots: 0. Nixon's humble beginnings cancelled out his suitlike attitude.

Height: -1. Nixon was slightly shorter than JFK, but he looked bad during the first debate.

Age: 1. Nixon was young, but didn't capture young hearts; he was experienced, but Eisenhower undercut his broader appeal.

Hair: -2. Nixon's widow's peak didn't hide his sweat during the first debate. His slicked-back hair and constant five o'clock shadow didn't help, either.

Beer Buddy: -4. Nixon seemed shifty and grim. You wouldn't want him on your bowling team.

Military: 1. Nixon served honorably in the navy.

Spouse: 2. Pat Nixon might have seemed like an ice queen, but she gave Nixon the all-American family image.

FINAL SCORE: -10%

So JFK had an image advantage of 70 percent. Why was 1960 such a narrow election? It was narrow because Nixon had the power of a popular incumbent president, Nixon had a terrific grasp of the issues, and Nixon was a tremendously energetic campaigner. If we take image out of the picture, Nixon clearly should have won the 1960 election over an inexperienced senator from Massachusetts who routinely missed committee meetings. The simple fact is that if Kennedy had been bald, he never would have been president.

Let's look at another close election: the election of 2000. Here are George W. Bush's image ratings vs. Al Gore's image ratings:

	Bush	**Gore**
Suits vs. Boots	4	1
Height	1	1
Age	2	2
Hair	2	2
Beer Buddy	4	-3
Military	-1	-1
Spouse	2	3
Total	14	5
Final Score	40%	14%

George W. Bush had a 26 percent image advantage, based primarily on the fact that Bush seemed like a genial guy, while Gore seemed stiffer than a two-by-four. Yet we spent a month after the election sorting out the winner. The tightness of the 2000 election testifies largely to the power of incumbency—the Clinton factor.

If Bush hadn't worn a cowboy hat, he would have lost the election. That's the power of image.

High image rating differentials, when combined with political advantages, lead to blowouts. We've already seen the ten best image candidates. Here, then, are the five worst:

1. HORACE GREELEY, 1872

Imagine a mole. Now add a neck beard, spectacles, and a surly disposition. You have just imagined Horace Greeley.

Suits vs. Boots: -5. Greeley was a lifelong New Englander and a lifelong newspaper man. Enough said.

Hair: -5. Greeley had the worst hair in presidential history. His giant bald pate was surrounded by long wisps of gray hair. Hair sprouted in great tufts from his neck; his face remained clean-shaven. It could have been worse—Greeley could always have braided his nose hair.

Beer Buddy: -5. Surly and temperamental, the grumpy editor went mad and died shortly after the 1872 election.

Military: -5. When Greeley, an original supporter of Lincoln and the Republican Party, received the Democratic nomination in 1872, the insanity began. Waving the bloody shirt—lumping Democrats together with Copperheads and Confederates—was all the rage. The unfortunate Greeley received the brunt of the attack.

FINAL SCORE: -100%

Running Greeley against Grant was about as smart as signing Martha Stewart to quarterback the 1986 Philadelphia Eagles. Both situations were bound to end in roadkill.

2. ADLAI STEVENSON, 1952 AND 1956

Adlai Stevenson was articulate, intelligent . . . and one of the worst presidential candidates in American history. And the Democrats nominated him twice.

Suits vs. Boots: -5. Stevenson was a suit, all the way. Though he attempted to shape his image as "The Man from Libertyville," he looked about as comfortable out of a suit as most people look in one.

Hair: -5. Stevenson was bald. So was Eisenhower. Eisenhower, however, did not embrace the egghead label. Stevenson did. "Eggheads of the world, unite!" he proclaimed. Not a winning slogan.

Age: 1. Eisenhower's age was an issue in both 1952 and 1956. Stevenson attempted to exploit it, but Eisenhower was simply too popular.

Beer Buddy: -4. Stevenson wasn't a bad guy, just a boring one. Going out for beers with Stevenson would have been like going out for beers with your geology professor and discussing sedimentary rock.

Military: -5. Normally Stevenson's military experience (or lack thereof) wouldn't have been an issue. Against Eisenhower, it was. Just as he had with his baldness, Stevenson embraced his civilian status, claiming that it made him more likely to pursue peace than his opponent. Hey, it was worth a shot.

Spouse: -5. Stevenson was the first divorced major party candidate in American history. His ex-wife suggested that he was a closeted homosexual.

FINAL SCORE: -77%

Eisenhower was a strong candidate. Stevenson was about as weak as they come. The result: two consecutive landslides.

3. MICHAEL DUKAKIS, 1988

Dukakis's opponent, George H. W. Bush, was not an unbeatable candidate. Dukakis just made him seem that way.

Suits vs. Boots: -5. Dukakis was an archetypal Massachusetts liberal. He sealed his suity fate when he calmly told a national television audience that if his wife were raped and murdered, he would still oppose the death penalty.

Height: -5. Dukakis, five-feet-eight-inches, looked like a shrimp next to the physically imposing six-feet-two-inch vice president.

Age: 1. Bush was sixty-four in 1988; Dukakis turned fifty-five just before the election.

Hair: 3. Dukakis's hair was quite underrated. He had a thick head of dark hair, nicely combed.

Beer Buddy: -4. Dukakis seemed like a nerdy stiff. As Neal B. Freeman of *National Review* put it in October 1988, "The nerd vote is a lock . . . [Dukakis] is, it appears, just about what he was in first grade—the smartest little guy in the class—and you find yourself liking him now just about as much as you liked him then."[14]

Military: -5. Dukakis foolishly reemphasized his weakness on national defense by staging a photo op riding in a tank. Dukakis looked like a bobblehead; the Bush campaign used the video from the tank photo op in their campaign commercials.

Spouse: 1. Kitty didn't play a big role in the campaign—which was a net positive for Dukakis, since Kitty was engaged in a frightening battle with alcoholism at the time.

FINAL SCORE: -40%

Dukakis was a rotten candidate; he also had to deal with the legacy of Reagan. Unsurprisingly, Bush won in a walk. Bush's weakness as a candidate would not be exposed until four years later.

4. HORATIO SEYMOUR, 1868

Horace Greeley with worse hair—seriously—and more political experience.

Suits vs. Boots: -5. A lifelong New Yorker and son of a banker. The human manifestation of a Hugo Boss suit.

Hair: -5. Just awful. Like Greeley, he sported a killer neck beard; his great curly sideburns met beneath his chin. Curly clumps of hair surrounded the top of his shiny dome. Acerbic cartoonist Thomas Nast pilloried Seymour, turning his strange haircut into devil ears.

Beer Buddy: 2. Seymour was generally described as good-natured.

Military: -5. Seymour's call for a peace treaty with the South, his support for the New York draft riots, and his defense of Copperhead congressman Vallandingham made him a prime target for Republicans waving the bloody shirt.

FINAL SCORE: -37%

Grant won the 1868 election by uttering four words: "Let us have peace." Seymour lost it by running.

5. BOB DOLE, 1996

In 1996, Bob Dole won the Republican Lifetime Achievement Award. After decades of running for the Republican nomination, he finally got his shot at the White House. There was only one problem. He was already seventy-three years old.

Suits vs. Boots: -1. Dole was from Kansas, which isn't suit territory, but he was also a career politician with a less-than-rugged reputation.

Age: -5. During World War II, Dole lost the use of his right arm, which made him look unhealthy from the start; his pale pallor and slight stoop accentuated his age. Falling off a stage and into a crowd of reporters in Chico, California, didn't help his cause. Next to Clinton, Dole seemed older than Methuselah.

Hair: -4. Dole's high forehead and receding hairline added five years.

Beer Buddy: -5. Though Dole would later prove funny and engaging, he showed little of those qualities during the 1996 campaign. He came off as a crotchety old man lecturing the youngsters.

Military: 1. Dole's military heroism was truly extraordinary, but it didn't avail him during the campaign. Running against the alleged draft-dodging incumbent, military issues simply didn't play.

Spouse: 3. Elizabeth Dole was surely the most impressive first lady candidate in American history. Secretary of labor under George H. W. Bush, secretary of transportation under Ronald Reagan, president of the American Red Cross, Dole was a true asset to her husband during the 1996 campaign.

FINAL SCORE: -34%

Clinton was a terrific image politician, by contrast, clocking in with a 48.5 percent image score. The image differential, combined with the power of incumbency, spelled doom for Senator Dole.

Honorable mentions include John Kerry, George McGovern, Thomas Dewey, William Jennings Bryan, Martin Van Buren, John Quincy Adams, and John Adams.

Where do the 2008 candidates stand? All in all, the 2008 presidential candidates look surprisingly weak.

HILLARY CLINTON: THE MAKEOVER QUEEN

Hillary is easily the most talked about presidential candidate since Teddy Kennedy in 1980. If she wins the nomination, however, she may suffer from image problems, some of them peculiar to being a woman.

Suits vs. Boots: -5. Hillary is a total suit. An Illinois native, she detoured to Arkansas with her husband before grabbing a Senate seat in New York. The leader of the pantsuit brigade, Hillary is not earthy or crunchy. She has little or no Southern appeal, despite her longtime Arkansas residence. When she adopted a horrifically fake Southern accent at a black church in Selma, Alabama, she provoked nationwide laughter.

Height: -3. Hillary stands five-feet-six-inches. How much does diminutive stature hurt a woman? It is difficult to tell. Certainly Hillary's smallish size benefited her in her 2000 senatorial run—during a debate with Republican Rick Lazio, she was able to convincingly play victim when the taller Lazio aggressively approached her onstage. Nonetheless, Hillary's size, combined with her high-pitched voice—she sounds particularly awful when she needs to project—makes her seem shrewish rather than feminine.

Age: 2. Hillary will turn sixty-one during the campaign. Her age, combined with her newfound political moderation, may help counter public perceptions that she is a 1960s-era radical.

Hair: -3. Hillary has tried more hairdos than Cher. Her best hair-cuts soften her face and make her look more, not less feminine. Her hair tends to thin if it lengthens beyond a certain point; her hair likely looked best during her 2000 senatorial run.

Beer Buddy: -5. Hillary projects arrogance; she seems hard as nails. Her profanity-laced, enraged tirades, aimed at her husband and her campaign aides, are the stuff of legend. Hillary ally Susan Estrich defended Hillary by asking, "Since when is being 'nice' the basis for being president? Since when does the nicest candidate win?"[15] And Estrich is right—the nicest candidate rarely wins. But the candidate who *seems* the nicest almost always wins. And Hillary can't even play-act "nice."

Military: -1. Unlike other candidates, Hillary will never have to answer questions about the Vietnam draft. Hillary *will* have to answer questions about her reported hatred for the military. Lieutenant Colonel Buzz Patterson, the man who carried the nuclear football during the Clinton Administration, reported that Hillary ordered military aides not to wear their uniforms.[16] This type of loathing for the military could come back to haunt the former first lady.

Spouse: 3. Bill Clinton's appeal is unmistakable. But will public perceptions of a power marriage damage Hillary? Will Bill's popularity overshadow Hillary's candidacy?

FINAL SCORE: -34%

Hillary has the potential to be a truly terrible image candidate. She can rescue herself by softening her image. She must smile more, try wearing a skirt on occasion, wear softer colors, soften her hair, and urge Bill to try standing by her side once in a while. Americans are ready and willing to elect a woman—but they are not willing to elect a woman masquerading as a man.

BARACK OBAMA: THE X-FACTOR

Barack Obama has seemingly emerged from nowhere to challenge Hillary Clinton for the Democratic nomination. How would Obama fare in a general election?

Suits vs. Boots: -5. Obama is less of a suit than Hillary, but not by much. He grew up in Hawaii and Indonesia, went to college at Occidental and Columbia, and then attended Harvard Law School. Many have already challenged the authenticity of his African American experience; he did not grow up in the inner city or face serious racism.

Height: 4. Obama is six-feet-two-inches and appears trim and healthy. He set politicos a-twitter when he appeared in *People* magazine emerging from the Pacific Ocean in a bathing suit. "We see his well-defined pecs, his perfectly hairless torso, just a bit of padding around the abs and a drawstring dangling from his form-fitting surfer trunks," Dana Milbank of the *Washington Post* wrote. "The aspiring presidential candidate splashes through the water and squints into the distance; he is transformed into Burt Lancaster in *From Here to Eternity*."[17]

Age: 3. Obama, who turns forty-seven in 2008, uses his age to his advantage, pledging to move beyond the politics of the 1960s, "the psychodrama of the Baby Boom generation—a tale rooted in old grudges and revenge plots hatched on a handful of college campuses long ago—played out on the national stage."[18] This is pap, of course, but it is effective pap. Still, his age could contribute to the perception that he isn't quite ripe for the presidency.

Hair: 3. Obama's haircut is close-shorn, giving him a younger look.

Beer Buddy: 4. Obama looks friendly. He has a winning smile and a confident manner. Obama's biggest danger is the growing perception that he is arrogant; he has a shockingly short resumé for a presidential candidate, which makes him seem ambitious. He gaffed regarding his role in his earlier Chicago organizing, maximizing his own role while ignoring the contributions of others. He must be careful about prevarications—he has already stepped into Al Gore territory once, falsely claiming that "Bloody Sunday" in Selma provided the impetus behind his parents' marriage (the march occurred in 1965; Obama was born in 1961).

Military: -2. Obama was too young to serve in Vietnam, which works to his advantage. He has blundered with regard to the military, however. He stated in an early campaign speech that soldiers who died in Iraq had "wasted" their lives.[19] If that statement was a symptom of Obama's distaste for the military, it will not be his last antimilitary gaffe. It looks more like a symptom than a simple slip of the tongue—Obama is clearly soft on terrorism, stating that "cynicism" is as much of a threat to peace in the Middle East as "just terrorists" or "just Hamas" or "just Hezbollah."[20]

Spouse: 2. Michelle Obama is a career woman and makes no bones about it. She is also a terrific campaign asset—she is energetic, intelligent, an excellent speaker. She must be careful not to intrude too much into her husband's spotlight, reminding Americans of Hillary circa 1996.

FINAL SCORE: 26%

Obama's profile is solid. Nonetheless, he's stuck between a rock and hard place. He must be wary of pinning himself down on policy—if he descends from his pedestal, he will be vulnerable to accusations about his inexperience and rather elite background. If he refuses to talk policy, however, he will have no ground on which to fight star power Republicans—candidates like Rudy Giuliani and John McCain, who have better policy credentials.

JOHN EDWARDS: THE POPULIST

John Edwards was 2004's Barack Obama: a relative no-name who struck gold. Edwards's 2004 vice presidential nomination would normally make him a frontrunner in 2008, but the presence of Clinton and Obama has stolen Edwards's thunder.

Suits vs. Boots: -3. Typically, Edwards's Southern roots and blue-collar past would have made him a boots candidate all the way. But Edwards is a wealthy trial lawyer and a conspicuous consumer. Edwards's palatial North Carolina estate, the largest in his county, spans 28,200 square feet.[21] Edwards talks about two Americas, but he's a member of the wealthier half.

Height: 3. At six feet tall, Edwards is telegenic and energetic.

Age: 2. Edwards turns fifty-five in 2008; he was just young enough to miss the Vietnam draft. Unfortunately for him, he can't claim that age translates into experience—he served just one term in the Senate.

Hair: -3. Edwards has the best hair of anyone running in 2008. His hair is so good that it's bad for his image; he's become known as the "Breck Girl." Edwards has already repeated John Kerry's crucial

$1,000 haircut blunder. In early 2007, he got *two* $400 haircuts at Torrenueva Hair Designs.[22] Many Americans believe that his hair is the sole basis for his popularity.

Beer Buddy: 4. Edwards is universally recognized as a nice guy—the only question to this point has been his inability to establish his gravitas.

Military: 0. Edwards has not blundered—but he hasn't strengthened his credibility on military issues, either.

Spouse: 5. Elizabeth Edwards is John's biggest asset. Her rediagnosis with cancer in March 2007 created a tremendous amount of sympathy for Edwards's candidacy. It made Edwards seem more serious—he was now facing a truly serious issue. "It's a helluva way to do it, but cancer may have closed the gravitas gap for John Edwards," noted Susan Estrich.[23]

FINAL SCORE: 23%

Edwards can boost his credibility by taking more substantive positions—and canceling a couple of his credit cards. His appeal is the appeal to the common man; if he loses that appeal, he is finished.

RUDY GIULIANI: THE WILD CARD

Rudy's image is entirely inconsistent. On some issues, he looks tremendous; on others, he looks downright awful. Will his strengths outweigh his weaknesses? Only if he can stop shooting himself in the foot.

Suits vs. Boots: 0. Rudy is a city boy, born and bred. He also poses as a tough guy. His decision to repeatedly quote *The Godfather*, imitating Marlon Brando, is a conscious—and smart—choice.

Height: 1. At five-feet-nine-and-a-half-inches, Rudy is hardly an imposing physical specimen. His moderate height is tempered by his pugnacious attitude, however. And to most Americans, Rudy remains a bigger than life figure.

Age: -1. Rudy turns sixty-four years old in 2008. He had prostate cancer back in 2000, a development that forced him to drop out of the 2000 New York senatorial race. Now he's clean, but questions about his health are sure to arise if he takes the Republican nomination.

Hair: 0. Rudy is bald—he would be the first bald presidential candidate since Gerald Ford in 1976. His cue-ball head would normally be a major drawback, but Americans are used to Rudy's face. Can Rudy make baldness cool?

Beer Buddy: 5. With the notable exception of certain firefighters, Americans see Rudy as a wonderful guy. He's rough and tough, but warm and caring. He was the kind of guy who attended both 9/11 funerals and 9/11 relatives' weddings. He has a muscular can-do optimism and a ready smile.

Military: 5. Giuliani did not serve during the Vietnam War; he received two deferments. As America's mayor, Giuliani shored up his military credentials. America sees Giuliani as a man who can stand up to terrorism—and they know he is a man who can endure under pressure.

Spouse: -3. Giuliani's checkered marital history—he has been married three times—is bound to hurt him. His third wife, Judith Nathan, has been married three times as well. Giuliani met Nathan while he was still married to his second wife. If Giuliani fails to keep Nathan out of the headlines, he may find himself in hot water.

FINAL SCORE: 20%

Rudy must continue to capitalize on his high-testosterone image while keeping his seedier side out of the tabloids. Rudy has been in the headlines since his election as mayor of New York in 1993, so many of his skeletons have already fallen out of the closet. He can only hope that the YouTube video of him in drag doesn't get mainstream play.

JOHN MCCAIN: THE MAVERICK

John McCain may have already taken his best shot when he ran for president in 2000. He will have difficulty making it through the Republican primaries. If he does, he will face imposing image issues.

Suits vs. Boots: 4. McCain's political maverick status is well-known. It also meshes well with his cowboy image. Born the scion of a military family in the American-controlled Panama Canal Zone, McCain ended up in Arizona, where he was eventually elected senator. And yes, he owns a ranch.

Height: -2. McCain stands only five-feet-seven-inches. His height may hurt him in presidential debates, depending on the height of his opponent. Americans will be surprised to see just how undersized McCain is.

Age: -3. McCain will turn seventy-two in 2008, making him the second-oldest nonincumbent candidate in American history, just behind Bob Dole. Unlike Dole, McCain still seems energetic and lively, but his hands are covered in liver spots; his stature and hair mean that he certainly looks his age. "He is visibly older, thinner, balder—and, yes, frailer—than he was just six years ago," observed

Vanity Fair reporter Todd Purdum. "Like his friend Bob Dole, he tries to minimize his disabilities, but they are serious."[24]

Hair: -3. McCain joins Giuliani in the bald category, but his is not a clean bald—it's a completely white comb-over. Rudy was always bald, but we remember when McCain wasn't; McCain has visibly aged.

Beer Buddy: 4. McCain is likable, but he is also overwhelmingly egotistic. He talks straight and throws in profanity for good measure. He handles the press expertly, but his "Straight Talk Express" may derail if he seems too concerned with press support. He walks a fine line between principle and pandering.

Military: 4. McCain's POW experience during the Vietnam War sets him apart from the other candidates. Unlike fellow Vietnam War vet John Kerry, however, McCain's support for the military is unquestioned.

Spouse: 1. McCain has been divorced, but that was thirty years ago. His current wife, Cindy, stays out of the spotlight.

FINAL SCORE: 14%

McCain's image remains powerful, but he will have to act decisively—as Reagan did in 1980—to counter perceptions that he is too old to govern.

MITT ROMNEY: A QUESTION OF TRUST

Unlike McCain and Rudy, Romney was nationally a virtual unknown before his 2008 run. As governor of Massachusetts, Romney was a liberal Republican; now he campaigns as the conservative candidate in a liberal Republican field. Can he broaden his appeal enough to win a general election?

Suits vs. Boots: -5. Romney was born in Detroit; his father was governor of Michigan and an unsuccessful presidential candidate, his mother an unsuccessful senatorial candidate. Romney is a businessman and lifelong politician. He blundered badly when he posed as a hunting expert, provoking guffaws of incredulous hunters the country over.

Height: 4. At six-feet-two-inches, Romney is athletically built and physically prepossessing.

Age: 0. Romney will turn sixty-one in 2008, and has no health problems. He doesn't have the kind of experience we expect of a man of sixty-one—he's a one-term governor of Massachusetts. If inexperience hurts Barack Obama, it hurts Mitt Romney.

Hair: 4. Romney is universally acknowledged to have the best hair in the field. His shock of thick black hair and gray patches at the temples give him a strongly presidential feel.

Beer Buddy: 3. "The man exudes niceness, which is one of the qualities that make him an unusually good retail politician," said John Miller of *National Review*. "He doesn't drink alcohol or coffee, smoke cigarettes, or swear—the closest thing to a curse word he'll ever utter is the adjective 'bloomin',' as in, 'Can you believe those bloomin' Democrats?' But he has to be really worked up before he'll say it."[25] If there's such a thing as *too* nice, Romney borders on it. Then there's the question of honesty: Romney has repeatedly shifted his positions on social issues. Does he have the passion or depth to grab the bull by the horns?

Military: 0. Romney never served; as governor of Massachusetts, he rarely commented on foreign policy. He stands in strong support of the military, however. He favors a dramatic increase in the military budget.

Spouse: 2. Romney is the only Republican in the field married just once. His wife, Ann, is a dedicated campaigner. "Ann Romney, though largely invisible back home in Massachusetts, is winning praise as a warm and witty sidekick as her husband begins to spread his name and promote his possible candidacy around the country," said Scott Helman of the *Boston Globe.*[26] Romney's monogamy may help squash the so-called "Mormon Problem." Ann's multiple sclerosis may become a campaign issue, but if it does, it will create sympathy for Romney.

FINAL SCORE: 23%

Romney looks good on paper—but he must show some fire if he wants to look anywhere near as good in reality. Romney's low profile may make it easy for opponents to pillory him as a flip-flopper; the last Republican to win the presidency without significant name recognition entering the election cycle was Warren G. Harding in 1920. Romney also looks better without an opponent—Democrat star power could easily overwhelm Romney in a general election.

FRED THOMPSON: STARRING AS RONALD REAGAN, PART DEUX

Fred Thompson is famous not for his governmental experience—he was a rather obscure one-term senator from Tennessee—but for his acting chops. Thompson made himself a nationally-known face in the late 1980s and early 1990s by playing governmental authority figures in movies like *Die Hard 2, The Hunt for Red October,* and *In the Line of*

Fire. After his Senatorial stint, he re-cultivated his celebrity status by joining the cast of *Law & Order.* He played President Ulysses S. Grant in 2007's cable production *Bury My Heart at Wounded Knee*— but will he be able to move into the real White House come January 2009?

Suits vs. Boots: 4. Thompson has done a tremendous job of polishing his boots image. Thompson is a former lobbyist and actor, but during his 1994 Tennessee Senatorial race, he drove a red 1990 Chevy pick-up around the state, wearing blue jeans and—you guessed it—"shabby boots."[26] Thompson's deep voice and slow, rumbling drawl only accentuate his cowboy image.

Height: 3. Thompson stands an imposing six-feet-five-inches. But will his massive height help him, as it did Lincoln, or hurt him, as it did Winfield Scott and John Kerry?

Age: –2. Thompson will turn 66 in 2008. He was diagnosed with lymphoma cancer in 2004; the cancer is now in remission. Nonetheless, when his increasing age and questionable health is paired with his naturally languid pace, Thompson seems older than his age. Without his *Law & Order* make-up, his campaign staffers should make sure there are no ultra-close-ups.

Hair: –1. Thompson habitually brushes back his thinning hair. Back in the early 1990s, there was more hair to brush.

Beer Buddy: 5. Thompson is a cigar-smoking, joke-telling good-ol'-boy. When Michael Moore challenged Thompson to a debate about healthcare, Thompson released a Youtube video. In it, Thompson puffs on a cigar, looks wryly into the camera, and drawls, "A mental institution, Michael—it might be something you ought to think about." Conservatives went wild.

Military: 2. Thompson doesn't have McCain's military experience or Rudy's high-profile terrorism-fighting skills. He does, however, act like a tough guy—and his image has benefited from his film roles as the tough but genial military man.

Spouse: –2. Thompson's personal life isn't as salacious as Rudy's, but it's still controversial material. Thompson has been divorced once, and he's currently married to Jeri Khen, 24 years his junior. Jeri, who is not averse to donning low-cut outfits, has already been labeled a trophy wife by many pundits.

FINAL SCORE: 26%

Reagan was a far more seasoned politician in 1980 than Thompson is today. For Thompson's Reagan impersonation to be successful, he must have a "Mr. Breen" moment—he must demonstrate that he's capable of getting riled up. He must also move beyond nice-sounding platitudes and offer hard-hitting solutions. While Thompson's supporters portray him as a bulldog, he must convince the rest of America that he's not all bark.

★ 9 ★

Should Image Matter?

IMAGE MATTERS. But should it? Why should JFK's hair convince us to vote for him over his more seasoned counterpart, Richard Nixon? Why should Gerald Ford's baldness have anything to do with Jimmy Carter's election? Why should Michael Dukakis's bobblehead have any impact on whether we choose him over George H. W. Bush? Why should Al Gore's patent inability to display any sort of spontaneity affect our decision to vote for George W. Bush?

We can make the question stronger. Doesn't image lie? Wouldn't we have been better off electing the older, unattractive, capable Winfield Scott rather than dashing, young, incompetent Franklin Pierce? Wouldn't we have done better with shiny-headed, short, chubby, experienced Martin Van Buren than we did with manufactured war hero William Henry Harrison?

And if image truly matters, what happens when terrific image masks a darker agenda? Democracies are not infallible—dictators have risen to power on the strength of their charisma and charm. Shouldn't we look, first and foremost, to policy?

No. Policy matters—but character matters more.

Politicians can say—and often do say—whatever is most politically convenient. They are motivated to do so by our republican system of government. Politics is a business of falsity—a politician may make a pledge for immediate political benefit, then renege. Just because a politician pledges to do something doesn't mean he'll do it. Electoral politics is about pleasing the people—until they vote. Afterward, who knows?

When we vote, then, we want to make sure that we know what we're getting after the ballots are counted. We want to know that our elected officials have the character to uphold their promises. That's why an AP-Ipsos poll showed 55 percent of Americans citing "honesty, integrity and other values of character the most important qualities they look for in a presidential candidate."[1] Only one-third cited policy positions. As Ken Mehlman, former chairman of the George W. Bush 2004 reelection campaign, explained, "Voters only look at policies as a lens into what type of person the candidate is."[2]

Which is why image matters. We judge politicians' honesty, integrity, and leadership quality the same way we judge everyone else's: by looking at them. Sometimes our eyes mislead us. In the vast majority of cases, however, the American people tend to be excellent judges of character. Whenever America has entered tempestuous waters, the American people have selected leaders to guide them through safely. We have spotted demagogues and blowhards, budding tyrants and weaklings—and, for the most part, we have done a remarkable job of weeding them out.

This isn't to say that image is the be-all end-all for voters. On rare occasions, policy trumps image. When Americans elected Nixon in 1968 and 1972, we knew what we were getting—an unscrupulous politician. As early as 1960, Democrats plastered the country with posters containing a caricature of Nixon, unshaven and greasy, accompanied by the slogan: "Would you buy a used car from this man?"[3] Still, in 1968, we chose a conservative who was short on character over a liberal backed by radicals. In 1972, we reelected Nixon amidst early allegations about Watergate—better a corrupt statesman, we thought, than an honest nut.

But Nixon's election is the exception rather than the rule. Most of the time, we vote based on our perception of the politician as a complete person—a mesh of issues and image. Voting for the candidate rather than the policies he or she publicly espouses is a time-honored tradition. It is a tradition that has its roots in the basic philosophy of republican representation.

Upon his election to Parliament in 1774, Edmund Burke stated:

> Certainly, gentlemen, it ought to be the happiness and glory of a representative to live in the strictest union, the closest correspondence, and the most unreserved communication with his constituents. Their wishes ought to have great weight with him; their opinion, high respect; their business, unremitted attention. It is his duty to sacrifice his repose, his pleasures, his satisfactions, to theirs, —and above all, ever, and in all cases, to prefer their interest to his own. But his unbiased opinion, his mature judgment, his enlightened conscience, he ought not to sacrifice to you, to any man, or to any set of men living. These he does not derive from your pleasure, —no, nor from the law and the Constitution. They are a trust from Providence, for the abuse of which he is deeply answerable. Your representative owes you, not his industry only, but his judgment; and he betrays, instead of serving you, if he sacrifices it to your opinion.[4]

When we elect candidates, we elect *people*, not agglomerations of policy positions. And people are not angels, as the founders were so quick to remind us.[5] People are susceptible to outside pressures; people are susceptible to passions; people's minds change. American voters have always understood that when they elect presidents, they elect complete individuals.

And that means that we worry about hair. We think about height. We contemplate whether a candidate is a suit or a boot. We ponder over candidates' military images. We worry about youth and inexperience, and we worry about age and decrepitude. We wonder about candidates' spouses. We ask ourselves whether the candidates are beer buddies or stiffs.

It all seems so trivial. It isn't. We turn the candidates inside out, handle them, inspect them for flaws and strengths. We want to get a complete picture of the men and women vying for the most powerful job on earth. The more we know about the candidates, the better our decisions will be.

So before we decry the nature of our politics, let us remember that we, the voters, are the deciders in chief. We are ultimately responsible for the decisions our leaders make—after all, we elect them. We have the obligation to consider every detail. Even details as seemingly insignificant as a single $1,000 haircut.

Notes

Introduction

1. Matt Drudge, "$1000 Haircut? Kerry Flies in Hairdresser for Touch-up Before 'Meet the Press,'" Drudgereport.com, 27 April 2004 12:59:04, http://www.drudgereportarchives.com/data/2004/04/27/20040427_175803_rcig.htm.

2. Brit Hume, James Rosen, and Brian Wilson, "Political Grapevine: Senator Kerry Has His Hair Styled by the Same Stylist As Senator Clinton," *Fox Special Report with Brit Hume* on Fox News Network, 28 April 2004.

3. Alan Murray, "Late-Night TV Hosts Comment on the News," *Capital Report* (7:00 p.m. ET) on CNBC, 21 May 2004.

4. "Unsubstantiated Drudge Rumor Echoed Through Media," Media Matters, 30 April 2004, http://mediamatters.org/items/200405020004.

5. Daniel Kurtzman, "John Kerry Jokes: Late-Night Jokes About John Kerry," About.com, http://politicalhumor.about.com/library/bljohnkerryjokes.htm.

6. "RNC Unveils New Kerryopoly Web Game," U.S. Newswire, 1 June 2004.

7. Richard B. Cheney and Lynne Cheney, "Richard B. Cheney Delivers Remarks Following a Victory 2004 Debate Watch Party," *Congressional Quarterly* Transcriptions, 13 October 2004.

8. Deborah McGregor, "Edwards Brings Energy to Help Fire Up Kerry on the Campaign Trail," *Financial Times* (London, England), 9 July 2004.

9. "Let Them Eat Ketchup," *New York Post*, 4 August 2004.

10. "Late Night Political Humor," *Frontrunner*, 9 August 2004.

11. Dana Milbank, "Steak Raises Stakes for Kerry in Philly," *Washington Post*, 13 August 2004.

12. James Kuhnhenn, "Kerry Displays His Athletic Prowess in New Hampshire," *Ventura County Star*, 26 January 2004.

13. Kate Zernike, "Who Among Us Does Not Love Windsurfing?" *New York Times*, 5 September 2004.

14. Eric Wargo, "How Many Seconds to a First Impression?" *Association for Psychological Science Observer*, Volume 19, Number 7, July 2006, http://www.psychologicalscience.org/observer/19/7/first_impression.

15. Lee Dye, "Study: First Impressions Really Matter," ABCNews.com, 22 September 2004, http://abcnews.go.com/Technology/print?id=69942.

16. Roger Ailes with Jon Kraushar, *You Are the Message: Secrets of the Master Communicators* (Dow Jones-Irwin, 1988), 22.

17. Kathleen Hall Jamieson, *Packaging the Presidency: A History and Criticism of Presidential Campaign Advertising* (Oxford University Press, 1996), 407.

18. Dave Barry, "What's Another Word for Donkey?" *Washington Post*, 21 September 2003.

19. James Carville, "Swamp Fever," Salon.com, 23 September 1996, http://www.salon.com/weekly/carville960923.html.

20. Bob Dole, *Great Presidential Wit . . . I Wish I Was in the Book: A Collection of Humorous Anecdotes and Quotations* (Scribner, 2001), 14.

21. Ailes, *supra* note 16 at 20.

22. Eric Sevareid, ed., *Candidates 1960: Behind the Headlines in the Presidential Race* (Basic Books, Inc., 1959), 11.

Chapter One

1. William Nisbet Chambers, "Election of 1840" in Arthur M. Schlesinger, Jr., ed., *History of American Presidential Elections 1789–1968: Volume I* (Chelsea House Publishers, 1971), 644.

2. Robert Gray Gunderson, *The Log-Cabin Campaign* (University of Kentucky Press, 1957), 73.

3. Chambers, *supra* note 1 at 665.

4. "Biography of Martin Van Buren," WhiteHouse.gov, http://www.whitehouse.gov/history/presidents/mb8.html.

5. Joel H. Silbey, "Election of 1836" in Schlesinger, *supra* note 1 at 580.

6. Chambers, *supra* note 1 at 659.

7. Gunderson, *supra* note 2 at 74.

8. Ibid., 76.

9. Ibid., 76–77.

10. Gunderson, *supra* note 2 at 167–171.

11. "The Speech That Toppled a President," AmericanHeritage.com, http://www.americanheritage.com/articles/magazine/ah/1964/5/1964_5_108.shtml.

12. Paul F. Boller, *Presidential Campaigns* (Oxford University Press, 1996), 69.

13. Gunderson, *supra* note 2 at 114.

14. Ibid.

15. Ibid., 121.

16. Boller, *supra* note 12 at 73.

17. Kathleen Hall Jamieson, *Packaging the Presidency: A History and Criticism of Presidential Campaign Advertising* (Oxford University Press, 1996), 11.

18. Gunderson, supra *note* 2 at 106.

19. Ibid., 266–273.

20. John Ferling, *Adams vs. Jefferson: The Tumultuous Election of 1800* (Oxford University Press, 2004), 71–72.

21. Ibid., 140.

22. Noble E. Cunningham, Jr., "Election of 1800" in Schlesinger, *supra* note 1 at 123.

23. Thomas Jefferson, *Notes on the State of Virginia*, The Avalon Project, http://www.yale.edu/lawweb/avalon/jevifram.htm.

24. Robert V. Remini, *The Life of Andrew Jackson* (Harper Perennial Modern Classics, 2001), 8.

25. "Declaration of Support for General Andrew Jackson: Philadelphia, October, 1823" in Schlesinger, *supra* note 1 at 399.

26. Boller, *supra* note 12 at 35.

27. "Jackson Delegate Ticket" (1828) in Bernard F. Reilly, Jr., *American Political Prints, 1766–1866: Catalog of the Collection in the Library of Congress*, http://loc.harpweek.com/LCPoliticalCartoons/DisplayCartoonMedium.asp?MaxID=25&UniqueID=14&Year=1828&YearMark=182.

28. Robert V. Remini, "Election of 1828" in Schlesinger, *supra* note 1 at 426–428.

29. Boller, *supra* note 12 at 48.

30. Robert V. Remini, "Election of 1832" in Schlesinger, *supra* note 1 at 511.

31. Gunderson, *supra* note 2 at 212.

32. Ibid., 214.

33. Boller, *supra* note 12 at 103.

34. Ibid., 103–104.

35. "'Taking the Stump' or Stephen in Search of His Mother" in Reilly, *supra* note 27, http://loc.harpweek.com/LCPoliticalCartoons/DisplayCartoonMedium.asp?MaxID=44&UniqueID=1&Year=1860&YearMark=1860.

36. "'Uncle Sam' Making New Arrangements" in Ibid., http://loc.harpweek.com/LCPoliticalCartoons/DisplayCartoonMedium.asp?MaxID=44&UniqueID=5&Year=1860&YearMark=1860.

37. "The Rail Candidate" in Ibid., http://loc.harpweek.com/LCPoliticalCartoons/DisplayCartoonMedium.asp?MaxID=44&UniqueID=38&Year=1860&YearMark=1860.

38. Boller, *supra* note 12 at 189–190.

39. Edmund Morris, *Theodore Rex* (Modern Library, 2002), 172–173.

40. Ibid., 174.

41. Edward J. Lordan, *Politics, Ink: How America's Cartoonists Skewer Politicians, from King George III to George Dubya* (Rowman & Littlefield Publishers, Inc., 2006), 57.

42. Morris, *supra* note 39 at 174.

43. Bob Dole, *Great Presidential Wit . . . I Wish I Was in the Book: A Collection of Humorous Anecdotes and Quotations* (Scribner, 2001), 113.

44. Edward Windsor Kemble, "It Takes Grit to Remove Grime," *Harper's Weekly*, 11 November 1911, http://elections.harpweek.com/1912/cartoon-1912-Medium.asp?UniqueID=2&Year=1912.

45. Edward Windsor Kemble, "The New Rider," *Harper's Weekly*, 13 July, 1912, http://elections.harpweek.com/1912/cartoon-1912-Medium.asp?UniqueID=19&Year=1912.

46. George E. Mowry, "Election of 1912" in Arthur M. Schlesinger, Jr., ed., *History of American Presidential Elections 1789–1968: Volume III* (Chelsea House Publishers, 1971), 2155.

47. Ronald J. Pestritto, *Woodrow Wilson: The Essential Political Writings* (Lexington Books, 2005), 18.

48. Alistair Cooke, ed., *The Vintage Mencken* (Alfred A. Knopf, Inc., 1955), 119.

49. Richard S. Kirkendall, "Election of 1948" in Arthur M. Schlesinger, Jr., ed., *History of American Presidential Elections 1789-1968: Volume IV* (Chelsea House Publishers, 1971), 3125–3127.

50. "Acceptance Speech by President Harry S. Truman at the Democratic National Convention: Philadelphia, July 15, 1948" in Ibid., 3191.

51. "Speech by President Harry S. Truman: Dexter, Iowa, September 18, 1948" in Ibid., 3198.

52. Ibid., 3198–3204.

53. David McCullough, *Truman* (Simon & Schuster, 1993), 590.

54. Ibid., 679.

55. Boller, *supra* note 12 at 276.

56. Jamieson, *supra* note 17 at 67.

57. McCullough, *supra* note 53 at 679.

58. Boller, *supra* note 12 at 272.

59. McCullough, *supra* note 53 at 669.

60. Boller, *supra* note 12 at 279.

61. Ibid., 286.

62. Susan Ratcliffe, ed., *People on People: The Oxford Dictionary of Biographical Quotations* (Oxford University Press, 2001), 119.

63. Gerald Gardner, *The Mocking of the President* (Wayne State University Press, 1988), 216.

64. Jamieson, *supra* note 17 at 61.

65. Schlesinger, *supra* note 1 at 3250.

66. "Acceptance Speech by Governor Adlai E. Stevenson" in Schlesinger, *supra* note 49 at 3295.

67. Ibid.

68. Mary McGrory, "Uneasy Politican: Adlai E. Stevenson" in Eric Sevareid, ed., *Candidates 1960: Behind the Headlines in the Presidential Race* (Basic Books, Inc., 1959), 232.

69. "Peace Is Non-Partisan," Stevenson-Kefauver Campaign Committee presentation, 1956, http://livingroomcandidate.movingimage.us/election/index.php?nav_action=election&nav_subaction=overview&campaign_id=166.

70. "Bio (Carter)," 1976, http://livingroomcandidate.movingimage.us/election/index.php?nav_action=election&nav_subaction=overview&campaign_id=171.

71. Edward J. Walsh, "Carter" in Richard Harwood, ed., *The Pursuit of the Presidency 1980* (Berkley Books, 1980), 239–240.

72. Jamieson, *supra* note 17 at 401.

73. Richard Harwood, "Labor Day 1980" in Harwood, *supra* note 71 at 279.

74. Lou Cannon, "Reagan" in Harwood, *supra* note 71 at 269.

75. "About the Reagan Ranch," Young America's Foundation, http://reaganranch.yaf.org/ranch/index.cfm.

76. Ronald Reagan, *An American Life* (Pocket, 1999), 275–276.

77. Floyd G. Brown, "At Home on the Reagan Ranch," National Review Online, 7 June 2004, http://www.nationalreview.com/comment/brown200406071022.asp.

78. Jamieson, *supra* note 17 at 431.

79. Lou Cannon, "Reagan" in Harwood, *supra* note 71 at 255.

80. Boller, *supra* note 12 at 366.

81. "'80 Presidential Debates: As Sponsored by The League of Women Voters Education Fund, Second Debate, Tuesday, 28 October, Official Transcriptional Record" in Harwood, *supra* note 72 at 384.

82. Ratcliffe, *supra* note 62 at 59.

83. Lou Cannon and William Peterson, "GOP" in Harwood, *supra* note 71 at 131–132.

84. David R. Runkel, ed., *Campaign for President: The Managers Look at '88* (Auburn House Publishing Company, 1989), 62.

85. Ryan J. Barilleaux, Mark J. Rozell, *Power and Prudence: The Presidency of George H. W. Bush* (Texas A&M Press, 2004), 18.

86. Runkel, *supra* note 84 at 205.

87. Ed. Stephen A. Smith, Preface to the Presidency: Selected Speeches of Bill Clinton, 1974–1992 (University of Arkansas Press, 1996), 214–215.

88. "The Third Clinton-Bush-Perot Debate Transcript," Commission on Presidential Debates, 19 October 1992, http://www.debates.org/pages/trans92c.html.

89. Michael Kranish, "Taking High Hopes to Iowa; GOP Front-Runner Bush Works the Crowds, Outlines Broad Agenda," *Boston Globe*, 13 June 1999.

90. Tim Nickens, "The Bush Family // America's New Dynasty," *St. Petersburg Times*, 31 May 1999.

91. Sam Attlesey, "Texans Rise or Fall on the Range; Whether Prop or Pitfall, Ranch Tours a Political Tradition," *Dallas Morning News*, 13 August 2000.

92. Editorial, "Campaign Notebook; On the Road in Crawford, Texas," *Dallas Morning News*, 6 July 2000.

93. Susan Page, "Each Hopes to Set Himself Apart, Above Gore Aims to Show He's a Candidate with Vision," *USA Today*, 17 May 1999.

94. Katharine Q. Seelye, "The Unbuttoning of Al Gore: Act 1," *New York Times*, 15 June 1999.

95. Muriel Dobbin, "Pundits, Feminists Criticize Gore for Paying Naomi Wolf for Advice," *Minneapolis Star Tribune*, 3 November 1999.

96. Maureen Dowd, "Campaign Trumps Baseball When It Comes to Hormones," *Milwaukee Journal Sentinel*, 26 October 2000.

97. Mark Steyn, "Kerry Can't Shoot Deer or Stop Terror," *UK Telegraph*, 27 July 2004.

98. Lois Romano, "Kerry Hunting Trip Sets Sights on Swing Voters," *Washington Post*, 21 October 2004.

99. Jodi Wilgoren, "Kerry on Hunting Photo-Op to Help Image," *New York Times*, 22 October 2004.

100. "Chris Matthews: Bush's F#&!*n' Ranch!," NewsMax.com, 7 February 2007, http://www.newsmax.com/archives/ic/2007/2/7/82213.shtml.

101. Boller, *supra* note 12 at 68.

102. Tim Reid, "'I can't believe I'm losing to this idiot': The Democratic Challenger Repeatedly Shot Himself in the Foot," *Times* (UK), 5 November 2004, http://www.timesonline.co.uk/tol/news/world/article1076657.ece.

Chapter Two

1. Paul F. Boller, *Presidential Campaigns* (Oxford University Press, 1996), 108.

2. Robert Bendiner, "Charisma? Washington? Madison? Jefferson?" *New York Times*, 28 August 1984.

3. William E. Huntzicker, *The Popular Press, 1833–1865* (Greenwood Press, 1999), 108.

4. David Herbert Donald, *Lincoln* (Simon & Schuster, 1996), 132.

5. Harold Holzer, *Lincoln at Cooper Union: The Speech That Made Abraham Lincoln President* (Simon & Schuster, 2004), 113.

6. Donald, *supra* note 4 at 427.

7. Ibid., 237.

8. Burkhard Bilger, "The Height Gap," *New Yorker*, 5 April 2004, http://www.newyorker.com/fact/content/articles/040405fa_fact?040405fa_fact.

9. William E. Huntzicker, *The Popular Press, 1833-1865* (Greenwood Press, 1999), 108.

10. Robert W. Johannsen, *Stephen A. Douglas* (University of Illinois Press, 1997), 4.

11. Ibid., 446–447.

12. "[Lincoln & Douglas in a presidential footrace]. No. 1. 1860." (1860) in Bernard F. Reilly, Jr., *American Political Prints, 1766-1866: Catalog of the Collection in the Library of Congress,* http://loc.harpweek.com/LCPoliticalCartoons/DisplayCartoonMedium.asp?MaxID=44&UniqueID=9&Year=1860&YearMark=1860.

13. Johannsen, *supra* note 10 at 781.

14. "Stephen Finding 'His Mother' " (1860) in Reilly, *supra* note 12, http://loc.harpweek.com/LCPoliticalCartoons/DisplayCartoonMedium.asp?MaxID=44&UniqueID=30&Year=1860&YearMark=1860.

15. Susan Page, "Election-Predicting Tools Point Both Ways," *USA Today*, 24 June 2004.

16. Steven E. Landsburg, "Short Changed: Why Do Tall People Make More Money?" Slate.com, 25 March 2002, http://www.slate.com/id/2063439/.

17. "Tall Men 'Top Husband Stakes,'" BBC News, 14 August 2002, http://news.bbc.co.uk/1/hi/health/2190461.stm.

18. Steven E. Landsburg, "Short Changed: Why Do Tall People Make More Money?" Slate.com, 25 March 2002, http://www.slate.com/id/2063439/.

19. Bob Dole, *Great Presidential Wit . . . I Wish I Was in the Book: A Collection of Humorous Anecdotes and Quotations* (New York: Scribner, 2001), 142.

20. Eric Burns, *Infamous Scribblers* (PublicAffairs, 2006), 289.

21. Susan Ratcliffe, ed., *People on People: The Oxford Dictionary of Biographical Quotations* (New York: Oxford University Press, 2001), 355.

22. Marvin Kitman, *The Making of the Prefident 1789* (Grove Press, 1989), 245.

23. Bilger, *supra* note 8.

24. Libby Copeland, "Buffing Up the Image of George Washington," *Washington Post*, 30 August 2005.

25. Dole, *supra* note 19 at 138.

26. Richard Brookhiser, "What Today's Students Should Know About George Washington," *Social Studies*, Vol. 88, 1997.

27. Boller, *supra* note 1 at 4.

28. David McCullough, *John Adams* (Simon & Schuster, 2001), 18.

29. R. B. Bernstein, *Thomas Jefferson* (Oxford University Press, 2003), 50.

30. "Physical Descriptions of Thomas Jefferson," Monticello.org, http://www.monticello.org/reports/people/descriptions.html.

31. Noble E. Cunningham, Jr., "Election of 1800" in Arthur M. Schlesinger, Jr., ed., *History of American Presidential Elections 1789-1968: Volume I* (Chelsea House Publishers, 1971), 124.

32. Evan Cornog, *The Birth of Empire: DeWitt Clinton and the American Experience, 1769-1828*, 6.

33. Ralph Ketcham, *James Madison: A Biography* (University of Virginia Press, 1990), 89.

34. Robert Bendiner, "Charisma? Washington? Madison? Jefferson?" *New York Times*, 28 August 1984.

35. Robert Allen Rutland, *The Presidency of James Madison* (University Press of Kansas, 1990), 21.

36. "James Madison," Whitehouse.gov, http://www.whitehouse.gov/history/presidents/jm4.html.

37. Dole, *supra* note 19 at 202.

38. Norman K. Risjord, "Election of 1812" in Schlesinger, *supra* note 31 at 253.

39. Mary W. M. Hargreaves, *The Presidency of John Quincy Adams* (University Press of Kansas, 1985), 22.

40. Dole, *supra* note 19 at 198.

41. Robert V. Remini, *The Life of Andrew Jackson* (Harper Perennial Modern Classics, 2001), 140.

42. Andrew Burstein, *The Passions of Andrew Jackson* (Knopf, 2003), 134.

43. "A Foot-Race" (1824) in Bernard F. Reilly, Jr., *American Political Prints, 1766-1866: Catalog of the Collection in the Library of Congress*, http://loc.harpweek.com/LCPoliticalCartoons/DisplayCartoonLarge.asp?MaxID=25&UniqueID=4&Year=1824&YearMark=182.

44. Stephen W. Sears, *George McClellan: The Young Napoleon* (Da Capo Press, 1999), 45.

45. Ibid., 71.

46. Ibid., 95.

47. John C. Waugh, *Re-Electing Lincoln: The Battle for the 1864 Presidency* (Crown Publishers, Inc.), 28.

48. Dole, *supra* note 19 at 35.

49. Sears, *supra* note 44 at 334.

50. Donald, *supra* note 4 at 330.

51. Waugh, *supra* note 47, at 11.

52. Ibid., 13.

53. Ibid., 273.

54. Ibid., 301–302.

55. "A Little Game of Bagatelle, Between Old Abe the Rail Splitter & Little Mac the Gunboat General" (1864) in Reilly, *supra* note 12, http://loc.harpweek.com/LCPoliticalCartoons/DisplayCartoonMedium.asp?MaxID=44&UniqueID=3&Year=1864&YearMark=1864.

56. "This Reminds Me of a Little Joke," *Harper's Weekly*, 14 September 1864, http://elections.harpweek.com/1864/cartoon-1864-Medium.asp?UniqueID=32&Year=1864.

57. "The Two Platforms: Columbia Makes Her Choice," *Frank Leslie's Budget of Fun*, 1 December 1864, http://elections.harpweek.com/1864/cartoon-1864-Medium.asp?UniqueID=35&Year=1864.

58. Frank Bellew, "Long Abraham Lincoln a Little Longer," *Harper's Weekly*, 26 November 1864, http://elections.harpweek.com/1864/cartoon-1864-Medium.asp?UniqueID=56&Year=1864.

59. Anita Manning, "Study Raises Doubts about FDR's Polio," *USA Today*, 30 October 2003.

60. Fred I. Greenstein, *The Presidential Difference: Leadership Style from Roosevelt to Clinton* (Free Press, 2000), 15.

61. Jonathan Alter, *The Defining Moment: FDR's Hundred Days and the Triumph of Hope* (Simon & Schuster, 2006), 52.

62. Ibid.

63. Ibid., 256.

64. Ibid., 58.

65. Ibid., 87.
66. Steven Neal, *Happy Days Are Here Again: The 1932 Democratic Convention, the Emergence of FDR—And How America Was Changed Forever* (William Morrow, 2004), 78.
67. Alter, *supra* note 63 at 58.
68. Ibid., 85.
69. Ibid., 84–85.
70. Neal, *supra* note 66 at 295–296.
71. Herbert Hoover, "My Personal Relations with Mr. Roosevelt," 26 September 1958 in Timothy Walsh and Dwight M. Miller, eds., *Herbert Hoover and Franklin D. Roosevelt: A Documentary History* (Greenwood Press, 1998), 210.
72. Boller, *supra* note 1 at 262.
73. David McCullough, *Truman* (Simon and Schuster, 1993), 331.
74. Boller, *supra* note 1 at 266.
75. Carol Felsenthal, *Princess Alice: The Life and Times of Alice Roosevelt Longworth* (St. Martin's Griffin, 2003), 219.
76. Mark Leibovich, "The True Measure of a Man," *Washington Post*, 14 March 2002.
77. Felsenthal, *supra* note 75.
78. Leon Friedman, "Election of 1944" in Arthur M. Schlesinger, Jr., ed., *History of American Presidential Elections 1789-1968: Volume IV* (Chelsea House Publishers, 1971), 3021.
79. "Crucial Week," *Time*, 2 October 1944, http://www.time.com/time/magazine/article/0,9171,933080-2,00.html.
80. McCullough, *supra* note 73 at 326.
81. Ibid., 379.
82. Ibid., 712.
83. Ibid., 668.
84. Pete Hamill, *A Drinking Life: A Memoir* (Back Bay Books, 1995), 107.
85. Ibid., 108.
86. Boller, *supra* note 1 at 353.
87. John Robert Greene, *The Presidency of Gerald R. Ford* (University Press of Kansas, 1995), 62.
88. Ibid.
89. Yanik Mieczkowski, *Gerald Ford and the Challenges of the 1970s* , 49.
90. Greene, *supra* note 87.
91. Mieczkowski, *supra* note 89.
92. Ibid., 53.
93. Sally Quinn, "Nancy Reagan on the Road to the Realm," *Washington Post*, 1 May 1980.
94. Haynes Johnson, "Reagan Finds Himself Racing Clock," *Washington Post*, 4 February 1980.
95. Edward J. Walsh, "Carter" in Richard Harwood, ed., *The Pursuit of the Presidency 1980* (New York: Berkley Books, 1980), 233.
96. William French, "Height: The Long and Short of It THE HEIGHT OF YOUR LIFE," *Globe and Mail* (Canada), 10 July 1980.
97. Garrett Epps, "How Carter Won (On November 4, 1980)," *Washington Post*, 4 November 1979.
98. PR Newswire, 6 November 1980.
99. Times Staff Writers, "Convention Notebook," *Los Angeles Times*, 19 July 1988.
100. "The Next President: David Frost Interviews Governor Dukakis," Federal News Service, 6 November 1988.
101. Barry Stavro, "Take the Presidency . . . Please," *Los Angeles Times*, 16 July 1988.
102. Jay Mathews, "Other Views: Here's the Long and Short of a Giant Issue," *Los Angeles Times*, 8 August 1988.
103. William Safire, "Remember the Forgotten Question," *Chicago Tribune*, 9 September 1988.

104. Maureen Dowd, "Campaign Trail," *New York Times*, 22 September 1988.

105. Maureen Dowd, "The Presidential Debate," *New York Times*, 26 September 1988.

106. Walter Shapiro, "Bush Scores A Warm Win," *Time*, 24 October 1988.

107. Lee May, "At Voter Rallies, Confident Reagan Refers to Bush as 'Next President,'" *Los Angeles Times*, 5 November 1988.

108. Colin MacKenzie, "No Biz, Just Show Biz as Democrats Gather," *Globe and Mail* (Canada), 18 July 1988.

109. Bud Newman, "GOP Dishes Out Zingers as Good as the Democrats," United Press International, 20 August 1988.

110. James Gerstenzang, "Bush Warns That 'Cold War Is Not Over,'" *Los Angeles Times*, 30 June 1988.

111. "Republican Ticket of Bush and Quayle Nominated," *Facts on File World News Digest*, 19 August 1988.

112. Marilyn Goldstein, "A Short Story About Tall Tales," *Newsday* 31 October 1988.

113. David R. Runkel, ed., *Campaign for President: The Managers Look at '88* (Auburn House Publishing Company, 1989), 62.

114. Clarence Page, "Poor George Can't Seem to Stand Tall Even Though He Is," *Chicago Tribune*, 3 February 1988.

115. Maureen Dowd, "Transition Watch," *New York Times*, 4 December 1988.

116. Rick Horowitz, "Staying on Top Is a Tall Order," *Cleveland Plain Dealer*, 21 November 1999.

117. "Offbeat," *Sunday Telegraph* (UK), 3 October 2004.

118. Tom Shales, "From Telegenic to Telegeneric," *Washington Post*, 1 November 2004.

119. Samuel 9:1–2 (*JPS Hebrew-English Tanakh*).

120. Samuel 10:22–24 (*JPS Hebrew-English Tanakh*).

121. William Manchester, *The Last Lion: Winston Spencer Churchill, Visions of Glory* (Little, Brown and Company, 1983), 755.

Chapter Three

1. Marvin Kitman, *The Making of the Prefident 1789* (Grove Press, 1989), 15.

2. Ibid., 20.

3. Ibid.

4. James Thomas Flexner, *Washington: The Indispensable Man* (Back Bay Books, 1994), 17.

5. Kitman, *supra* note 1 at 62.

6. Flexner, *supra* note 4 at 24–27.

7. Kitman, *supra* note 1 at 16.

8. Joseph Ellis, *His Excellency: George Washington* (Random House Large Print, 2004), 119.

9. Kitman, *supra* note 1 at 96.

10. Ibid., 168.

11. Marcus Cunliffe, "Elections of 1789 and 1792" in Ed. Arthur M. Schlesinger, Jr., *History of American Presidential Elections 1789-1968: Volume I* (Chelsea House Publishers, 1971), 8–9.

12. Susan Ratcliffe, ed., *People on People: The Oxford Dictionary of Biographical Quotations* (Oxford University Press, 2001), 355.

13. Michael Moore, "Recruit the Chickenhawks," MichaelMoore.com, http://www.michaelmoore.com/books-films/dudewheresmycountry/chickenhawks/index.php.

14. "Some Account of Some of the Bloody Deeds of General Jackson" (1828) in Bernard F. Reilly, Jr., *American Political Prints, 1766-1866: Catalog of the Collection in the Library of Congress*, http://loc.harpweek.com/LCPoliticalCartoons/DisplayCartoonLarge.asp?MaxID=25&UniqueID=21&Year=1828&YearMark=182.

15. Robert V. Remini, *The Battle of New Orleans: Andrew Jackson's and America's First Military Victory* (Penguin, 2001), 1–2.

16. Robert V. Remini, *The Life of Andrew Jackson* (Perennial Classics, 2001), 3.
17. Ibid.
18. Ibid., 4.
19. James F. Hopkins, "Election of 1824" in Schlesinger, *supra* note 11 at 362.
20. Kathleen Hall Jamieson, *Packaging the Presidency: A History and Criticism of Presidential Campaign Advertising* (Oxford University Press, 1996), 6.
21. Paul F. Boller, *Presidential Campaigns* (Oxford University Press, 1996), 45.
22. Ibid., 47.
23. Edwin David Sanborn, Daniel Webster, and Fletcher Webster, *The Private Correspondence of Daniel Webster* (Little, Brown, 1857), 371.
24. Ratcliffe, *supra* note 12 at 187.
25. Bob Dole, *Great Presidential Wit . . . I Wish I Was in the Book: A Collection of Humorous Anecdotes and Quotations* (Scribner, 2001), 192.
26. Florence Weston, *The Presidential Election of 1828* (The Ruddick Press, 1938), 145.
27. Lyndon B. Johnson, "Remarks at the War Memorial Building in Nashville," 9 October, 1964 as quoted at The American Presidency Project, http://www.presidency.ucsb.edu/ws/print.php?pid=26582.
28. John Sugden, *Tecumseh: A Life* (Owl Books, 1999), 232–236.
29. Robert Gray Gunderson, *The Log-Cabin Campaign* (University of Kentucky Press, 1957), 112.
30. Ibid., 124.
31. Ibid., 128.
32. Ibid., 142.
33. Ibid., 101.
34. Ibid., 221.
35. Ibid.
36. Ibid., 222.
37. Holman Hamilton, "Election of 1848" in Arthur M. Schlesinger, Jr., ed., *History of American Presidential Elections 1789-1968: Volume II* (Chelsea House Publishers, 1971), 865–866.
38. Dole, *supra* note 25 at 209.
39. K. Jack Bauer, *Zachary Taylor: Soldier, Planter, Statesman of the Old Southwest* (Louisiana State University Press, 1993), 214.
40. Hamilton, *supra* note 37 at 867.
41. Dole, *supra* note 25 at 210.
42. Hamilton, *supra* note 37 at 889.
43. "Original Pictorial Rough and Ready Melodies, No.3. Old Zack Taylor Is the Man!" (1848) in Reilly, *supra* note 14, http://loc.harpweek.com/LCPoliticalCartoons/DisplayCartoonMedium.asp?MaxID=89&UniqueID=50&Year=1848&YearMark=1846.
44. Hamilton, *supra* note 37 at 867.
45. "The Nation's Choice for the 12th President of the U.S. Genl. Z. Taylor and His Battles" (1847) in Reilly, *supra* note 14, http://loc.harpweek.com/LCPoliticalCartoons/DisplayCartoonMedium.asp?MaxID=89&UniqueID=24&Year=1847&YearMark=1846.
46. "An Available Candidate. The One Qualification of a Whig President." (1848) in Ibid., http://loc.harpweek.com/LCPoliticalCartoons/DisplayCartoonMedium.asp?MaxID=89&UniqueID=31&Year=1848&YearMark=1846.
47. "Zachary Taylor," WhiteHouse.gov, http://www.whitehouse.gov/history/presidents/zt12.html.
48. Ibid.
49. John S. D. Eisenhower, *Agent of Destiny: The Life and Times of General Winfield Scott* (University of Oklahoma Press, 1999), 18–19.
50. Ibid., 111–114.
51. Ibid., 329.

52. Ibid., 223–225.

53. See, e.g. "A Dish of 'Black Turtle'" (1852) in Reilly, *supra* note 14, http://loc.harpweek.com/LCPoliticalCartoons/DisplayCartoonMedium.asp?MaxID=74&UniqueID=22&Year=1852&YearMark=1850.

54. Eisenhower, *supra* note 49 at 96.

55. Ibid., 329.

56. Ibid., 328–329.

57. Ibid., 328.

58. "Gas and Glory" (1852) in Reilly, *supra* note 14, http://loc.harpweek.com/LCPoliticalCartoons/DisplayCartoonMedium.asp?MaxID=74&UniqueID=33&Year=1852&YearMark=1850.

59. "Loco Foco Hunters Treeing a Candidate" (1852) in Reilly, *supra* note 14, http://loc.harpweek.com/LCPoliticalCartoons/DisplayCartoonMedium.asp?MaxID=74&UniqueID=39&Year=1852&YearMark=1850.

60. James M. McPherson, *Battle Cry of Freedom: The Civil War Era* (Oxford University Press, 1988), 365.

61. Ibid., 364.

62. "The Lincoln Catechism," New York, 1864 in Arthur M. Schlesinger, Jr., ed., *History of American Presidential Elections 1789-1968: Volume III* (Chelsea House Publishers, 1971), 1214–1237.

63. David Herbert Donald, *Lincoln* (Simon & Schuster, 1996), 387.

64. Ibid., 537–538.

65. See, e.g., "The Commander-in-Chief Conciliating the Soldier's Votes on the Battle Field" (1864) in Reilly, *supra* note 14, http://loc.harpweek.com/LCPoliticalCartoons/DisplayCartoonMedium.asp?MaxID=44&UniqueID=33&Year=1864&YearMark=1864.

66. Donald, *supra* note 63 at 387.

67. "Editorial by Benjamin Wade from the Cincinnati *Gazette*," 25 October 1864, in Schlesinger, *supra* note 62 at 1197–1203.

68. "The White Man's Banner . . . Seymour and Blair's Campaign Song" (1868) in Reilly, *supra* note 14, http://loc.harpweek.com/LCPoliticalCartoons/DisplayCartoonMedium.asp?MaxID=35&UniqueID=25&Year=1868&YearMark=1866.

69. Frank Bellew, "'Tis But a Change in Banners," *Harper's Weekly*, 26 September 1868, http://elections.harpweek.com/1868/cartoon-1868-Medium.asp?UniqueID=9&Year=1868.

70. John Hope Franklin, "Election of 1868" in Schlesinger, *supra* note 62 at 1262.

71. Jean Edward Smith, *Grant* (Simon & Schuster, 2002), 458.

72. "The Modern Gulliver Among the Lilliputians," *Harper's Weekly*, 12 September 1868, http://elections.harpweek.com/1868/cartoon-1868-Medium.asp?UniqueID=6&Year=1868.

73. William S. McFeely, *Grant: A Biography* (W.W. Norton & Company, 2002), 280.

74. Franklin, *supra* note 70 at 1260.

75. McFeely, *supra* note 73 at 283.

76. Barton J. Bernstein, "Election of 1952" in Arthur M. Schlesinger, Jr., ed., *History of American Presidential Elections 1789-1968: Volume IV* (Chelsea House Publishers, 1971), 3224.

77. Jamieson, *supra* note 20 at 46.

78. "Speech by General Dwight D. Eisenhower," *New York Times*, 25 October 1952, in Schlesinger, *supra* note 76 at 3326.

79. Ratcliffe, *supra* note 12 at 119.

80. Michael O'Brien, *John F. Kennedy: A Biography* (Thomas Dunne Books, 2005), 128–153.

81. Ibid., 171.

82. Christopher J. Matthews, *Kennedy and Nixon: The Rivalry That Shaped Postwar America* (Free Press, 1997), 116.

83. Ibid., 131.

84. Jamieson, *supra* note 20 at 138–139.

85. Ibid., 136.

86. Ibid., 137.

87. Dole, *supra* note 25 at 81.

88. "Transcript #134," CNN Newsmaker Sunday, 11 October 1992.

89. "1992 Debate Transcript," Commission on Presidential Debates, 11 October 1992, http://www.debates.org/pages/trans92a1.html.

90. Susan Page, "The First Debate," *Newsday*, 12 October 1992.

91. "1992 Debate Transcript," Commission on Presidential Debates, 19 October 1992, http://www.debates.org/pages/trans92c.html.

92. Robert L. Jackson, "Clinton 'Simply Doesn't Tell the Truth,' Quayle Charges," *Los Angeles Times*, 11 October 1992.

93. "Transcript #134," CNN Newsmaker Sunday, 11 October 1992.

94. A. L. May, "Bush Making an Issue of Clinton's Vietnam Stand," *Atlanta Journal and Constitution*, 9 October 1992.

95. "1992 Debate Transcript," Commission on Presidential Debates, 19 October 1992, http://www.debates.org/pages/trans92c.html.

96. "Text of John Kerry's Acceptance Speech at the Democratic National Convention," *Washington Post*, 29 July 2004, http://www.washingtonpost.com/wp-dyn/articles/A25678-2004Jul29.html.

97. "Punchlines from the Political Road," Cox News Service, 1 February 2004.

98. "This Morning," *Hotline*, 8 March 2004.

99. Nikki Finke, "Does Mr. Middle-of-the-Road Lean Left?" *LA Weekly*, 17 September 2004.

100. Joshua Muravchik, "Kerry's Cambodia Whopper," *Washington Post*, 24 August 2004.

101. James Hebert, "Party Lines," *San Diego Union-Tribune*, 1 November 2004.

102. Donald, *supra* note 63 at 411–412.

103. David McCullough, *John Adams* (Simon & Schuster, 2001), 236–237.

Chapter Four

1. Haynes Johnson, "Reagan Finds Himself Racing Clock," *Washington Post*, 4 February 1980.

2. Allan J. Mayer, Gerald C. Lubenow, James Doyle, and Stryker McGuire, "Ronald Reagan Steps up His Pace," *Newsweek*, 11 February 1980.

3. Paul F. Boller, *Presidential Campaigns* (Oxford University Press, 1996), 363.

4. Ibid., 366.

5. Lou Cannon and William Peterson, "GOP" in Richard Harwood, ed., *The Pursuit of the Presidency 1980* (Berkley Books, 1980), 139.

6. Allan J. Mayer, Gerald C. Lubenow, James Doyle, and Stryker McGuire, "Ronald Reagan Steps up His Pace," *Newsweek*, 11 February 1980.

7. Cannon and Peterson, *supra* note 5.

8. Lou Cannon, "Reagan Is Feted for His Birthday During N.H. Tour," *Washington Post*, 6 February 1980.

9. Roger Ailes with Jon Kraushar, *You Are the Message: Secrets of the Master Communicators* (Dow Jones-Irwin, 1988), 78.

10. Ronald Reagan, *An American Life* (Pocket, 1999), 212.

11. "1980—Ronald Reagan," The New Hampshire Political Library, http://clients.bn24.com/portals/NHPL/Default.aspx.

12. Ailes, *supra* note 9.

13. Reagan, *supra* note 10 at 213.

14. Kathleen Hall Jamieson, *Packaging the Presidency: A History and Criticism of Presidential Campaign Advertising* (Oxford University Press, 1996), 455–456.

15. "The Second Reagan-Mondale Presidential Debate," Commission on Presidential Debates, 21

October 1984, http://www.debates.org/pages/trans84c.html.

16. Ailes, *supra* note 9 at 20.
17. "The Second Reagan-Mondale Presidential Debate," Commission on Presidential Debates, 21 October 1984, http://www.debates.org/pages/trans84c.html.
18. Michael Stokes Paulsen, "Is Bill Clinton Unconstitutional?" *Constitutional Commentary*, 22 December 1996.
19. Marvin Kitman, *The Making of the Prefident 1789* (Grove Press, 1989), 201–202.
20. Ibid., 202.
21. Joseph Ellis, *His Excellency: George Washington* (Random House Large Print, 2004), 253.
22. Matthew Spalding, "The Man Who Would Not Be King," *Heritage Foundation*, 5 Feburary 2007, http://www.heritage.org/Press/Commentary/ed020507c.cfm.
23. Kitman, *supra* note 19 at 202.
24. Paul Johnson, *George Washington: The Founding Father* (Eminent Lives, 2005), 122.
25. Eric Burns, *Infamous Scribblers* (PublicAffairs, 2006), 354.
26. Bob Dole, *Great Presidential Wit . . . I Wish I Was in the Book: A Collection of Humorous Anecdotes and Quotations* (Scribner, 2001), 139–140.
27. David McCullough, *John Adams* (Simon & Schuster, 2001), 452.
28. John Whitcomb and Claire Whitcomb, *Real Life at the White House* (Routledge, 2000), 13.
29. McCullough, *supra* note 27 at 544.
30. Joseph J. Ellis, *American Sphinx: The Character of Thomas Jefferson* (Vintage, 1998), 259–260.
31. *United States v. Callender* (1800), 25 F. Cas. 239 (Circuit Court, D. Virginia).
32. Burns, *supra* note 25 at 381.
33. "Letter of Alexander Hamilton on John Adams" (1800) in Arthur M. Schlesinger, Jr., ed., *History of American Presidential Elections 1789-1968: Volume I* (Chelsea House Publishers, 1971), 154.
34. Dole, *supra* note 26 at 138.
35. Richard Brookhiser, *Alexander Hamilton: AMERICAN* (Free Press, 2000), 187.
36. McCullough, *supra* note 27 at 565.
37. Robert Gray Gunderson, *The Log-Cabin Campaign* (University of Kentucky Press, 1957), 74.
38. Ibid., 220.
39. Jamieson, *supra* note 14 at 13.
40. Gunderson, *supra* note 37 at 97.
41. Jamieson, *supra* note 14 at 13.
42. Ibid., 164.
43. Ibid., 165.
44. Ibid.
45. Ibid., 167.
46. Ibid., 171.
47. William Nisbet Chambers, "Election of 1840" in Arthur M. Schlesinger, Jr., ed., *History of American Presidential Elections 1789-1968: Volume I* (Chelsea House Publishers, 1971), 659.
48. Gunderson, *supra* note 37 at 171.
49. Chambers, *supra* note 47.
50. D. W. Bartlett, *The Life of General Frank Pierce of New Hampshire, The Democratic Candidate for President of the United States* (Derby & Miller, 1852), 242–243.
51. Roy and Jeannette Nichols, "Election of 1852" in Arthur M. Schlesinger, Jr., ed., *History of American Presidential Elections 1789-1968: Volume II* (Chelsea House Publishers, 1971), 938.
52. Dole, *supra* note 26 at 224.
53. Edward Deering Mansfield, *The Life of General Winfield Scott, Commander of the United States Army* (A. S. Barnes & Co., 1852), 193–194.
54. John S. D. Eisenhower, *Agent of Destiny: The Life and Times of General Winfield Scott* (University of

Oklahoma Press, 1999), 329.

55. Allan Peskin, *Winfield Scott and the Profession of Arms* (Kent State University Press, 2003), 214.

56. Dole, *supra* note 26 at 225.

57. Gilbert C. Fite, "Election of 1896" in Schlesinger, *supra* note 51 at 1808.

58. Ibid., 1809–1810.

59. Ibid., 1811.

60. William Jennings Bryan, *The First Battle: A Story of the Campaign of 1896* (Kessenger Publishing, 2005), 459.

61. Ibid., 484.

62. Dole, *supra* note 26 at 172.

63. Paul F. Boller, *Presidential Campaigns* (Oxford University Press, 1996), 174.

64. Bryan, *supra* note 60 at 492.

65. William Allen Rogers, "The Deadly Parallel," *Harper's Weekly*, 29 August 1896, http://elections.harpweek.com/1896/cartoon-1896-Medium.asp?UniqueID=17&Year=1896.

66. Bryan, *supra* note 60 at 492–493.

67. Alistair Cooke, ed., *The Vintage Mencken* (Alfred A. Knopf, Inc., 1955), 165–167.

68. Gerald Gardner, *The Mocking of the President* (Wayne State University Press, 1988), 230.

69. Boller, *supra* note 63 at 287.

70. Gardner, *supra* note 68 at 230.

71. Jamieson, *supra* note 14 at 46.

72. Ibid., 85.

73. Gardner, *supra* note 68 at 216.

74. Eric Sevareid, "The Ideal Candidate" in Eric Sevareid, ed., *Candidates 1960: Behind the Headlines in the Presidential Race* (Basic Books, Inc., 1959), 12.

75. Jamieson, *supra* note 14 at 106.

76. Ibid., 105–106.

77. Ibid., 107.

78. Ibid., 99.

79. Ibid., 111.

80. Ibid., 110.

81. Ibid., 107.

82. Eric Sevareid, ed., *Candidates 1960: Behind the Headlines in the Presidential Race* (Basic Books, Inc., 1959), 13.

83. Fletcher Knebel, "Pulitzer Prize Entry: John F. Kennedy" in Ibid., 209.

84. Jamieson, *supra* note 14 at 139–140.

85. Ibid., 140.

86. Ibid., 139.

87. Boller, *supra* note 63 at 299.

88. Susan Ratcliffe, ed., *People on People: The Oxford Dictionary of Biographical Quotations* (Oxford University Press, 2001), 201.

89. Allan Louden and Kristen McCauliff, "The 'Authentic Candidate'" in Kenneth L. Hacker, ed., *Presidential Candidate Images* (Rowman and Littlefield Publishers, Inc., 2004), 98.

90. "The First Clinton-Bush-Perot Debate Transcript," Commission on Presidential Debates, 11 October 1992, http://www.debates.org/pages/trans92a1.html#c-experience.

91. Chris Black, "Bush Faces a New Generation," *Boston Globe*, 18 January 1992.

92. "Big Step for Clinton, Network," *Chicago Sun-Times*, 6 July 1992.

93. Christine Hagstrom, "Campus Correspondence," *Los Angeles Times*, 21 June 1992.

94. Jeff Greenfield, "The Baby-Boom White House," *USA Today*, 17 January 1992.

95. William Schneider, "The Savage Struggle for Power," *Los Angeles Times*, 26 January 1992.

96. Larry Tye, "They're Fit for Office," *Boston Globe*, 16 February 1992.

97. Peter Applebome, "Bill Clinton's Uncertain Journey," *New York Times*, 8 March 1992.

98. David Lightman, "Generation Difference May Decide Race Between Bush and Clinton," *Hartford Courant*, 20 April 1992.

99. Colin MacKenzie, "Republicans Find Ray of Hope in Latest Polls Bush Gaining Ground, but Clinton Far Ahead in Electoral College Vote," *Globe and Mail*, 31 October 1992.

100. Edward Walsh, "Clinton Picks Gore To Form A 'New Generation' Ticket," *Washington Post*, 10 July 1992.

101. Bob Dole, *Great Political Wit: Laughing (Almost) All the Way to the White House* (Doubleday, 1998), 187–189.

102. "The Cheney-Edwards Vice Presidential Debate," Commission on Presidential Debates, 5 October 2004, http://www.debates.org/pages/trans2004b.html.

103. "Chattanooga Weekend," *Chattanooga Times Free Press*, 9 July 2004.

Chapter Five

1. Andrea Comer, Nicholas Goldberg, and Joseph W. Queen, "Wisconsinites Stage Whine, Cheese Protest," *Newsday*, 17 July 1992.

2. Bob Hohler, "Clinton Lifts a Glass in Dorchester Pub," *Boston Globe*, 26 September 1992.

3. " 'Pit Bull' Dan Quayle," *Seattle Post-Intelligencer*, 2 December 1991.

4. Bob Dole, *Great Presidential Wit . . . I Wish I Was in the Book: A Collection of Humorous Anecdotes and Quotations* (Scribner, 2001), 153.

5. David Lauter, "Clinton Team Is Reflective of Its Boss," *Los Angeles Times*, 27 October 1992.

6. Timothy Clifford, "Democratic Duo Stumps Together," *Newsday*, 12 July 1992.

7. Tom Baxter and Carrie Teegarden, "Campaign '92 Whips into Final Frenzy," *Atlanta Journal and Constitution*, 1 November 1992.

8. Mitchell Locin, "As the Race Winds Down, Clinton Steps up His Pace," *Chicago Tribune*, 1 November 1992.

9. Susan Feeny, "A Campaign with Different Voices," *Dallas Morning News*, 28 October 1992.

10. Susan Page, "Campaign Countdown," *Newsday*, 22 October 1992.

11. Michael Kelly, "The 1992 Campaign: The Democrats; Clinton Says Bush Is Afraid of Debating 'Man to Man,'" *New York Times*, 19 September 1992.

12. Mitchell Locin, "Clinton Says President Promotes Intolerance," *Chicago Tribune*, 24 August 1992.

13. Jeffrey Stinson, "State Dept.'s Searching of Mom's Files Riles Clinton," *Chicago Sun-Times*, 23 October 1992.

14. Steve Berg, "The Moment Was His, and He Seized It," *Minneapolis Star Tribune*, 21 August 1992.

15. Michael Kranish and Scot Lehigh, "Insults Fly as Clinton, Bush Travel to Key States," *Boston Globe*, 30 October 1992.

16. "Bush: 'Bush Comes on Strong,'" *Hotline*, 29 October 1992.

17. M. O'Neill, "Bush on His Last Chance," *Sunday Herald Sun*, 11 October 1992.

18. Martin Kasindorf, "Bush Sticks to Updated Truman Track," *Newsday*, 24 August 1992.

19. Catherine Crier, "Keys to the White House—A Glimpse of the Race," CNN Transcript, 6 September 1992.

20. Ann Demaris, Ph.D., and Valerie White, Ph.D., *First Impressions: What You Don't Know About How Others See You* (Bantam, 2004), 27–28.

21. Dole, *supra* note 4 at 137.

22. Ibid., 203.

23. Ibid., 193.

24. Robert Gray Gunderson, *The Log-Cabin Campaign* (University of Kentucky Press, 1957), 124.

25. Paul F. Boller, *Presidential Campaigns* (Oxford University Press, 1996), 69.

26. Gunderson, *supra* note 24 at 123.

27. Ibid., 125.

28. Ibid., 167.

29. Ibid., 139.

30. Ibid., 139–140.

31. Ibid., 129.

32. Ibid., 133.

33. Ibid., 126.

34. Dole, *supra* note 4 at 15.

35. Bob Dole, *Great Political Wit: Laughing (Almost) All the Way to the White House* (Doubleday, 1998), 18–19.

36. James C. Humes, *The Wit and Wisdom of Abraham Lincoln* (Gramercy, 1999), 162–163.

37. Ibid., 136.

38. Ibid., 162.

39. David Herbert Donald, *Lincoln* (Simon & Schuster, 1996), 217.

40. Dole, *supra* note 4 at 14.

41. Ibid., 31.

42. Donald, *supra* note 39 at 259.

43. "This Reminds Me of a Little Joke," *Harper's Weekly*, 17 September 1864, http://elections.harpweek.com/1864/cartoon-1864-Medium.asp?UniqueID=32&Year=1864.

44. J. F. Feeks, "Hey! Uncle Abe, Are You Joking Yet? Tune- 'Johnny Cope.' J. F. Feeks, 26 Ann Street, and 636 Broadway, New York. [n. d.]." (1864) *America Singing: Nineteenth-Century Song Sheets*, Library of Congress. http://memory.loc.gov/cgibin/ampage?collId=amss&fileName=as1/as105320/amsspage.db&recNum=0&itemLink=D?amss:2:./temp/~ammem_UU50::.

45. Dole, *supra* note 4 at 38–39.

46. Dole, *supra* note 4 at 56.

47. Chris Matthews, *American: Beyond Our Grandest Notion* (Free Press, 2002), 97.

48. Dole, *supra* note 4 at 59.

49. Edmund Morris, *Theodore Rex* (Modern Library, 2002), 233.

50. Dean Keith Simonton, *Greatness: Who Makes History and Why* (The Guilford Press, 1994), 350.

51. Morris, *supra* note 49 at 244–245.

52. Hugh Sidey, "Puritan in the Cabinet Room," *Time*, 16 November 1981.

53. Peter McGrath, "The President's President," *Newsweek*, 7 September 1981.

54. Alan Brinkley, "Calvin Reagan," *New York Times*, 4 July 1981.

55. Alistair Cooke, ed., *The Vintage Mencken* (Alfred A. Knopf, Inc., 1955), 220–222.

56. Dole, *supra* note 35 at 56.

57. Malcolm Lee Cross, "Calvin Coolidge" in William C. Spragens, ed., *Popular Images of American Presidents* (Greenwood Press, 1988), 301.

58. Ruth Tenzer Feldman, *Calvin Coolidge* (Lerner Publishing Group, 2005), 47.

59. John Hiram McKee, *Coolidge Wit and Wisdom: 125 Short Stories About "Cal"* (Frederick A. Stokes Company, 1933), 4.

60. Henry Mitchell, "Presidential Levity and the Old Coolidge Try," *Washington Post*, 16 January 1981.

61. Dole, *supra* note 4 at 67.

62. McKee, *supra* note 59 at 75.

63. Ibid., 92.

64. Dole, *supra* note 4 at 72.

65. McKee, *supra* note 59 at 9.

66. Ibid., 35–36.

67. Henry Mitchell, "Presidential Levity and the Old Coolidge Try," *The Washington Post*, 16 January 1981.

68. Dole, *supra* note 4 at 67.

69. McKee, *supra* note 59 at 123.
70. Ibid., 125.
71. Ibid., 124.
72. Dole, *supra* note 4 at 70.
73. McKee, *supra* note 59 at 99.
74. Boller, *supra* note 25 at 236.
75. Jonathan Alter, *The Defining Moment: FDR's Hundred Days and the Triumph of Hope* (Simon & Schuster, 2006), 108.
76. Conrad Black, *Franklin Delano Roosevelt: Champion of Freedom* (Public Affairs, 2003), 284.
77. "Acceptance Speech by Governor Franklin D. Roosevelt, Chicago, July 2, 1932" in Arthur M. Schlesinger, Jr., ed., *History of American Presidential Elections 1789-1968: Volume III* (Chelsea House Publishers, 1971), 2791.
78. Alter, *supra* note 75 at 90.
79. "Speech by President Franklin D. Roosevelt, Washington, September 23, 1944" in Ed. Arthur M. Schlesinger, Jr., *History of American Presidential Elections 1789-1968: Volume IV* (New York: Chelsea House Publishers, 1971), 3081.
80. Alter, *supra* note 75 at 263–264.
81. Black, *supra* note 76 at 276–277.
82. Alter, *supra* note 75 at 221.
83. Dole, *supra* note 4 at 77–78.
84. Michael O'Brien, *John F. Kennedy: A Biography* (Thomas Dunne Books, 2005), 423–424.
85. Dole, *supra* note 4 at 81.
86. Ibid., 423.
87. Ibid., 424.
88. Philip Potter, "Political Pitchman: Richard M. Nixon" in Eric Sevareid, ed., *Candidates 1960: Behind the Headlines in the Presidential Race* (Basic Books, Inc., 1959), 69.
89. Frank Holeman, "The Curious Quaker: Richard M. Nixon" in Ibid., 134.
90. Dole, *supra* note 4 at 78.
91. Gerald Gardner, *The Mocking of the President* (Wayne State University Press, 1988), 203.
92. Boller, *supra* note 25 at 306.
93. Ibid., 306–307.
94. Potter, *supra* note 88 at 71.
95. Kathleen Hall Jamieson, *Packaging the Presidency: A History and Criticism of Presidential Campaign Advertising* (Oxford University Press, 1996), 257, 293–301.
96. Christopher J. Matthews, *Kennedy and Nixon: The Rivalry That Shaped Postwar America* (Free Press, 1997), 117.
97. Dinesh D'Souza, *Ronald Reagan: How an Ordinary Man Became an Extraordinary Leader* (Free Press, 1999), 72.
98. Ibid., 71.
99. Ibid., 72.
100. Ibid., 71.
101. Edward J. Walsh, "Carter" in Richard Harwood, ed., *The Pursuit of the Presidency 1980* (Berkley Books, 1980), 252.
102. Richard Harwood, "Labor Day 1980" in Harwood, *supra* note 101 at 285.
103. Ibid.
104. Jamieson, *supra* note 95 at 410.
105. Richard Harwood, "October" in Harwood, *supra* note 101 at 296.
106. Boller, *supra* note 25 at 361.
107. Ronald Reagan, *An American Life* (Pocket, 1999), 221.
108. Boller, *supra* note 25 at 366.

109. D'Souza, *supra* note 97 at 67.

110. Ibid., 82.

111. Dole, *supra* note 4 at 235.

112. "Will Americans be Voting for Lesser of Two Evils Come Election Day?" *The O'Reilly Factor* Transcript, Fox News Channel, 24 October 2000.

113. Ciro Scotti, "Chill George. It's Kerry's Turn," *Business Week Online*, 29 October 2004.

114. Noemie Emery, "John Kerry Is Different from You and Me," *Weekly Standard*, 2 August 2004.

Chapter Six

1. Joe Mitchell Chapple, *Life and Times of Warren G. Harding: Our After War President* (Kessinger Publishing, 2004), 282.

2. Malcolm Gladwell, *Blink: The Power of Thinking Without Thinking* (Little, Brown, and Company, 2005), 72–73.

3. "Biography of Warren G. Harding," WhiteHouse.gov, http://www.whitehouse.gov/history/presidents/wh29.html.

4. Bob Dole, *Great Presidential Wit . . . I Wish I Was in the Book: A Collection of Humorous Anecdotes and Quotations* (Scribner, 2001), 211.

5. Eugene P. Trani and David L. Wilson, *The Presidency of Warren G. Harding* (University Press of Kansas, 1977), 25.

6. Dole, *supra* note 4 at 213.

7. George Weigel, "Mencken Trouble," *The Weekly Standard*, 4 November 2002.

8. Chapple, *supra* note 1 at 123–124.

9. Trani and Wilson, *supra* note 5.

10. Chapple, *supra* note 1 at 126.

11. Harry M. Daugherty, *The Inside Story of the Warren G. Harding Tragedy* (Kessinger Publishing, LLC, 2005), 299.

12. Bo Emerson, "Losing It in Atlanta," *Atlanta Journal-Constitution*, 3 November 2003.

13. Gladwell, *supra* note 2 at 76.

14. James Brown and Bruce Tucker, *James Brown: The Godfather of Soul* (Thunder's Mouth Press, 2003), 88.

15. "American Experience: John and Abigail Adams: Part Two," *PBS* Transcript, http://www.pbs.org/wgbh/amex/adams/filmmore/pt_2.html.

16. Henry Adams, *History of the United States During the Second Administration of Thomas Jefferson: Volume I* (New York: Charles Scribner's Sons, 1908), 452.

17. David McCullough, *John Adams* (Simon & Schuster, 2001), 537.

18. Eric Burns, *Infamous Scribblers* (PublicAffairs, 2006), 354.

19. John T. Morse, *Thomas Jefferson* (Houghton, Mifflin and Company, 1899), 4.

20. Adams, *supra* note 16 at 453.

21. John T. Morse, *John Quincy Adams* (Houghton, Mifflin and Company, 1882), 229–230.

22. Cyrus Townsend Brady, *The True Andrew Jackson* (J.B. Lippincott Company, 1906), 136.

23. Sean Wilentz, *Andrew Jackson* (Times Books, 2005), 1.

24. John William Ward, *Andrew Jackson: Symbol for an Age* (Oxford University Press, 1962), 182.

25. Robert Vincint Remini, *The Life of Andrew Jackson* (Harper Perennial Modern Classics, 2001), 87.

26. Ibid., 149.

27. "Some Account of Some of the Bloody Deeds of GENERAL JACKSON" (1828) in Bernard F. Reilly, Jr., *American Political Prints, 1766-1866: Catalog of the Collection in the Library of Congress*, http://loc.harpweek.com/LCPoliticalCartoons/DisplayCartoonLarge.asp?MaxID=25&UniqueID=21&Year=1828&YearMark=182.

28. Remini, *supra* note 25 at 164.

29. Roger Bruns, *Almost History: Close Calls, Plan B's, and Twists of Fate in America's Past* (Hyperion, 2000), 49–51.

30. Paul F. Boller, *Presidential Campaigns* (Oxford: Oxford University Press, 1996), 107.

31. Paul F. Boller, *Presidential Campaigns* (Oxford University Press, 1996), 107–108.

32. Ibid.

33. Allan Peterkin, *One Thousand Beards: A Cultural History of Facial Hair* (Arsenal Pulp Press, 2001), 35–36.

34. Bruns, *supra* note 29.

35. Thomas Nast, "Leaders of the Democratic Party," Library of Congress (1868), http://elections.harpweek.com/1868/cartoon-1868-Medium.asp?UniqueID=8&Year=1868.

36. Thomas Nast, "Time, Midnight. – Scene, New York City Hall," *Harper's Weekly*, 5 September 1868, http://elections.harpweek.com/1868/cartoon-1868-Medium.asp?UniqueID=20&Year=1868.

37. Thomas Nast, "Lead Us Not into Temptation," *Harper's Weekly*, 19 September 1868, http://elections.harpweek.com/1868/cartoon-1868-large.asp?UniqueID=21&Year=1868.

38. Thomas Nast, "The Democratic Hell-Broth," *Harper's Weekly*, 31 October 1868, http://elections.harpweek.com/1868/cartoon-1868-Medium.asp?UniqueID=23&Year=1868.

39. Hamlin Garland, *Ulysses S. Grant: His Life and Character* (Doubleday & McClure Co., 1898), 227.

40. William Conant Church, *Ulysses S. Grant and the Period of National Preservation and Reconstruction* (G. P. Putnam's Sons, 1897), 219.

41. "Victory!" *Harper's Weekly*, 3 October 1868, http://elections.harpweek.com/1868/cartoon-1868-large.asp?UniqueID=36&Year=1868.

42. Matthew Hale Smith, *Sunshine and Shadow in New York* (J. B. Burr and Company, 1869), 654-655.

43. Boller, *supra* note 30 at 129.

44. Thomas Nast, "Let Us Clasp Hands Over the Bloody Chasm," *Harper's Weekly*, 21 September 1872.

45. Thomas Nast, "H.G. 'Let Us Clasp Hands Over the Bloody Chasm,'" *Harper's Weekly*, 19 October 1872.

46. Boller, *supra* note 30 at 129.

47. Peterkin, *supra* note 32 at 67.

48. Sir Harry Lauder, *Roamin' in the Gloamin'* (Kessinger Publishing, 2005), 218.

49. Robert Sobel, *Coolidge* (Regnery, 2000), 161.

50. John A. Barnes, *John F. Kennedy on Leadership: The Lessons and Legacy of a President* (AMACOM, 2005), 56.

51. Michael O'Brien, *John F. Kennedy: A Biography* (Thomas Dunne Books, 2005), 310.

52. Ibid., 328.

53. Ibid.

54. Ibid., 330–331.

55. Neil Steinberg, *Hatless Jack: The President, the Fedora, and the History of American Style* (Plume, 2004), 20–21.

56. Ibid.

57. Ibid.

58. Barnes, *supra* note 49.

59. John Hellman, *The Kennedy Obsession: The American Myth of JFK* (Columbia University Press, 1997), 94.

60. Kathleen Hall Jamieson, *Packaging the Presidency: A History and Criticism of Presidential Campaign Advertising* (Oxford University Press, 1996), 139.

61. Steinberg, *supra* note 54 at 21.

62. Ibid., 22.

63. Jamieson, *supra* note 57 at 158–159.

64. Carolyn L. Funk, "Candidate Images When Things Go Sour" in Kenneth L. Hacker, ed., *Presidential Candidate Images* (Rowman and Littlefield Publishers, Inc., 2004), 69.

65. Steinberg, *supra* 54 at xix–xxi.

66. Ibid., 282.

67. Jack McCallum, "Reagan Did a Number on Counter-Culture Generation," *Morning Call*, 13 June 2004.

68. Dottie Ashley, "When Clothes Were the Sign of the Times," *Post and Courier*, 20 February 1998.

69. Walter R. Mears, *Deadlines Past: Forty Years of Presidential Campaigning: A Reporter's Story* (Andrews McMeel Publishing, 2003), 112.

70. Mike Royko, "Poof! Go the Democrats; Candidate with Poofiest Hair Usually the Party's Nominee," *Orlando Sentinel*, 4 October 1991.

71. Jamieson, *supra* note 57 at 324.

72. Richard Harwood, "October" in Richard Harwood, ed., *The Pursuit of the Presidency 1980* (Berkley Books, 1980), 291.

73. Karon K. Skinner, Ronald Reagan and Martin Anderson, *Reagan: A Life in Letters* (Free Press, 2003), 79.

74. Michael K. Deaver, *A Different Drummer: My Thirty Years with Ronald Reagan* (HarperCollins, 2001), 14.

75. George F. Will, "The Joy of Politics," *Newsweek*, 26 November 1979.

76. "Leading Man," *Newsweek*, 1 October 1979.

77. Lawrence Martin, "On the Road with Reagan: The Jelly Beans Tell the Story," *Globe and Mail*, 13 September 1980.

78. Michael Kernan, "Toupee or Not Toupee," *Washington Post*, 17 September 1980.

79. "A Man of Parts," *Newsweek*, 7 May 1979.

80. Howard Wilkinson, "Kerry, Edwards Claim They Have Better Ideas—and Hair," *Enquirer*, 8 July 2004.

81. Joe Blundo, "With Edwards in Race, Voters Might Split Hairs," *Columbus Dispatch*, 15 July 2004.

82. "Cheney: Preserving Freedom, Security 'Greatest Challenge of Our Time,'" CNN.com, 2 September 2004.

83. Roger Ailes with Jon Kraushar, *You Are the Message: Secrets of the Master Communicators* (Homewood, Illinois: Dow Jones-Irwin, 1988), 22.

Chapter Seven

1. Sol Barzman, *The First Ladies* (Cowles Book Company, Inc., 1970), 198.

2. H. P. Jeffers, *An Honest President: The Life and Times of Grover Cleveland* (Perennial, 2002), 106–108.

3. Ibid., 108.

4. Ibid., 110.

5. Alyn Brodsky, *Grover Cleveland: A Study in Character* (St. Martin's Press, 2000), 92.

6. Ibid., 93–94.

7. Barzman, *supra* note 1 at 199.

8. Ibid., 200–202.

9. William Ewart Gladstone, Roger Quarles Mills, James Gillespie Blaine, and Lloyd Stephens Bryce, *Life of Hon. Grover Cleveland* (1892), 90.

10. Barzman, *supra* note 1 at 203.

11. William Cowper Brann, *The Complete Works of Brann, the Iconoclast: Volume X* (The Brann Publishers, 1898), 6–7.

12. Barzman, *supra* note 1 at 4–5.

13. Ibid., 92–100.

14. Ibid., 110–118.
15. "Biography of Harriet Lane," WhiteHouse.gov, http://www.whitehouse.gov/history/firstladies/hl15.html.
16. Barzman, *supra* note 1 at 146–147.
17. Ibid., 59–61.
18. Paul F. Boller, *Presidential Campaigns* (Oxford University Press, 1996), 46.
19. Paul F. Boller, *Presidential Wives* (Oxford University Press, 2006), 65–66.
20. Carl Sferrazza Anthony, *First Ladies: The Saga of the Presidents' Wives and Their Power (1789–1961)* (Perennial, 2003), 111.
21. Boller, *supra* note 19 at 66.
22. Robert V. Remini, *The Life of Andrew Jackson* (Harper Perennial Modern Classics, 2001), 169.
23. Ibid., 169–170.
24. David A. Smith, *Presidents from Adams Through Polk, 1825–1849: Debating the Issues Pro and Con Primary Documents* (Greenwood Press, 2005), 37.
25. Robert Vincent Remini, *Henry Clay: Statesman for the Union* (W.W. Norton & Company, Inc., 1991), 340.
26. Angus McLaren, *Sexual Blackmail: A Modern History* (Harvard University Press, 2002), 81.
27. Conrad Black, *Franklin Delano Roosevelt: Champion of Freedom* (PublicAffairs, 2003), 98.
28. Mary Winget, *Eleanor Roosevelt* (Lerner Publications Company, 2001), 47.
29. Black, *supra* note 27.
30. Ibid., 904.
31. Douglas Brinkley and David Rubel, *World War II: The Axis Assault, 1939–1942* (Times Books, 2003), 303.
32. John Kenneth Galbraith, *Name-Dropping: From FDR On* (Houghton Miffling Company, 1999), 50.
33. Steve Neal, ed., Eleanor Roosevelt, Gloria Steinem, *Eleanor and Harry: The Correspondence of Eleanor Roosevelt and Harry S. Truman* (Kensington Publishing Corp., 2004), 17.
34. Betty Houchin Winfield, *FDR and the News Media* (University of Illinois Press, 1990), 61.
35. Barzman, *supra* note 1 at 302.
36. Rodger Streitmatter, ed., Eleanor Roosevelt, *Empty Without You: The Intimate Letters of Eleanor Roosevelt and Lorena Hickok* (Da Capo Press, 2000), 8.
37. Russell Freedman, *Eleanor Roosevelt: A Life of Discovery* (Clarion Books, 1993), 93.
38. Eleanor Roosevelt, *The Autobiography of Eleanor Roosevelt* (Da Capo Press, 1992), 163.
39. Barzman, *supra* note 1 at 303.
40. Ibid., 304–305.
41. "The Graceful Loser," *Time*, 23 July 1965.
42. Jean H. Baker, *The Stevensons: A Biography of an American Family* (W.W. Norton & Company, Inc., 1997), 331.
43. Ibid., 329.
44. Ibid., 329–330.
45. Ibid., 330.
46. Ibid., 331.
47. Ibid., 430.
48. Boller, *supra* note 19 at 352.
49. Ibid., 343–345.
50. Kathleen Hall Jamieson, *Packaging the Presidency: A History and Criticism of Presidential Campaign Advertising* (Oxford University Press, 1996), 108.
51. Ibid.
52. Barzman, *supra* note 1 at 332.
53. Fletcher Knebel, "Pulitzer Prize Entry: John F. Kennedy" in Eric Sevareid, ed., *Candidates 1960: Behind the Headlines in the Presidential Race* (Basic Books, Inc., 1959), 199.

54. Michael O'Brien, *John F. Kennedy: A Biography* (Thomas Dunne Books, 2005), 328.

55. Ibid., 293.

56. Ibid., 299–300.

57. Ibid., 300.

58. Ibid., 302.

59. Ibid., 695–696.

60. Knebel, *supra* note 53 at 199–200.

61. Carl Sferrazza Anthony, *As We Remember Her: Jacqueline Kennedy Onassis, in the Words of Her Family and Friends* (Perennial, 2003), 122.

62. Randall Woods, *LBJ: Architect of American Ambition* (Free Press, 2006), 205.

63. Ibid., 290.

64. Ibid., 288.

65. Ibid., 666.

66. Ibid., 288.

67. Ibid., 103.

68. Ibid., 406.

69. Barzman, *supra* note 1 at 345.

70. Gary A. Donaldson, *Liberalism's Last Hurrah: The Presidential Campaign of 1964* (M. E. Sharpe, 2003), 273.

71. Ibid., 276.

72. Jennifer Steinhauer, "Back in View, a First Lady with Her Own Legacy," *New York Times*, 31 December 2006.

73. Boller, *supra* note 19 at 417–418.

74. Elizabeth Peer, "Woman of the Year," *Newsweek*, 29 December 1975.

75. John Robert Greene, *Betty Ford: Candor and Courage in the White House* (University Press of Kansas, 1994), 79.

76. Neely Tucker, "Betty Ford, Again Putting on a Brave Face," *Washington Post*, 29 December 2006.

77. Elizabeth Peer, "Woman of the Year," *Newsweek*, 29 December 1975.

78. Betty Boyd Caroli, *First Ladies* (Oxford University Press, 1995), 259–260.

79. Jennifer Steinhauer, "Back in View, a First Lady with Her Own Legacy," *New York Times*, 31 December 2006.

80. Boller, *supra* note 19 at 441.

81. Rosalynn W. Carter, *First Lady from Plains* (University of Arkansas Press, 1994), 148.

82. Jamieson, *supra* note 50 at 364.

83. Elizabeth Peer, "Woman of the Year," *Newsweek*, 29 December 1975.

84. "Governor and Mrs. Bill Clinton Discuss Adultery Accusations," *60 Minutes*, CBS, 26 January 1992.

85. "Bill Clinton Allegations Aftermath," *Nightline*, ABC News, 27 January 1992.

86. "Stand by Your Woman: Hillary as Campaign Issue," *The Hotline*, 17 March 1992.

87. "Hillary Clinton: Attorney, Activist, Political Wife," *All Things Considered*, NPR, 30 March 1992.

88. Marjorie Williams, "FIRST Ladies," *Washington Post*, 1 November 1992.

89. "GOP versus Hillary: Your Move, Mr. Bond," *Hotline*, 13 August 1992.

90. "Transcript #641," *Crossfire*, CNN, 18 August 1992.

91. "GOP Leaders Ask Speakers to Soften Attacks on Hillary," *Seattle Post-Intelligencer*, 20 August 1992.

92. Bill Plante, "Democrats Deflect Attacks Against Hillary Clinton," *CBS Morning News*, CBS, 20 August 1992.

93. "Overheard," *Newsweek*, 31 August 1992.

94. John Aloysius Farrell and Michael Kranish, "GOP Sees Its Stress on Values Backfire," *Boston Globe*, 27 August 1992.

95. Carolyn Barta, "The Candidate's Counselor and Confidante," *Dallas Morning News*, 13 August 2000.

96. Ibid.

97. Lance Morrow, "Gore's Kiss Is So '60's—and Probably Fake," CNN.com, 28 August 2000, http://archives.cnn.com/2000/ALLPOLITICS/stories/08/28/morrow8_28.a.tm/index.html.

98. Nick Gillespie, "Being Al Gore: The 'Real' Appeal of The Kiss," *Reason*, November 2000.

99. "This Morning," *Hotline*, 21 August 2000.

100. "Late Night Political Humor," *Bulletin's Frontrunner*, 21 August 2000.

101. "Laugh Lines," *Los Angeles Times*, 27 August 2000.

102. Ibid.

103. "Gore's Revival Sealed with a Kiss," *News & Record* (Greensboro, NC), 31 August 2000.

104. Bonna M. de la Cruz, "Energetic Gore Courts Vital Midwest States," *Tennessean*, 31 October 2000.

105. Andrea Koppel, Paula Zahn, Candy Crowley, and Kyra Phillips, "A Profile of Teresa Heinz Kerry, Laura Bush," *CNN People in the News* (CNN), 30 October 2004.

106. Lowell Ponte, "Cash-and-Kerry," Frontpagemag.com, 27 January 2004, http://frontpagemag.com/Articles/ReadArticle.asp?ID=11939.

107. "This Morning," *Hotline*, 30 April 2004.

108. "This Morning," *Hotline*, 3 May 2004.

109. "This Morning," *Hotline*, 17 June 2004.

110. "This Morning," *Hotline*, 24 March 2004.

111. James Hebert, "Party lines," *San Diego Union-Tribune*, 1 November 2004.

112. Mark Leibovich, "The Heart of Politics," *Washington Post*, 2 June 2002.

113. Lisa de Moraes, "Pop Goes the Psychology: The Dr. Phils Meet the Kerrys," *Washington Post*, 7 October 2004.

114. Mike Sunnucks, "Heinz Kerry Helps Democrats Raise $1M at Phoenix Event," *Business Journal of Phoenix*, 23 September 2004.

115. Dan Balz, "Heinz Kerry Has Retort for Bush Fans," *Washington Post*, 3 August 2004.

116. "Laura Bush Brushes Aside Heinz Kerry's Remarks," CNN.com, 21 October 2004, http://www.cnn.com/2004/ALLPOLITICS/10/21/laura.teresa/index.html.

117. "Teresa Heinz Kerry: Democratic National Convention," PR Newswire, 27 July 2004.

118. "Teresa Heinz Drops 'Kerry,'" *Pittsburgh Tribune-Review*, 6 February 2005.

Chapter Eight

1. Joe Mitchell Chapple, *Warren G. Harding—The Man* (Chapple Publishing Company, 1920), 58.

2. Elaine Landau, *Warren G. Harding* (Lerner Publications Company, 2000), 83.

3. Marvin Kitman, *The Making of the Prefident 1789* (Grove Press, 1989), 202.

4. William A. Degregorio, *The Complete Book of U.S. Presidents* (Wings Books, 1991), 389.

5. Edmund Lester Pearson, *Theodore Roosevelt* (The MacMillan Company, 1920), 76.

6. Hamlin Garland, *Ulysses S. Grant: His Life and Character* (Doubleday & McClure Co., 1898), 404.

7. Degregorio, *supra* note 4 at 118.

8. Ibid., 110.

9. John Derbyshire, "The SOB Factor," *National Review Online*, 12 March 2007, http://article.nationalreview.com/?q=MTlmMTEwN2VhMWY5ZjVlMTg0MGQyYTc2ZTNkODU3NDg=.

10. Bob Dole, *Great Presidential Wit . . . I Wish I Was in the Book: A Collection of Humorous Anecdotes and Quotations* (Scribner, 2001), 225.

11. Nathaniel Hawthorne, *The Life of Franklin Pierce* (1852), http://www.eldritchpress.org/nh/fp01.html.

12. Max J. Skidmore, *Presidential Performance: A Comprehensive Review* (North Carolina: MacFarland & Company, Inc., 2004), 114.

13. James Carville, Paul Begala, *Take It Back: Our Party, Our Country, Our Future* (Simon & Schuster, 2006), 14.
14. Neal B. Freedman, "Wimp Thrashes Nerd," *National Review*, 28 October 1988.
15. Susan Estrich, "Meanie for President," Creators.com, 2 March 2007, http://www.creators.com/opinion/susan-estrich/meanie-for-president.html.
16. Buzz Patterson, *Dereliction of Duty* (Regnery, 2003), 93.
17. Dana Milbank, "At Newsstands Everywhere, the Honorable Beach Babe from Illinois," *Washington Post*, 9 January 2007.
18. Ben Shapiro, "Is Barack Obama the Messiah?" Townhall.com, 31 January 2007, http://www.townhall.com/columnists/BenShapiro/2007/01/31/is_barack_obama_the_messiah.
19. Lynn Sweet, "Obama Regrets Saying Soldiers' Lives 'Wasted,'" *Chicago Sun-Times*, 13 February 2007.
20. Susan Estrich, "Obama, Israel and Al Sharpton," Yahoo! News, 16 March 2007, http://news.yahoo.com/s/uc/20070316/cm_uc_crsesx/op_392228.
21. Don Carrington, "Edwards Home County's Largest," *Carolina Journal*, 26 January 2007.
22. Ben Smith's Blog, "The Hair's Still Perfect," 16 April 2007, http://www.politico.com/blogs/bensmith/0407/The_Hairs_Still_Perfect.html.
23. Susan Estrich, "Can Cancer Close the Gravitas Gap?" Creators.com, 6 April 2007, http://www.creators.com/opinion/susan-estrich/can-cancer-close-the-gravitas-gap.html.
24. Todd S. Purdum, "Prisoner of Conscience," *Vanity Fair*, February 2007.
25. John J. Miller, "Matinee Mitt," *National Review*, 20 June 2005.
26. Scott Helman, "Ann Romney's Time," *Boston Globe*, 27 February 2006.
26. Noam Scheiber, "Popular Mandate," *TNR Online*, 27 April 2007.

Chapter Nine
1. Ron Fournier and Trevor Tompson, "Poll: Character Trumps Policy for Voters," Associated Press, 11 March 2007, http://www.usatoday.com/news/washington/2007-03-11-candidate-traits_N.htm.
2. Ibid.
3. David E. Johnson and Johnny Ray Johnson, *A Funny Thing Happened on the Way to the White House: Foolhardiness, Folly, and Fraud in Presidential Elections, from Andrew Jackson to George W. Bush* (Taylor Trade, 2004), 121.
4. Conor Cruise O'Brien, *The Great Melody: A Thematic Biography of Edmund Burke* (University of Chicago Press, 1994), 75.
5. James Madison, "Federalist #51" in *The Federalist Papers* (Penguin Books, 1987), 319.

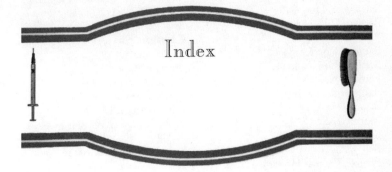

Index